Museums of the Mind

Magritte, *Legend of the Centuries*. The Menil Collection, Houston.

Museums of the Mind

Magritte's Labyrinth and Other Essays in the Arts

Ellen Handler Spitz

Yale University Press   New Haven and London

Designed by Sonia L. Scanlon
Set in Bodoni type by Tseng Information Systems, Inc.
Durham, North Carolina.
Printed in the United States of America by Edwards
Brothers, Ann Arbor, Michigan.

Library of Congress Cataloging-in-Publication Data
Spitz, Ellen Handler
    Museums of the mind : Magritte's labyrinth
and other essays in the arts / Ellen Handler
Spitz.
        p.   cm.
    Includes bibliographical references and
index.
    ISBN 0-300-06029-7
    1. Psychoanalysis and the arts. 2. Magritte,
René, 1898–1967—Criticism and interpretation. 3. Surrealism—Belgium.   I. Title.
NX180.P7S66   1994
700′.1′05—dc20   94-12347
                        CIP

A catalogue record for this book is available from the
British Library.
The paper in this book meets the guidelines for permanence
and durability of the Committee on Production Guidelines for
Book Longevity of the Council on Library Resources.

10 9 8 7 6 5 4 3 2 1

With abiding love and admiration
I dedicate these pages
to the memory of two courageous women
my mother
Beulah Hoffberg Handler
and
my mentor in Part One of this book
Martha Wolfenstein

Contents

Contents

Illustrations

Plates

Following page 16

1. Magritte, *Girl Eating Bird*, 1946. Private Collection. Giraudon/Art Resource, New York.

2. Magritte, *The Spirit of Geometry*, 1937. Tate Gallery, London/Art Resource, New York.

3. Magritte, *Titanic Days*, 1928. Private Collection. Giraudon/Art Resource, New York.

4. Magritte, *Dangerous Relationships*, 1936. Private Collection. Giraudon/Art Resource, New York.

5. Magritte, *Attempting the Impossible*, 1928. Private Collection. Giraudon/Art Resource, New York.

6. Magritte, *When the Hour Will Strike*, 1964. Private Collection. Herscovici/Art Resource, New York.

7. Magritte, *The Human Condition*, 1933. Private Collection. Herscovici/Art Resource, New York.

8. Magritte, *The Blank Signature*, 1965. Collection of Mr. and Mrs. Paul Mellon. National Gallery of Art, Washington, D.C.

Figures

Frontispiece. Magritte, *Legend of the Centuries*, 1952. The Menil Collection, Houston. © 1994 C. Herscovici, Brussels/ Artists Rights Society (ARS), New York. Photograph by F. W. Seiders.

Following page 36

Illustrations

1.10. Magritte, *Philosophy in the Boudoir*, 1947. Gouache. Private Collection. Giraudon/Art Resource, New York.

Following page 40

1.11. Flier for *Core Questions in Philosophy: A Text with Readings* by Elliott Sober (New York: Macmillan College Publishing Company, 1991.) Reproduced with the permission of Macmillan College Publishing Company.

1.12. Magritte, *This Is Not an Apple*, 1964. Private Collection. Herscovici/Art Resource, New York.

1.13. Advertisement. Copyright 1990. Minolta Corporation.

1.14. Magritte, *The Great War*, 1964. Private Collection. Giraudon/Art Resource, New York.

1.15. Magritte, *The Unexpected Answer*, 1933. Musées Royaux des Beaux-Arts de Belgique, Brussels. Art Resource, New York.

1.16. Rivi Handler-Spitz, age seven, Lunch bag drawing in crayon based on *The Great War*.

1.17. Rivi Handler-Spitz, age seven, Lunch bag drawing in crayon based on *The Pleasure Principle*.

1.18. Magritte, *The Pleasure Principle*, 1937. Edward James Foundation, Sussex. Bridgeman/Art Resource, New York.

1.19. Magritte, *Hegel's Vacation*, 1959. Private Collection. Herscovici/Art Resource, New York.

What men have seen they know;
But what shall come hereafter
No man before the event can see,
Nor what end waits for him.
Sophocles, *Ajax*

Preface

The chorus in a Greek tragedy always reminds us that although
we must live our lives facing forward, we can only look back.
The psychoanalyst does just that with his or her patients: together
they gaze at aspects of life that have already gone by and seek
to discover recurring patterns there. Similarly, the writing of this
book has occasioned many returns. As thought and feeling have
flowed together on its pages, I have witnessed the surfacing of previously unnoticed currents and crosscurrents, doublings, signs,
and designs.

Once the psychoanalyst glimpses an emerging theme, however, there may be some reluctance to point it out. This reticence
sometimes stems from concern lest further revelation and discovery be stifled. In this preface, I am similarly reluctant to offer
a preemptive list of themes that could be traced in the pages
to come. *Museums of the Mind* was written associatively rather
than argumentatively; yet, it is not entirely without argument. It
is a work neither of art history nor aesthetics nor criticism, but
rather of contemplations and uneasily disciplined passions. Its
unnumbered chapters, like tributaries of a waterway, adjoining
chambers in a sprawling villa, or outcropping roots of an aged
tree, may be experienced in whatever order pleases the reader.

Borrowing both analytic reticence and the mystery of Magritte
as my models, I offer this preface then as "not a preface" but
rather an open invitation to a tour that may lead inward as well as
to the outside world.

To write with fervor about the power of works of art to mark and
shape our lives is not to shortchange the credit due our human en-

vironment, which is clearly preeminent. To endure the relentless incursions of life and loss, human sustenance is indispensable. Many wise and generous colleagues have offered their help to me, both direct and subtle, as this book was forming. Insofar as possible, I have tried to remember them individually within these pages. Here, however, I want to express my appreciation to a group of people whose support cannot easily be linked to one chapter or another. They are, nonetheless, the people upon whom, in the profoundest ways, this book depends.

First I wish to acknowledge a vibrant young woman, my second-born daughter, Rivi Handler-Spitz, whose lifespan has coincided with my enchantment by Magritte. Rivi was born years after her maternal grandmother had passed away and just as Martha Wolfenstein was dying. Thus her meetings with those figures, each central, as is she, to my readings of his art, have occurred only in the realm of the surreal. As such, they are recorded in the pages of this work.

I want especially to remember here one friend and one colleague for whom mourning continues as these words are being written—Carol Goodman, formerly of Los Angeles, and Roy Ginsburg, formerly of Palo Alto, each of whom gave me the gift of belief in this project.

For their thoughtful readings of various incarnations of the manuscript, I wish to thank Patrick O'Brien, James E. B. Breslin, Norman Bryson, and, at the Yale University Press, my dedicated manuscript editor, Cynthia Wells, and my anonymous reader. I also wish to thank Janyce Beck at the Press for her patience and kindness. To Leon Botstein and Eugene Carr of the American Symphony Orchestra I extend my appreciation for arranging a concert to coincide with the Magritte retrospective at the Metropolitan Museum of Art in 1992, and for the invitation to lecture at Avery Fisher Hall as well as at the Museum, thus stimulating me to consider the topic of surrealism and music. Susan Davidson and Mary Kadish of the Menil Collection made paintings available to me that I had not seen before, and for that I am most grateful.

To all my children—Jennifer Beulah Lew and Paul Nathan Foster, Nathaniel Geoffrey Lew, and Rivi Handler-Spitz, to my dear friends Joanna and Peter Strauss, Anne Griffin and Jay Lefer, Yael S. Feldman, Joan Baudouine, Peter Jelavich, Ramsay and James E. B. Breslin, Sheila and John Gilmour, to my beloved aunt, Sylvia Hoffberg Franklin, and to my nonpareil editor Gladys Topkis, I give my heartiest and most resounding thanks. To Patrick I give all of that and more.

Part One

In the Labyrinth of René Magritte

Magritte

Martha   Mourning

Metamorphosis

Museum   Murder

Mind   Memory

Mystery

Magic   Music

Meaning

Maze   Minotaur

Mother

Unhappy woman! How? By her own hand. The worst of what
was done you cannot know. You did not see the sight.

. . .

Do not seek to be master in everything, for the things you
mastered did not follow you throughout your life.
Sophocles, *Oedipus Rex*

Collective Inventions

In late spring of 1912, the year in which after troubling dreams,
Franz Kafka awoke one morning in Prague to tell the proto-surreal
story of Gregor Samsa, "The Metamorphosis"—a tale of turnings
away from both life and death—the mother of the future surrealist
artist René Magritte committed suicide by drowning in the river
Sambre in Belgium. Magritte was not yet fourteen. Like Kafka,
who opposed pictorial versions of his literary work, Magritte ada-
mantly opposed verbal attempts to explicate his cryptic imagery.
Kafka, when told an artist was to make a drawing for the title page
of "The Metamorphosis," protested: "Not that, please not that!
The insect itself cannot be illustrated. It cannot even be shown
from a distance" (Hayman, 1981). Magritte wanted his work to
remain mysterious.

In this book, however, I have rebelliously disobeyed the manifest command of the artist, trusting that to do so might serve an
even deeper, albeit unacknowledged, desire—or perhaps a different kind of truth. For, despite the artist's fears, the images
discussed in these pages will surely survive my interpretations.
Their visual qualities will stand firm against any assaults made on
them by verbal signs.

My design is to negotiate a labyrinth of paintings by means of
tangled psychoanalytic threads. We shall enter a maze that also
contains a masterpiece by Pieter Breughel in which there is a
turning away from death. This sixteenth-century canvas, *Landscape with the Fall of Icarus* (fig. 1. 20), deeply imprinted the
psyches of several twentieth-century artists, including not only
the painter Magritte but also the poets W. H. Auden and William

Carlos Williams, who tried to create verbal equivalents for it. Its breath-taking coupling of fresh air with death recalls to us the ending of "The Meta-morphosis," where Gregor Samsa's demise by starvation sends his family outdoors into the pleasant countryside. The painting's layered repetitions and counterpointed images remind us of those that crowd the strongest works by Magritte. Its ironies strike us slowly—inscribed as they are in both time and space. We learn, by careful looking, that our own lives and deaths (and our ambivalently cherished traditions) are both seen and not seen, seen but not noticed, noticed but not comprehended, comprehended but strenuously ignored.

Opening his seminal essay on "thick interpretation," a wonderfully sensuous term borrowed from Gilbert Ryle, Clifford Geertz (1973) notes that although grand new ideas may at first seem like shining keys to the universe (see Magritte's *Smile of the Devil* [*Le Sourire du diable*], 1966 [fig. 1.1]), they must inevitably recede as we confront inherent limitations on their usefulness. He speaks of such ideas as the second law of thermodynamics and the principle of natural selection as well as the psychoanalytic notion of unconscious motivation. But to become aware of dawning limitations on their applicability is hardly to render them obsolete. To acknowledge their failure to supply us with a *via regia* to all physio/bio/cultural knowledge and eventuality is not to deny them an enduring role in our thought. In particular, psychoanalysis, or more precisely certain of its constituent notions, while unable to explain everything, certainly explains *some*thing. It therefore continues, in concert with other grand ideas, to serve as a guide in our interpretive and critical endeavors.

This book asks whether and how psychoanalysis might whisper to us in our private moments with works of art. Paradoxically, the interpretations that follow are all, in a certain sense, communal. This is because works of art are experienced by individuals only in terms that include in important ways the insights and responses of others, even though such contributions—apparently accretions or secretions of the works themselves—often go unnoticed. Every work, in other words, expands to include the residues of previous readings and viewings. In this sense, all responses may be taken as more or less cooperative, for one breathes in and consumes the dispositions of others, and one's own apparently spontaneous reactions are in turn completed, embellished, and distorted by those who take hold of them. Filtered through the scrims of one's own and others' scotomas, perceptions circulate in a protean swirl.

Psychologically minded or not, most people spend time and energy considering their relationships with other human beings. For some individuals, however, the visual arts and literature assume an importance comparable to that of the live human environment that surrounds them. In such cases, attachments to and kinship with works of art become central to a life history. Ties to them possess distinct narratives, much as do all loves between human beings. In some cases, they prove enduring; in other instances, transient; they are variously turbulent and tranquil, quiescent and engrossing. In every instance, the course of the relationship reflects changes wrought by personal growth, knowledge, mental states, fantasy and dreams, even the vicissitudes of physical health, and, equally, by a wide range of external circumstances.

Art criticism, in my view, is always a contingent practice consisting of negotiations among idiosyncratic individuals and objects. What follows in these pages is thus unavoidably personal as well as public. Situated in front of Magritte's paintings, my own gaze riveted on and by them, I have never been able to help becoming, in the words of Marion Milner, strangely "mixed up with them" (1957, p. 10).

Each of the paintings of René Magritte continues to swell in meaning as a result of psychoanalytic understanding, and likewise each one continues to exert pressure on the scaffolding fashioned for it, so that whatever amount of energy my colleagues and I expend continues to be replaced. Writing across the disciplines, writing across spaces that open and close, thus feels like a kinetic, an athletic enterprise. Dynamic, vibrant, and quintessentially cooperative, criticism is always work in progress. Its goals, as I see them, are to stimulate fresh bursts of awareness, to clarify the shape of fading memories, to alter—even momentarily—the margins of understanding.

But, cavorting with psychoanalysis in the darkling woods and playgrounds of the visual and literary arts, I sometimes wonder why its lenses, so powerful when focused on the psyches of individuals who are artists, seem less so when trained on works. Paintings, for example, have a maddening habit of marching past psychoanalytic critics like the eight kings and Banquo's ghost in *Macbeth*. They unsettle or provoke while remaining tenebrous. This matters. For unless the psychoanalytic critic can bring delicacy, depth, and directness to bear on actual works and in so doing address them in the fullness of their impact on beholders, this unique approach will not survive as a viable critical tool. My project, then, aims at realizing at least a few moments of this species of rhetorical, Breughelian truth.

In staging this project (a relevant expression for Magritte, who was obsessed with both theatrical and symbolic curtains), I have taken the risk of recreating a species of surreal experience by referring to a number of pictures not illustrated in these pages. From the surrealists themselves, I have borrowed the format of collage. Like theirs, my mode has been speculative. Moreover, the experiment as a whole plays on an endemic feature of psychoanalytic process, namely, that, out of the plethora of words that tumble pell-mell into an imaginary space that opens between therapist and patient, meanings gradually come into focus. As they are broached, labeled, and questioned, they magnify and proliferate. Something similar happens, I believe, with respect to the oeuvre of visual artists. We walk through museums as through a maze. Wandering, we notice that some themes vanish only to reappear, whereas others dissipate like dandelion puffs at a child's breath. My goal, therefore, is to open an analogous space between us as beholders and Magritte's paintings, with psychoanalytic thought as a beacon that occasionally blinds us or misses the mark but that always continues to search.

The phrase "museums of the mind" came to me in response to a passage in Claes Oldenburg's 1960s manifesto *Store Days*, which I revisited in connection with a 1991 project on New York City subway-car graffiti (*1991*). Oldenburg, whose whimsical works still proclaim the influence of surrealism, once provocatively announced that art should have "a starting point of zero," should do "something other than sit on its ass in a museum." Moved by but resisting the seductiveness of that passionate plea for absolute beginnings, I prefer to argue for the existence of a *museum of the mind*— a place where images from the past are preserved in an inner cache or treasure trove from which none of us, artist or otherwise, can escape.

Psychoanalysis acquaints each of us with our own intrapsychic museum by guiding us gently, despite our protests, on tours through rooms we have tried to forget. Reluctantly, we are made to behold, in varying degrees of ruin or curatorial repair, the pictured traces of our earliest relations—all we once loved, hated, feared, tried to destroy or give up. We learn that, try as we might to shut out awkward sketches, snapshots, and postcards of past life, our metaphoric museums of the mind, even when split radically from consciousness, remain with us. Illuminated or enshrouded, these permanent collections stay put—even as temporary exhibits pass kaleidoscopically before our dreaming and waking eyes.

The painted puzzles of Magritte, populating my own intrapsychic museum for so many years, seem to attract philosophers, psychoanalysts, and advertising artists even more than art historians. Is this because they are questions as well as paintings, or paintings as questions? Is it because they illustrate links between the abstract and the personal, the paradoxical and the perverse? Because they connect childhood trauma with recurrent obsessions about seeing and knowing and seeing as knowing? Viewed through the crystalline psychoanalytic prisms wrought by the late Martha Wolfenstein, they seem to merge with her interpretive work. Like all trenchant exegeses, her insights have bonded with, altered, and reshaped the boundaries of these aesthetic objects. My discursive panorama juxtaposes her vision with mine as it does the metaphors of *museum* and *maze*.

The Exquisite Corpse

My passion for the work of René Magritte owes its being to Martha
Wolfenstein (1911–1976), a psychologist and psychoanalyst who,
in the early 1970s, did the first psychoanalytic studies of this artist. My private dialogues with the paintings evoked in these pages
would be unimaginable without her guidance.

To have known Wolfenstein during the time of her intense involvement with the paintings of Magritte was to have had contact
with a woman of incisive and subtle intellect. I had been aware
for years of her sterling reputation as a teacher, a coveted clinical supervisor, and a writer with unusually wide-ranging cultural
interests, which included a collaboration with Margaret Mead.
Her deep engagement with the work of Magritte, however, came
as a complete surprise. I will never forget my *frisson* one wintry
evening after arriving at her apartment for dinner. As she opened
her closet door nonchalantly to hang up my coat, I had to suppress
a gasp. There against the wall in semi-darkness was propped
an oversized color print of Magritte's *Legend of the Centuries*
(*La Légende des siècles*), 1952 (see frontispiece)—the portrait of
a titanic, Ozymandias-like stone chair upon which a tiny chair
silently "sits." The sight stunned and, as I remembered it, dizzied
me. I could not expunge the image. The whole encounter took
on an uncanny aspect. It was just as Freud had intimated when
he used the term *unheimlich* and spoke of the "return of the repressed"—that queasy sensation, almost like nausea or panic,
that arises when some object, person, or place seems strange and
alien but at the same time palpably familiar. Magritte's strongest
paintings, as I subsequently came to learn, are invariably ablaze

with this uncanniness, even literally so, as for example his glowing fiery tuba, *The Discovery of Fire* (*La Découverte de feu*), 1936.

Wolfenstein's attraction to the art of Magritte derived from her longstanding clinical interest in bereaved children, specifically children who had suffered the death of a parent (1966, 1969). She had written on Magritte and on the English poet A. E. Housman from that perspective in an essay entitled "The Image of the Lost Parent" (1973) and on children's reactions to the death of a president following the assassination of John Kennedy (see Wolfenstein and Kliman, 1965). She left two unpublished manuscripts on Magritte, one the text of a lecture delivered to the Margaret S. Mahler Symposium in Philadelphia in 1974, "The Past Recaptured in the Work of René Magritte," the other a long unedited text posthumously called "The Man in the Bowler Hat" (referred to in these pages as "MS"). My analysis in the following pages is deeply indebted to all these sources.

Our lives had crossed many years earlier when I was a little girl and she had been doing research at the Vassar Summer Institute; on the occasion of my discovery of her closeted Magritte, Wolfenstein was only slightly older than my mother would have been at that time if she had not died of cancer. This disease was very soon to claim the life of Wolfenstein herself; thus, her conversations with me about Magritte's tragic loss of his mother took place in the context of her own steadily worsening condition. Both her words and his images revived the pain of my own unencompassable maternal bereavement. Past and pending, personal and remote, these absences and omens formed an emotional palimpsest for my initial encounters with Magritte's paintings—a background that reinforced the structure of many of the works themselves and persistently intruded as foreground to upset whatever objective stance I was struggling to maintain toward them. After visiting Wolfenstein in the hospital shortly before her death, I successfully put these experiences behind me for several years. But the images had already gouged themselves into my psyche. They returned; they would not be repressed.

By now, after so many years of looking, conjuring, and recollecting, my perceptions have blended not only with hers but with those of other sensitive and suggestive viewers of Magritte's paintings, notably writers, critics, and art historians such as Michel Foucault, Suzi Gablik, David Sylvester, and Sarah Whitfield, but also family members, colleagues, students, and friends. My contribution, in dialogue with all of them, draws freely on

9

their prior and ongoing work—much like that surrealist game, the "corps exquis," in which an unpredictable composition is made by a number of artists drawing sequentially on folds of the same sheet, which, when it is opened, reveals a composite picture often eerie and compelling albeit incongruous. Additive rather than agonistic, what is offered here represents a threaded pathway through the maze, a way for some beholders to negotiate the labyrinth formed by these pictures.

Preeminently, my mode is psychoanalytical. Mary Ann Caws, for one, has written stunningly (see her 1989 essay "Ladies Shot and Painted") on the surrealists' propensity to devalue women, and Marianne Hirsch (1989) has demonstrated the programmatic denigration of mothers throughout the arts. Both of these are approaches that matter for an understanding of the oeuvre of Magritte; yet, my own emphasis is somewhat different. Drawing on the insights of Wolfenstein, I see his cold canvases, his panorama of erotically idealized but outrageously distorted, unavailable women, as drawing energy also from a developmental imperative, namely, the necessity to push away and to push hard—to force distance, never mind how—into that first hot bond between mother and self, a necessity that affects both sexes, so that the pictures, in all their horror, catch and hold. The circumstances of Magritte's early life—particularly its nodal point of sudden, dramatic, self-inflicted parental death—shortcircuited a normally protracted path of separation. Thus, his gallery of bizarre women can be read as figuring the gamut of emotions a child may have and continue to feel toward an untimely maternal bereavement.

The notion of safety also concerns me. By thwarting our confident expectations, by teasing, shocking, and repelling us, Magritte knows how to destabilize our visual environment. He can make us feel insecure. By recreating the perversities of his (and our own) traumas, he induces in us a reexperience of the disbelief that occurs when unforeseen disaster assaults our tenuous grip on a benevolent reality. Simultaneously, he achieves something else. Because he relies on a constricted repertoire of symbols and formal pictorial devices, he is able to pull an uneasy stasis over the breaking ground. His paintings, especially en masse, can on this account bore as well as provoke. They can irritate us with their facility—their hurry to ward off the strong feelings they elicit and/or to elicit those feelings for the inconclusive purposes of scorn or for the defensive but more adaptive purposes of wit. To feel perfectly safe with such pictures might indeed mean having given up on something important, might mean having become jaded and blasé, yet contrariwise, to feel unsafe and nervous among them does not necessarily betoken a state of greater empathy or understanding.

Not all of us lose our mothers to death in our childhood or adolescence, but we do lose them symbolically in the sense that we must relinquish (never without pain) the all-encompassing, all-absorbing love that characterizes, in a unique blend of reality and fantasy, that first human bond. Moreover, each of us must come to terms with the palette of feelings, vivid to gray, this loss entails. For me, Magritte's images, cold and hard, are signs of a lifelong struggle with this loss. They strive on many levels to deny its occurrence, to touch and hide its sadness, to recapture states associated with it, to mark and disavow its absence, to create substitutes while simultaneously devaluing them, to vent and contain rage, to doubt any project of reparation, to replay the shattering moments of final trauma, and, encompassing all of these postures, to comment darkly on art, on vision, and on the entrapment that constitutes human life. Magritte's most gripping pictures are not easy to look at, despite their wit. Their absurdity stings. They produce shocks and afterpains. These pains, these throbbings, stay with us; they have caused me to write and lecture on Magritte's work.

Beauty will be convulsive or it will not be.
André Breton

Surreal Sounds and Illicit Images

Imagine silence and a cold indigo sky with a pregnant cloud that lowers over a landscape of uncanny imagery. Unpredictably, the cloud bursts. Air and space fill with discordant sound, unintelligible words, perpetual motion that expends energy but takes objects nowhere. Torrents appear ready to cascade: slit bells and burning tubas, violins with bowties, great jagged boulders poised to smash, groaning bleeding falling birds, panes of splintered glass, cracking surfaces at the point of coming apart, severed body parts, loaves of tooth-shattering bread. And below this eerily fertile sky, against stretches of insipid sand, waves break incessantly, loud in their indifference.

Surrealism erupts into our space, even today, so many years after its birth between the world wars. It floods our ark of security. It retains its capacity to jar and unsettle us like an unexpected downpour, to thwart our plans and make us successively—or simultaneously—angry, irritable, bemused, tolerant, even merry. The world we had always recognized shifts, so that what we think ought to come next never does. We are discomforted and discomfited. The art, poetry, music of surrealism all strive not to lull but to intercept, not to entertain but to infuriate, not to soothe but to baffle, and to goad.

And yet, the intervening time since its inception has produced ironies of its own, so that to view or hear surrealist art or music from our current vantage point is also to sense a certain preciosity or false fervor. It is to meet the absurd with the sardonic. For us today, after Auschwitz, Hiroshima, Vietnam, Cambodia, Bosnia, Somalia, and a postmodern computer/audio/video technology that alters sound and image at will, the shock value of a sewing machine meeting an umbrella on a dissecting table has decrescendoed. What remains is a strident theatricality to which we must choose our response.

One possible anchor for the slippery origins of surrealism and its disjointed history is the appearance of André Breton's first *Manifesto of Surrealism* in 1924. Breton, disillusioned with Dada, that anarchic response of so many intellectuals and artists to the senseless carnage of World War I, saw the movement as capitulating gradually to institutionalism and as sloughing off its revolutionary warhead. He felt it necessary to supplant it with a notion he defined as permanently, incessantly defiant, namely, the "surreal," which he described as beyond all control of reason—as automatic, accidental, concerned utterly with chance and nonconformity, and with the marvelous and the absurd, as is the domain of dreams.

Surrealism, then, initially a profusion of sproutings from and critiques of Dada, advanced upon the scene of European culture. It can be viewed with hindsight as in part a prolonged but well-disguised reaction to war, a smarting counterattack, a revolution against the status quo that supposedly had caused the dislocations of these artists' youth. In the early 1930s, a number of its adherents, all associates of Magritte (among them Breton, Paul Éluard, Louis Aragon), briefly espoused Communism, but surrealist agendas meshed with other currents in European intellectual life as well, with trends in contemporary philosophy and psychology, particularly the advent and aura of psychoanalysis, structural linguistics, phenomenology, and existentialism.

Most fascinating of all, surrealism, with its slurring of the stops between illusion and reality, hallucination and perception, lent itself in highly differentiated ways to the diverse personalities of its cadre of devotees. Take, as an example, their varying attitudes toward the art of music. Breton distrusted music, and his distaste was shared by Giorgio de Chirico, who said, "One never knows what music is about. . . . There is no mystery in music. . . . [Music] is something one takes before the meal or after, but which is not a meal in itself" (quoted in Jean, 1980). Curiously, these sentiments may well have been acceptable to Freud, a major source of inspiration for the surrealists, for he found music the most unfruitful of all the arts for his own type of investigation. Such negative sentiments were, however, uncongenial to Magritte, who otherwise revered de Chirico, and to his circle of Belgian surrealists, who printed music in their publications, used

13

musical symbols in their paintings, and sponsored concerts. André Souris, composer, conductor, and member of this Brussels group, published with such friends of Magritte as Paul Nougé and Louis Scutenaire and under their auspices performed his aleatoric music. In fact, one evening in January of 1929, Souris conducted a concert of modernist works in a hall hung about with paintings by Magritte.

Magritte himself made dazzling use of musical symbols—the tuba, the disembodied scroll and pegs of a violin, or its strings alone, an uncanny gramophone, multitudinous slit spherical bells suspended in strange locations. He cut out of and into sheet music and overpainted it for his collage works. Furthermore, despite the stasis and silence pervading so much of his work, the suggestion of sound, if not precisely of music per se, is momentous there: even his lifeless, sometimes mutilated, birds betoken an absence of joy *as* music. He paints the crash of thunder, the thud of raindrops, the crackle of flames. And in shrill images like *The Secret Double* (*Le Double Secret*), 1927, in which a woman's skin is peeled away to reveal her insides filled with bells, or *The Listening Chamber* (*La Chambre d'écoute*), 1959 (fig. 1.2), where an enormous apple disturbingly fills an entire room, the notion Magritte conveys is that sound is absolutely primal and inescapable. His pictures elict a jangle of pleasure and repugnance and a recognition of the absurd.

We might recall here that the word *absurd* literally means "hard to hear." *Surdus* in Latin is "deaf" or "unwilling to listen," and Cicero used the expression *absurde canere* for "to sing jarringly, disharmoniously." So that to feel assaulted, to encounter a measure of disequilibrium, may be a sign that one is, in the case of surrealist art, truly listening (or looking)! As we ponder the mix of emotional and cognitive assonances and dissonances evoked by the works themselves, we may find ourselves brought to crises of Sartrean malaise or to spells of Rabelaisian delight, while at the same time we teeter on the precipice of chasms gouged by the grim realities of our late twentieth-century world.

Magritte, along with other surrealists who worked in the 1920s, 1930s, and in his case through World War II and even into the 1950s and 1960s, programmatically strove to disrupt what has always seemed and still seems a desideratum in the arts—namely, that deliciously smooth process whereby we allow ourselves to slip into, to become caught up in, an aesthetic experience—be it a particular work of visual art, music, or film. One might think, for example, of Buñuel's *Un Chien andalou* (1929), which is contemporaneous with Magritte's most brilliant early works and with musical pieces by the surrealist composers Varèse, Souris, and Poulenc. Surrealism disallows that utterly pleasurable, almost magical process by which we lose ourselves temporarily in a work, abandon ourselves to it unproblematically, and then return refreshed to our habitual modus operandi, somewhat more removed, more critical perhaps, more controlled. We expect that such states will alternate within us as we sit quietly in a concert hall, listening, or move through the galleries of a museum, looking.

The surrealist artist does not permit us this idiosyncratic, alternating flow of being, of merging imperceptibly with the experience and then pulling back from it. He refuses to play along with our relaxed familiarity, our sense that we have grasped the realms of image, sound, and verbal language. Rather, he plans aggressively to manipulate our closeness and distance to objects—and to ourselves—to challenge and repeatedly to thwart our presumedly unexamined assumptions. This is done with malice aforethought—the agenda being, in part, to assault our easy supposition that we know what we are doing when we visit a museum or attend a concert. To this, the surrealist artist says in part: I will shake you out of your complacency, and by doing so, by giving you a hard time, by making problems for you, I will rescue you from banality. I will push you over the brink into a new place from which you will have to figure out where to go and—very important—what to feel, or how to feel, what and whether it is even possible to feel. I am even perhaps going to give you a chance to encounter new perspectives on art and life more generally.

Thus, our wish to remain captive to art, to linger over some aspect, to feel attuned to it so that we can intuit and confidently expect what is coming next—all of this is strenuously denied us by the surrealist project. Again, however, it is done—successfully or not—with the purpose of opening new possibilities and liberating its audience from what has been taken as a stultifying and defunct tradition.

Of course, the surrealists never abandoned tradition. They played on and with it. Their project reminds me sometimes of a friend's little Jack Russell terrier, who, if you hold out a sock to him, will play with you fiercely, purposefully, highly aggressively, though harmlessly. Shaking frantically, he will keep trying to pull the sock out of your hand. He will growl agitatedly and never give up, yet, all the while, he will manage to convey the distinct

15

impression that he knows perfectly well that what he has in his mouth is not an actual rat!

Surrealism trades on our eternal thralldom to childhood, our refusal to abandon that early delicious sense of terror, which churns dream and reality into a froth of ecstasy, which brings exaggerated feelings of strength, even of omnipotence, and at the same time an awareness of abject helplessness. This delicious terror, I am certain, constitutes a quintessential pleasure afforded by surrealist art. Surrealism, as Donald Kuspit (1988) has pointed out, internalizes just enough convention to render resistance feasible—in the sense that for resistance to take place there must be something to push against. It is this recognition of revolution as a compromise between old and new that constitutes the most enduring contribution of surrealism. And a certain cheer, a certain hopefulness, may occasionally inhere—an implicit notion that change *is* indeed possible. In this sense, the whole movement can be seen as a last gasp of Romanticism, a set of transformations and transfigurations performed to demonstrate that life and art are inexhaustible, that they (and we) cannot be encompassed or eclipsed by banality. Even dark acts of violence, such as those articulated by Breton and painted by Magritte, are, on a manifest level, often intended to convey hope by demonstrating the possibility of freedom.

1. Magritte, *Girl Eating Bird*.

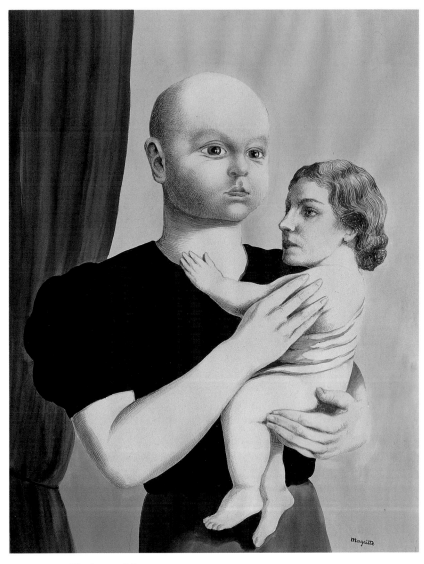

2. Magritte, *The Spirit of Geometry.*

3. Magritte, *Titanic Days*.

4. Magritte, *Dangerous Relationships*.

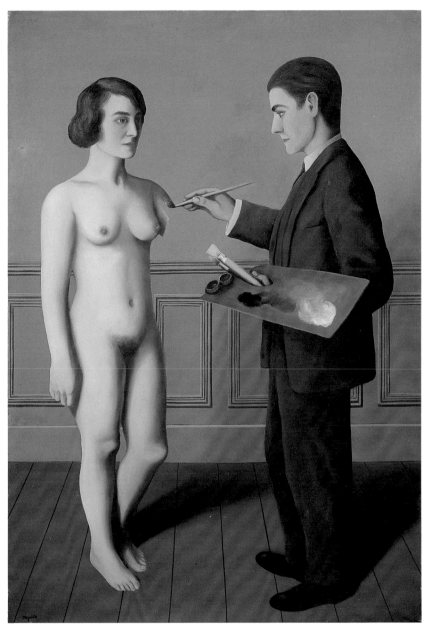

5. Magritte, *Attempting the Impossible*.

6. Magritte, *When the Hour Will Strike*.

7. Magritte, *The Human Condition*.

8. Magritte, *The Blank Signature*.

The eye is never satisfied with seeing; endless are the desires of the heart. *Gates of Repentance* (**Shaarei Teshuvah**)

Optical Appetites

Complex and prolific, René Magritte invented schemata for representing his own (and our own) intrapsychic conflicts in visual terms. These terms were consonant with but not merely parasitic on surrealism, the new movement in the arts that coincided historically with his artistically formative years and, importantly, with the emergence and dissemination of psychoanalysis.

Remarkable for having forged an unusual fit between his internal and external worlds, Magritte devised visual strategies for co-opting the philosophical preoccupations of his moment in history and used them to express the unacknowledged confusions that beset him and that are endemic to the human project of growing up—that is, of exchanging (and never completely) a child's for an adult's body and mind. Thus, while sketching links between the works and their maker, my greater concern is to emphasize the lines that stretch between these works and us, their contemporary beholders, lines that transverse the general realms of experience we share.

Magritte's existential puzzles concern life and art, words and pictures; they are highly conscious and sophisticated and at the same time related to primitive questions—to riddles that admit of no final answers. They concern massively defended puzzles about how women are different (and are not different) from men; whether and how good, protective mothers can abandon their children (a theme often conveyed by means of oral and aerial imagery around birds and eggs both in and out of nests and cages); how people can be here with us in the evening and then gone by morning (absent and present simultaneously in pictorial condensation);

how things living differ (and yet do not differ) from things dead; how important objects can appear small and insignificant (while others, when charged
with strong feeling, loom large); how looking differs from experiencing; how
art differs from life; how the same object that frightens and angers us at one
moment can seem funny or absurd the next; how the concrete can become
suddenly abstract and the abstract all too horribly concrete.

Because he functioned on such a high level, cognitively as well as artistically, and because the emotional impact of his paintings depends on parallels and perpendiculars between the lines of his own manifest and latent
themes (and those of others) and between these and the intellectual puzzles
of his time and ours—above all, because the ambiguities with which he
deals endure—the paintings themselves, at least the strongest of them,
reward reflective contemplation and an application of empathic skill and
cognitive mettle.

To imitate a gesture characteristic of the artist himself, we must disclaim
a historical frame while at the same time being bound by one: "This is not a
pipe!" To view images through psychoanalytic lenses that include an understanding of child development and trauma, especially the denial of loss, is
to engage with only one of many possible discourses. Yet psychoanalysis
does seem singularly apt here, in that many of the most trenchant of the
artist's works were painted during Freud's lifetime.

Preferring, as he often said, to preserve the *mystery* of his paintings,
Magritte chose—with great ambivalence, as we shall see—to think of himself as a kind of sorcerer, conjurer, or magician. In this connection, we
might ourselves attempt to conjure up his 1951 painting entitled *The Magician (Le Sorcier)*. There, he portrays himself as able, by means of additional
hands, simultaneously to pour wine, convey bread to his lips, and cut the
meat on his plate! Unlike those of the Hindu god Shiva, Magritte's additional limbs do not enable him to perform prodigious feats but merely allow
him to eat more rapidly. Thus, the image forces us to wonder how magic
might be connected with feeding and with taking in, with making external
substances part of the self by destroying them, with needing and wanting
more than one's two hands can manage, with never having enough. Surely
the mysteries of such a work, emanating as they do from unanswerable
riddles, stand fast against the ravages of any interpretation, psychoanalytic
or otherwise.

Moreover, I believe with Wolfenstein that, while Magritte's images surely do probe our capacity for tolerating epistemological uncertainty, emotional ambiguity, and the lure of forbidden knowledge, especially knowledge gained by forbidden *looking*, all these abstractions must be linked with the exigencies of development and the aftermath of childhood trauma.

With respect, for example, to Magritte's obsession with blocked looking, with blindness, as it were, and with invisibility, several thoughts come to mind. Recurrently, we note Magritte's radical elimination of the face in his imagery, his painted heads that are covered up or turned away, the eyes that are closed or occluded (as by an apple) or transparent (as in his 1929 painting entitled *The False Mirror* [*Le Faux Miroir*])—portrayals in every case of an inability to see or to be seen. For Freud, blindness (as in Oedipus) is interpretable as the symbolic equivalent of castration, this being in turn the punishment visited upon those who seek, desire, and consummate an incestuous intimacy with the mother. The compensation, however, for this self-inflicted punishment (as in the fantasied renunciations of puberty) is not the prize of the mother per se but rather another woman like her, her literal replacement. For Magritte, perhaps, we can see this replacement as taking the form in both life and art of Georgette Berger, the woman he saw for the first time in his youth just after his mother had died and who became, after he married her, his sole female companion—his lover, model, the woman to whom he remained attached until the moment of his own death. In his representations of her on canvas, she became deeply implicated, as we shall see, in his conflicts over looking.

Recent studies of trauma in childhood and adolescence report needs that may develop for extreme closeness to one person to the exclusion of others and even the propensity for early marriage, as well as the constriction and inhibition of affect (a kind of defensive blindness) due to fears of being overwhelmed by intense emotion (Greenberg and van der Kolk, 1987; Pynoos and Nader, 1990). All this is supremely relevant for Magritte, whose daily life was highly routinized and who chose, like Bluebeard, not to open the door to his own past. Pynoos and Nader (1990) speak also of the disparity between such constriction and a rich creative capacity in some individuals, an observation also strikingly apt for Magritte. These authors suggest in particular that children who have suffered parental suicide may be at special risk for self-destructive behaviors, a risk often warded off by the maintenance of rigidly predictable behaviors (this may be present in Magritte's stubborn clinging to conventional means of pictorial representation rather than exploring the more radical unrealities of modern abstraction). These limitations bespeak a species of willed blindness, a protective failure to see.

Likewise, consider the hide-and-seek figured by his attitude toward eyes and face, as in *The Son of Man* (*Le Fils de l'homme*) of 1964, where just one eye peeks out from behind a large green apple that obscures both the other eye and all other facial features of that inscrutable, emblematic bowler-hatted man we have come to know as the artist's ubiquitous alter ego. Greenberg and van der Kolk (1987) describe in detail a posttraumatic patient who, artistically gifted like Magritte, also sought symbolic invisibility as a result of the particular trauma she had suffered. Richly overdetermined, this game of concealment and revelation, so highly charged in those who have suffered sudden tragedy, harks back for all of us to early childhood and to the first games we played with our mothers to establish the safety of our world. These experiences often begin with the mother putting her hands over her eyes and thus "hiding" teasingly from the baby, always unexpectedly to reappear with a smile. They progress to the stage when the young toddler him- or herself runs off and disappears (often to explore the world) and thus "hides" temporarily, intentionally or not, from the (sometimes frantic) mother. In effect, what is passively endured becomes actively pursued, and in every variant on these playful interludes, a minidrama of loss and restoration, of danger and safety, is enacted, experienced, and joyfully survived.

To "fight the face" (as Martin Bergmann [1993] once put it) is to avert the eyes; it is to conceal one's own gaze while refusing to return the gaze of the other. It is, moreover, to dread the consequences of one's own aggression (as well as, secondarily, the aggression of the other). Avoidance too, we recall, belongs among the earliest and remains among the most primitive of defenses, the one available to even the youngest of infants. Thus, to eliminate the face is to engage problematically with (while at the same time fleeing) both sexuality and aggression. These paradoxical themes, overlaid with a hyperintellectual philosophical doubt and with satire, and often displaced from the human body to inanimate objects, recur throughout the oeuvre of Magritte.

Returning now to our metaphoric museum of the mind, received psychoanalytic wisdom would probably derive the pictures we discover there from internalized primary objects (that is to say, from mother and father) by means of a proliferating labyrinth of increasingly remote displacements:

the oedipal triangle, in other words, as originative. But to say this would be to downplay the shaping of our inner worlds by the arts and culture. It would be to minimize the role of visual templates that vivify not only mental imagery but theoretical concepts as well. Psychoanalysis, wedded to a transhistorical, highly abstract taxonomy, all too often shortchanges the cultural framing and reframing of its own core concepts. It tends to elevate, unproblematically, word over image. However, even so-called transparent psychoanalytic constructs draw nourishment from, are dwarfed or expanded by, specific images—images that may be colorful, dramatic, and sensuous.

Magritte makes us know that when we look at a painting we are looking at ourselves, just as, to make a musical analogy, John Cage enforces a silence upon us that makes us hear all the sounds of our own bodies. (Think of Cage's *4'33"* of 1952, the first of his works to employ that technique.) Likewise, when we gaze at a Magritte, it returns that gaze: it bites us back. In *The Month of the Grape Harvest* (*Le Mois des vendanges*, fig. 1.3), 1959, for example, a bevy of bowler-hatted men looks inside a window yet simultaneously out at us, thus drawing us in (E. H. Spitz, 1991). Seeing and being seen, they remain anonymous—and the French *mois*, "month," puns on the splitting of the self (*moi*) into many "me's." A harvest for the *mouth* (grapes) shifts to a harvest for the *eyes* (material for intense looking). This is, however, a substitution that can never quite work. Fond relatives may have told us that they "love[d] us so much they could simply eat us up," but we know as adults what we were not so entirely sure of as children— namely, that eyes can never do precisely what mouths and teeth can do. Nevertheless, the conflictual nature of such thoughts, that is, the equation of looking and devouring, must at the same time be suppressed. In this vein, Magritte's multiplicity of gazing eyes reminds us of the multiplicity of writhing snakes that crown the head of the gorgon Medusa and both warn of and ward off castration (see Freud, 1922).

This eye-mouth equation functions, we shall see, as a central metaphor for Magritte, who fantasized that he had seen his mother's corpse immediately after her suicide—and, in fact, it pervades our Western way of understanding. Mouth and eye. ("You are the apple of my eye"; "you look good enough to eat.") A painting such as this forces us to behold ourselves as beholders. Mirroring the gaze of the bowler-hatted men, we are denied an objective position outside the work of art. Confronted with the enforced splitting of our own subjectivity, we must observe ourselves being observed by the objects of our gaze—an experience, eerie and unsettling, that matters to Magritte's personal project, to surrealism more broadly conceived, and ultimately to the project of art itself.

Magritte's repetitive imagery constitutes a pictorial swirl, the analogue of that nebula of words which envelops analyst and patient. Engulfed by it, we may find ourselves at sea, awash in an undecidable flow of image, idea, fantasy, memory, percept, concept, and event. Gazing at his paintings induces wishes for something stable to catch on to lest we drown—a feeling Magritte provokes and simultaneously defends against by clinging to external objects. But something untoward has always happened to these objects—something violent and surprising. The paintings also create desires for something to *move*—for something to happen, rather than for things just to stand still, the absence of a future perspective being a symptom common to victims of childhood trauma (Terr, 1991). For the victim, there is no future time, no confident expectation, only arrest and stasis.

Stillness and immobility of forms signal a guarded stance, as if some potential action is being strenuously arrested. Transfixedness into hard outlines and frozen shapes conspires to achieve a visual realm from which temporal sequence has been banished. When, therefore, deeply buried affects do erupt, they blaze with intensity. A 1938 painting actually called *Time Transfixed* (*La Durée poignardée*) seems to instantiate the need to stave off conscious awareness of, and perhaps thus reexposure to, an overpowering memory. It suggests those vivid moments in dreams when we feel desperate to escape some danger but, despite all our efforts, remain immobilized. Freud attributed this sensation to the presence of intrapsychic conflict so intense that the opposing forces of desire and defense are evenly matched, and impasse results.

Time Transfixed portrays a toy engine going nowhere, suspended midair in a permanently disfunctional hearth. Nevertheless, it casts a shadow and belches smoke. In the eternal present of this image, narrative sequencing is short-circuited. All history, including the psychosexual, is annihilated: anal expulsion, conflated with phallic penetration, in the form of the toy train, is arrested. The candlesticks on the mantlepiece are candleless; the fireplace emits no warmth. The result: an astonishing portrait of intense inner conflict with strong affective links to other Magrittes despite alterations in manifest content. Rendered according to pictorial rules long hallowed in Western art, rules of perspective and foreshortening, pictures such as this both parody and preserve that representational tradition. Thus, Magritte manages to have his cake and eat it, to affirm and to deny—as he does in a related painting of 1955 called *Where Euclid Walked* (*Les Promenades d'Euclide*, fig. 1.4), where a conical tower and a street vanishing into the distance are paralleled with one another—seemingly indistinguishable shapes, but one figures a presence, whereas the other denotes an absence. In this manner, Magritte's objects are flotsam on waves of doubt, ambiguity, absurdity, and what Patrick Waldberg (1965) called "panic laughter."

At once attractive and repellent, they comment brilliantly on the topic of oral aggression. *The Explanation* (*L'Explication*) of 1952 recalls Karl Abraham's 1924 psychoanalytic treatise on oral erotism, which distinguished two successive stages in infancy—the oral incorporative stage (sucking) and the oral sadistic stage (biting). Reading from left to right, Magritte's painting depicts three large objects placed on a foreground table: a carrot, a black glass bottle, and what appears to be a black bottle turning into a carrot. Beyond them the hills and sky seem indistinct and far away. Thus a typical surrealist theme, metamorphosis, has been exploited not only to challenge the relations between animate/vegetable (carrotlike) things and inanimate/mineral (bottlelike) things but to return us to our most primitive relations with the breast of the mother—the breast which gives or withholds and which a newborn infant first sucks and later attempts to bite—the good and bad breast of Kleinian description. In Magritte's presentation, if we were to bite the bottle, we might get a mouthful of glass, whereas if we were to try to drink the carrot, we would choke.

Frustration persists to another developmental level, for, if we interpret the image as a convergence of male and female symbolism, what we discover is a lurid, mesmerizing hybrid with dubious power to provide any pleasure whatsoever. Thus the very notion of "explanation" is itself parodied by this painting; if this is clarification, Magritte implies, what, pray tell, is obfuscation?

Among his other works devoted to the theme of oral erotism, perhaps the most ghastly is *Girl Eating Bird* (*Jeune fille mangeant un oiseau*), a motif of which Magritte painted versions in 1927 and in 1946. This picture, to which we shall return, portrays a little girl calmly devouring a live bird (plate 1).

Margaret Mahler's (1968) notion of *infantile symbiosis* (the fused interdependent bonding of infant with mother) and D. W. Winnicott's (1965) concept of *good-enough mothering* are expanded and at the same time taken to task by a painting Magritte first called *Motherhood* but then retitled *The Spirit of Geometry* (*L'Esprit de la géométrie*). There are two versions, painted in 1936 or 1937 (see plate 2), and according to Sarah Whitfield (1992), it is not certain which came first. In both, the transposition of heads from one body to another creates an unsettling psychological equation by suggesting that a mother's dependence on her child may be coequal with the child's reliance on her.

As so often in Magritte's work, the painful laughter evoked by the image creates a distance that protects against its disorienting effects and the unwelcome truth it proclaims. As if to underscore this distance and inscribe it within the image per se, Magritte directs the gazes of the two figures away from each other and away, as well, from us. A coldness pervades the canvas, a forbidding air that contrasts dramatically with the tender tradition of mother-child images in Western art—with the venerable Christian cult of the Madonna. And as that tradition is evoked, the reversal of heads takes on an added meaning, for, with Mary and baby Jesus, it is the mother who must one day watch as her son dies a horrible and untimely death; the faraway gaze so often depicted on her face thus betokens her foreknowledge of this loss. Magritte's image, by contrast (but also in continuity), signifies an entirely different sort of self-sacrifice. In the artist's own life, it was he, the son, who had to witness and bear the unforeseen demise of his mother. The curtain drawn back to the left in the painting is, as in so many of Magritte's pictures, a conventional prop but somehow in this context especially unsettling and malapropos.

The Flood (*L'Inondation*) of 1928 presents us with the spectacle of a woman nude from the waist down, her upper parts merging into the sky. The lower, sexual parts of her body are accompanied by a phallic horn, a great tuba, one of Magritte's favorite images, and by a detached arm that appears incongruously heavy and muscular, masculine in size and proportion. The scene is set against a watery background in which a building and tree seem partially submerged in the distance. This image, striking and repugnant, not only dehumanizes the woman by robbing her of any presence other than as a sexual object but also seems to illustrate the Freudian notion of female body as lack, as castrated, and as in need of some appendage or completion by a male-coded form.

Yet another psychoanalytic notion, that of the *primal scene*, springs vividly to life in a 1928 painting Magritte first called *Fear of Love* (*La*

Peur d'amour) before changing it to *Titanic Days* (*Les Jours gigantesques*, plate 3). Concretizing the typical childhood fantasy that sexual intercourse consists of exciting and potentially dangerous acts perpetrated by a physically stronger father against an unwilling, protesting mother, the male figure here seems pasted on the woman's flesh so that her push cannot prevail against him. At the same time, however, with typical ambivalence, Magritte renders the image so that the male figure, entirely contained within the shape of the female, is, as it were, controlled by her. While his face is positioned as if to lunge greedily at her left breast, she angrily pushes him away. A rape scene then perhaps, but also a poignant portrait of the hungry adult male desperately seeking what he craved in infancy, and being denied. Formally, the image recalls a jigsaw puzzle piece, a symbol associated with childhood perplexity. Thus the riddle of parental relations, of adult heterosexuality, is here pictorially captured. The male and female figures themselves, glued permanently together, instantiate the enigma of human sexuality that cannot be unstuck.

This phenomenon, then, of an image *unwittingly* enlivening a given theoretical construct or calling it into question occurs ubiquitously not only in the labyrinths of Magritte but in the realm of the arts more generally and in the psychiatric consulting room, where patients' vivid word-pictures often serve to reanimate the abstractions of theory. In surrealism as a movement, we see and hear attacks on complacency and elitism. And, turning back to Freud (1900, 5:553), we remember the so-called ghoulish ghosts from the underworld of the *Odyssey* who, as he put it, awaken to new life each time they taste blood. Thus Magritte, in his boldest pictures, teaches us to rethink our cherished shibboleths while at the same time he visualizes them for us and affords us a consummate arena for applying and testing them.

No amount of telling seems ever to do justice. . . .
There are never enough words or the right words,
there is never enough time or the right time, and never
enough listening or the right listening. **Dori Laub**

Testimony through Painting

Regina Bertinchamps Magritte committed suicide by drowning
when her eldest son, René, was thirteen and a half years old. Yet,
as Wolfenstein (1973) has taught us, the trauma persists in his art
like "an ever-bleeding wound." Young, sensitive, ambivalently
attached to a mother who had made previous attempts against her
own life, so that, shortly before the suicide, her husband had
taken to locking her up in her bedroom at night (Sylvester, 1992),
the future artist was at the time very unlikely to have been able to
mourn, psychic shock and a host of personal and developmental
factors interfering, as Wolfenstein (1969) and Terr (1991) have
described, with gradual healing. That is to say, he was probably
unable to undergo the slow process Freud describes in "Mourning
and Melancholia" (1917), to relinquish the beloved object piece-
meal over time, grieving over each fresh reminder of her absence,
each object, each spot, each trace associated with her. Rather,
indicative perhaps of the severity of his conflict and his need to
keep it at bay, Magritte assiduously avoided all conversation about
his mother's death, even with his wife, who served, it seems, in
the role of a replacement object, for he kept her near him and
did not wish to leave her side. In *Memory* (*La Mémoire*) of 1945
(fig. 1.5) and its earlier versions, Magritte quotes de Chirico's
1914 *Song of Love*, an image he encountered with a shock of uncanny recognition in the mid-1920s, just before his own mature
style of painting was to develop.

Surveying forty years of his paintings, one senses a driven, repetitive quality—emblematic of conflicts that continue to seethe
and boil. Sophisticated surrealist agendas fuse with an archaic

inner splitting: a young person's need and wish and hope, perhaps, for his mother's return and the implacable intellectual knowledge that she could, in fact, never return. Through Wolfenstein's lenses (1966, 1969, 1973, 1974, MS), we can see the disavowed anger, rage at being abandoned, a subsequent denial of rage, and its transformation into mockery. We hear bitter laughter that restrains tears. We witness a painting project that restages and denies the trauma that induced it.

Even the horrors of murder may be invoked to belie the shame of suicide. This defense surfaces in a painting entitled *The Menaced Assassin* (*L'Assassin menacé*) of 1927, which purveys, as do so many of Magritte's pictures, the aura of a nightmare. Suzi Gablik (1976) and others have made much of the influence on Magritte during the 1920s, the time he painted this image, of a series of popular novels detailing the adventures of Fantomâs, a diabolical criminal who is never captured—and of the realm of detective novels and silent films and of Lautréamont's *Les Chants de Maldoror*, a mid-nineteenth-century novel in verse which trumpets the delights of a bizarre and brutal irrationality and became a standard resource for other surrealist artists, including Breton and Max Ernst.

Pervaded with a gray sense of the sinister, Magritte's *Menaced Assassin* unmistakably suggests the scene of a mysterious crime. A woman, her head and neck severed from her body, is stretched on a chaise longue, a prop we shall see again. She bleeds from the mouth, which is interesting in light of Magritte's ongoing preoccupation with oral aggression and the mechanism he occasionally employs of projecting that sadism onto the woman against whom it is initially directed by the child (see *Girl Eating Bird*, plate 1). Tying this image to a later one entitled *The Rape* (*Le Viol*) (fig. 1.6), which exists in several versions, we may interpret the bleeding from the mouth here as displaced genital bleeding, the woman seen as a victim of rape, a casualty of some horrible sexual crime. With her head and body separated by a swath of cloth, she has been deprived of any mental capacity (as also in *Collective Invention* [*L'Invention collective*] of 1935 [fig. 1.7], where the woman has been given the brain of a fish). Furthermore, her eyes are closed so that, although we can observe her at our leisure, she cannot return our gaze. She is, in effect, thoroughly disempowered.

The white cloth that separates her head from her torso can be read, perhaps, as a reference to the white nightgown Magritte (in his one recorded recitation of the story of his mother's suicide [Scutenaire, 1947]) said he

27

saw when Regina's corpse was retrieved from the river. In detaching the woman's head from her body here, Magritte reminds us of his claim, in the narrative recorded by Scutenaire, that his drowned mother's face was covered by her gown, so that only her headless body was visible to him. Through a window, in a scene reminiscent of *The Month of the Grape Harvest* (fig. 1.3), three intense male faces stare into the room, reminding us that Magritte and his two young brothers all lived at home and all suffered maternal abandonment at the time of the drowning. Their faces gaze fixedly at the scene before them, which is also before us. Again, they mirror our gaze and place us willy-nilly into the scene with them as mesmerized and bewildered voyeurs.

Spatially, this painting evokes those early Netherlandish pictures by Pieter de Hooch and Jan Vermeer where one partially enclosed area gives out on another, which leads to a third, and so on. The one-point perspectival composition, however, also stimulates eerie associations to the religious paintings of the high Renaissance. Cold, lifelessly colored, and geometric, each compartment conveys in visual terms the discrete, hyperrational, but unintelligible component of a dream sequence. Robert Liebert's (1983) brilliant analysis of Michelangelo's *Doni Tondo* springs to mind as an analogy here. Liebert likens each spatial unit of the painting to a temporal unit of a dream and to a different developmental and dynamic conflict in the artist's life. Gripped by this juxtaposition of strange objects and inexplicable actions and by the fact that each figure occupies a separate space and none makes eye contact with any of the others or with us, we catch from the picture a sense of malevolence and claustrophobia. Under the calm, carefully painted grays of this canvas steams a cauldron ready to explode. The composition also suggests a stage set where the director has suddenly bellowed, "Freeze!" or the game children sometimes play called Statues, where, at the height of exuberant activity, everything suddenly stops dead.

Each image both cries and suppresses (numbs) its cries. Sometimes this is effected by mockery, as in *Collective Invention* (fig. 1.7), a painting of a reversed mermaid which Magritte called his "solution to the problem of la mer" (mer/mère:mother/sea). Here, as Wolfenstein points out (MS), the bereft child asks the mother why she was so stupid as to believe she was a fish who could breathe under water. In depicting her this way, the artist also degrades her sexually, turning her into what has been called a "practical man's mermaid" and denying his own erotic longings toward her by portraying her as repugnant. The fish face of this mermaid has a glazed eye that stares reproachfully at its beholders, so that we too are implicated in her misery. Her belly is slightly distended; could it be the beginnings of an aborted pregnancy, one wonders, a motherhood prematurely stopped—in any case, a strange life violently arrested?

Each painting similarly stages a battle between mind and body, memory and desire. The conflict between the need to remember and the longing to forget is concretized in *The Daydreams of a Solitary Walker* (*Les Rêveries d'un promeneur solitaire*) of 1926, where a bowler-hatted man looks away from a naked, floating, strangely hermaphroditic corpse. Here we see the temporal metaphor (*I want to put the past behind me*) translated into a spatial one. Dangerous looking, forbidden looking, blocked looking, and looking away—all can be seen as relating in part to Magritte's presumed fantasy about the trauma and the aggressive role he may have wished to play in it and thus feared he had actually played. The rigid, deathlike pose of both figures and especially the hermaphroditic appearance of the corpse also suggest a deep identification of the artist with the drowned mother. Thus, the imagery of this painting can be linked with Magritte's interest in the mythical drowned boy Icarus, who appears in the title of another of his paintings, *The Childhood of Icarus* (*L'Enfance d'Icare*) of 1960, and both river and bridge may be read as direct quotations from the Scutenaire account of the mother's suicide in the river Sambre. An atmospheric softness envelops this image, playing against the sharp outlines of its principal shapes. As in so many of the finest examples of his work, Magritte portrays the altered state of dreams.

The temptation to look versus the impulse to turn away is evoked by *The Glass House* (*La Maison de verre*) of 1939 (fig. 1.8), which suggests that, if one cannot relinquish the past, one is condemned to look in both directions at once, to live in a state where psychic borders are transparent and frangible. This painting, as titled, resonates with a particularly intrusive kind of narcissistic relation that can obtain between a mother and child. An analytic patient described it as follows: "I lived in a glass house into which my mother could look at any time. In a glass house, however, you cannot conceal anything without giving yourself away, except by hiding it under the ground. And then you cannot see it yourself either" (Miller, 1981, p. 21). Thus, in looking away, the figure hides also from himself—

a recurrent theme in the paintings of Magritte. Apropos of the image of glass, Wolfenstein reports the case of a fifteen-year-old girl whose mother died suddenly and who felt, after her initial grief, a sense of frozenness and emptiness. "A glass wall," she said, seemed to descend between her and all that was going on in the present (Wolfenstein and Kliman, 1965, p. 71). One thinks too of the "bell jar" of Sylvia Plath.

Control versus fragmentation is conveyed by *Dangerous Relationships* (*Les Liaisons dangereuses*) of 1936 (plate 4). In this disjointed image, its title the same as that of the intimate and wicked 1782 *roman à lettres* by Pierre Choderlos de Laclos, a nude woman with downcast, possibly closed eyes holds a mirror that faces toward the viewer of the painting but reflects her own headless and legless body in profile, in reduced scale, and turned in the opposite direction from her face. At a quick glance, the buttocks seem to replace the belly, so that the impression given is that of a pregnant woman. Early on in the Magrittes' marriage, Georgette became pregnant (see Sylvester, 1992, p. 48; and E. H. Spitz [citing Wolfenstein], 1985, pp. 85–86). On suffering a miscarriage, she became ill (so ill that the couple decided to renounce all future attempts at generativity); hence, per- haps, the dangerousness of the liaisons mentioned in the title. By the time this painting was made, that decision must have been rapidly becoming irreversible.

The mirror, turned outward toward the viewer, reflects the woman's body to us as our own—an impossibility, since, in that case, we would have to be facing away from the painting. In its fragmentation and reassem- blage, it thus creates an incongruous image with bisexual aspects, such as the heavy brown hair which, falling below the figure's face, can be read simultaneously as a shaggy beard. Hermaphroditism is, not insignificantly, a recurrent and traceable theme throughout the oeuvre of Magritte; see, for example, *The Spirit of Geometry* (plate 2), and both *The Flood* and *The Daydreams of a Solitary Walker*, mentioned above.

Twisted, bending over with averted eyes in a posture closer to shame than pride, the figure in *Dangerous Relationships* betokens a traumatized victim by virtue of her dismembered body and in her aspect as one who closes her eyes, who cannot look steadfastly into the future. She recalls that scene from the eighth circle of Dante's *Inferno* in which sinners who pridefully try by forbidden arts to peer into the future are punished by having their heads turned backward on their bodies, so that the stream of their tears falls down between their buttocks.

Focusing on the awkwardness and discomfort of this image, Mary Ann Caws (1989) has pointed out that its mismatching pieces (in terms of both scale and position) display the division of woman against herself, her enforced identity as a mere sight for the delectation of others, and her knowledge of always being watched and thus of never enjoying the experience of being whole. Dismembered and reassembled by the male artist, the model is devoid of autonomy. At the same time, however, in holding these distortions up to us she is portrayed as being on some level complicitous with them. The female body parts, especially the thighs and buttocks but also the hair, breast, and fingers, possess a sensuality that is in a sense heightened by their detachment from the troublesome problematics of a mind. Thus, a frank eroticism emanates from this painting. In this way, Magritte both teases and troubles its beholders, male and female.

The mirror—time-honored symbol in Western painting of *vanitas*, redolent of death, a *memento mori*—reminds us of Freud's (1914) tendentious description of narcissism in beautiful women. Such women, Freud declared, "love [themselves] with an intensity comparable to that of the man's love for them. Nor does their need lie in the direction of loving, but of being loved. . . . The importance of this type of woman for the erotic life of mankind is to be rated very high" (p. 89). Although Magritte's model does not, contrary to the prevalent tradition of such images in Western art (Titian, Velásquez, Picasso, and endless others), gaze into the mirror at herself, she nonetheless clearly presents herself to us as the object of our gaze; we are, that is, to behold her. Thus, a hostility with complex roots emanates from the image—a double hostility directed against both the subject of the painting and its beholder. Closing her eyes, the woman holds up the mirror to us, displaying something, but not everything. She gives and withholds, acquiesces and refuses. Indeed, she *con*fuses. And perhaps above all it is the confusion of the image that spellbinds us, mirroring to us our own disavowed confusions, against which we erect idealized façades of integrity, autonomy, and perfection.

Like all Magritte's finest paintings, this one returns us to the scene of childhood—to a time when we saw our mothers as alternately frustrating and facilitating, welcoming and rejecting, returning and departing. Significantly, the eyes of the figure see nothing; shut within her divided world, she is only superficially available. Beyond the sensuous surface, she is gone. Beyond holding up her trick mirror in our faces, she does not care to occupy herself with us at all. Perhaps the dangerous liaison referred to in the title is

31

between her and us, as well as between her and a male consort, or between her different aspects—aspects that can be fitted together only by an act of violence. Or, perhaps, by art. But, in that case, art itself becomes a violent act. And this is, as we shall see, an ongoing vexation for Magritte.

The terrifying inscrutability of mothers and of women more generally is conveyed by *The Rape* (fig. 1.6), where Magritte, by superimposing nude body on face (or face on nude body), reveals (as Jacques Lacan has pointed out) the ubiquitous operation of desire at the level of the gaze. The point here is that since under normal circumstances only the face of a woman (mother) is naked and visible, while her body is hidden by her clothing, it is her face that must carry the allure of what is not seen: that is to say, desire is projected upward onto the face. Simultaneously, I believe, the image can be read as nuanced with associations to infantile experience, for, held by its mother and nursing at her breast, the baby gazes into her countenance and conflates its sensual and perceptual experience of her in a kind of *coanaesthesia* (R. Spitz, 1965) which can be at once passive and aggressive.

Further, the image richly evokes schematic drawings by very young children, whose human figures are ovals that stand simultaneously for face and body, the four limbs drawn as emerging from one combined form. Consider the so-called tadpole figures (Golomb, 1992), which are drawn, with variations, by young children cross-culturally and present a fascinating paradox closely related both to Magritte's image here and to his larger project. For, if small children are perception-bound—that is to say, prisoners of their senses—they should logically draw what they *see*, but clearly they do not. Furthermore, since they can accurately name—that is, refer verbally—to many body parts that never appear in their tadpole pictures, it would be equally false to say they draw what they *know*. To explain this discrepancy between pictorial and verbal performance, Rudolf Arnheim, explorer par excellence of art and perception, suggests that the tadpole be seen *not* as an inferior representation derived from immature reasoning or performance error but as a graphic schema that *simplifies* percept and memory in accordance with the bounds of a novice graphic vocabulary.

To be aware of this developmental stage is to interpret Magritte's image as more than an unmasking of the erotic male gaze at a woman's face. It is to sense something *in addition:* namely, that its uncanny queasiness is bred in part from overlays of earlier moments, that it evokes those first tentative efforts to represent the human figure in graphic terms—a momentous effort, we might presume, for children who will grow up to become visual artists.

Thus, the image condenses a temptation to merge and to regress with a powerful imperative to ward off that temptation, to fight it by attacking it at its source, to insist with strenuous hostility on sharp boundaries, on the maintenance of differentiation and distinction.

This painting and many others also evoke, in their play with revealing and concealing, one of the earliest games of childhood: "peek-a-boo," which, as discussed earlier, appears first in a passive and later in an active form. As Freud (1920) understood and taught in his famous passage on the *fort-da* game in *Beyond the Pleasure Principle*, such games are classic vehicles for enabling children to master loss and to bear separation.

Closely related to *The Rape* and to *Dangerous Relationships*, *The Eternally Obvious* (*L'Evidence éternelle*) of 1930 is a portrait of Magritte's wife in which her body has been divided into five segments, each framed separately with a few inches of space intervening. Taken as a whole, the image plays on the above-mentioned surrealist game of the "exquisite corpse" and commits aggression symbolically once again against the woman whose armless (disarmed) body is carved in pieces. Sexuality is of moment here, for in simultaneously arousing and repelling the viewer, the image figures a perverse eroticism—a realm of cruel pleasure, not tenderness.

If one looks closely at the arrangement of the pieces as they have been mounted on plexiglass in the Menil Collection (an arrangement, however, that may not reflect precisely the artist's original alignment), one notices that an invisible plumb line connects them, that an imaginary vertical relates the disparate body parts so that the whole does, as it were, hang together. The presence of this invisible plumb line serves here, as we have seen so often in Magritte's work, to connect what has been disconnected, to affirm what has been denied. The model sports, moreover, despite her dismemberment, an enigmatic smile, and just one of her eyes (the left) is visible in its entirety; likewise, only the left nipple is in full view; thus, as in *The Rape*, an equation between these body parts is implied.

When these works succeed, they trace patterns that etch themselves into the soft stuff of our minds and remain imprinted there as permanent templates for future experiences in life or art. But Magritte doubts his own enterprise. He calls into question the efficacy of his work, its power to restore and preserve. He undercuts its role, its apparent sorcery, as in a Pygmalion image called *Attempting the Impossible* (*Tentative de l'impossible*) of 1928 (plate 5), where he portrays himself in the dubious act of bringing a woman (again, his young wife) to life. The two figures, though posed face to face, avoid eye contact—as is usual in Magritte. Feature by feature they resemble one another: their serious expressions, straight noses, identically colored hair, well-defined chins, the slightly mannish stance of the model (even more mannish in an unfinished stage of the painting), all betoken the bonds of identification we notice between Magritte and his female figures. Aggression, along with hermaphroditism, enters in here as well: the active male with both arms intact and his brushes extended maintains hegemony over the passive one-armed female, who, though posed upright, possesses little volition and is as independent of action as a drowned mermaid or a floating corpse. The artist, therefore, can paint the woman accurately; he can portray, represent, re-envision, even actually re-member her; he cannot, however, breathe life into her static limbs.

Doubt also invades *Perspective: Mme Récamier by David* of 1951 (fig. 1.9), where, as we shall see, he discredits the project of portraiture, the task par excellence of preserving the memory of the dead through art.

Repeatedly, the tragedy of maternal suicide has been linked causatively to features of Magritte's art. This central story is condensed in a painting called exactly that. *The Central Story* (*L'Histoire centrale*) of 1928 displays a triad of mysterious forms that engage us: a large silent tuba, a sturdy valise, and a heavy-set woman, her face veiled by an opaque white cloth, her strangely masculine arm reaching toward her throat. Gazing at this canvas, I have pondered its links with *The Menaced Assassin*, *The Discovery of Fire*, in which a tuba burns but is not destroyed, and *The Flood*. In each case, the mammoth instrument emerges, and strains from the Requiem Mass fill my ears: "Tuba mirum, spargens sonum. . ." Magritte was raised in Catholic Belgium, but his painted world is silent. A suicide has no place in Paradise. Magritte's feelings toward religion were clearly negative by adulthood; how derisively he plays upon the notion of Resurrection, elevating every sort of odd object from bread to stone and situating it nonchalantly in the sky! Over a dozen times between 1929 and 1931 (Whitfield, 1992), he covered entire canvases with absolutely nothing but an azure cloud-laden sky to which his close friend and mentor Paul Nougé gave the title, *The Curse* (*La Malédiction*).

Curiously, the account of the suicide he told as an adult to his friend and biographer Scutenaire is not consistent with newspaper stories that appeared at the time of the event. Printed sources in Charleroi, Belgium, state that in late February 1912, at about four one morning, Mme Magritte disappeared from her family home in nearby Châtelet (Sylvester, 1978). About two weeks later, on March 12, at eleven in the morning, her corpse was recovered from the local river. Magritte claimed to have seen and recognized her drowned body immediately after the suicide. The journal report suggests that this would have been highly unlikely.

Scutenaire's text (1947), which Wolfenstein (1973, 1974) and others (Terr, 1987; Viederman, 1987) assumed to be accurate, relates that Magritte was roused in the middle of the night—an experience luminously and dramatically captured in an image entitled *The Empire of Lights* (*L'Empire des lumières*), which exists in more than twenty versions in both oil and gouache produced by the artist between 1949 and 1964 (Sylvester, 1992). In these pictures, day and night converge in an electrified house, a stunning metaphor for that pivotal moment in life when everything goes terribly, unpredictably awry. Magritte's youngest brother, according to this story, slept in his mother's room. It was he who awoke and realized she was missing. He alerted the other family members who searched the house for her in vain and, following her footprints to a bridge over the local river, discovered her body, her nightgown wrapped over her face.

This narrative, taken as memory rather than fantasy, forms the basis for persuasive psychoanalytical readings of Magritte's imagery. If it is mere fantasy or distortion, an erroneous tale, how can we make sense of its explanatory power? How shall we account for the ubiquitous conflicts over looking, the white cloths and nightgowns, the transpositions of heads and missing faces, the hidings and spyings, the multiple bodily distortions and violations to women in his paintings? One thinks, for example, of versions of *Philosophy in the Boudoir* (*La Philosophie dans la boudoir*) of 1947 (fig. 1.10), a headless body of a woman metamorphosing into a white nightdress—or is it the other way around? And of the decapitated female form on a beach in *When the Hour will Strike* (*Quand l'heure sonnera*) of 1964 (plate 6). A gap opens here, and shadows fall between event and image, history and fiction. But the dilemma is not peculiar to Magritte. Rather, it is an intensification of a problem endemic to all studies of life and art—namely, the problematic move from private inner space to the domain of public knowledge. And even to state this dichotomy is to miss the public aspect that inheres in Magritte's own retrospective statement to a friend who was also a biographer and the inherent formal constraints and margins of error that inhere in any newspaper story.

Wolfenstein's own death having preceded Sylvester's work, she never grappled with the juxtaposition of the two narratives about the suicide, and the discrepancy between them does seem to matter. Or does it? If we balk at labeling one account "true" and the other "false," would we be ready to call only one "real"? Why is it that the so-called private account tallies with dozens of images in ways that the so-called public account does not? And what relevance do such questions have for longstanding theoretical debates over the status of the seduction theory in psychoanalysis (an especially important question for the treatment of alleged child-abuse victims and the prosecution of perpetrators), where, similarly, the effects of actual and imagined experience have proven hard to unravel? As in Magritte's own painted puzzles, the questions proliferate as they are posed and admit of no easy answers.

Yet current psychiatric research informs us that victims of trauma may well experience visual hallucinations that recur vividly for years (Terr, 1991; see also Caruth, 1991; Laub, 1991). "Horror over the circumstances of a violent death may result in misleading explanations or conspiracies of silence," report Pynoos and Nader (1990). The experience of trauma may, these authors continue, create "ongoing confusion for the child," and "actual images of the [deceased] may not be the only intrusive images that persist—the media coverage and [other] individuals may introduce distortions, rumors, or inaccuracies as well as new intrusive images. Children are often troubled by imagined images if they did not see the body" (p. 342). This finding is relevant for Magritte through its reference to the visual and its address to his refusal throughout his lifetime to speak openly about his mother's suicide except, apparently, to Scutenaire. All statements such as these, however, while relating directly and helpfully to the painted oeuvre of Magritte, fail to approach the crucial issue of artistry: that is, they cannot tell us precisely why or how one particular form of hallucination occurs rather than another. In his revisioning, his selectivity, his artfulness, Magritte remains, as he would have wished, mysterious. Furthermore, it is these very "distortions" of the circumstances of his mother's death, if indeed they were distortions, that motivated his most original and memorable paintings.

1.1. Magritte, *The Smile of the Devil.*

1.2. Magritte, *The Listening Chamber* (II).

1.3. Magritte, *The Month of the Grape Harvest.*

1.4. Magritte, *Where Euclid Walked.*

1.5. Magritte, *Memory.*

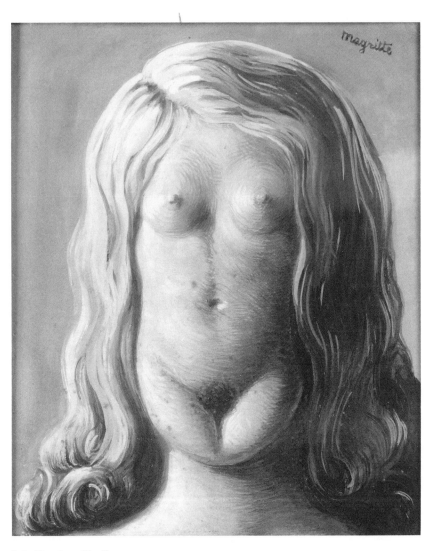

1.6. Magritte, *The Rape.*

1.7. Magritte, *Collective Invention*.

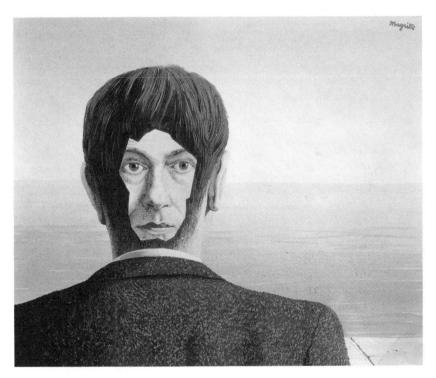

1.8. Magritte, *The Glass House*.

1.9. Magritte, *Perspective: Madame Récamier by David.*

1.10. Magritte, *Philosophy in the Boudoir.* (Variant in gouache.)

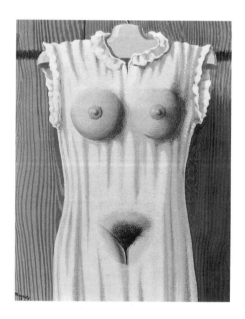

> . . . the Queen was in a furious passion
> and went stamping about, and shouting,
> "Off with his head!" or "Off with her head!"
> about once in a minute.
> **Lewis Carroll,** *Alice's Adventures in Wonderland*

Mimicry and Media

Staggeringly prolific, Magritte left work that has been widely reproduced and appropriated, both mimetically and parodically,
since his death. His impact, like that of many of his fellow surrealists, should by now be somewhat clouded. Yet his work continues
to circulate in popular culture and to bewitch new generations
of beholders. His paintings have been reproduced, for example,
on the jackets of recent publications in philosophy. *Core Questions in Philosophy: A Text with Readings* by Elliott Sober (1991;
see fig. 1.11) purloined (with a twinkle) Magritte's *This Is Not an
Apple* (*Ceci n'est pas une pomme*) of 1964 (fig. 1.12). A flier for a
book entitled *The Absent Body* by Drew Leder (1990) reproduces
Magritte's *The Pilgrim* (*Le Pèlerin*) of 1966. There, an apparently
bowler-hatted man, visible from the waist up, faces us against a
solid neutral ground. Curiously, his face from neck to forehead
has migrated several inches to the left of the rest of him—if indeed the painted hat and suit may be said to "be" him at all since
they both, on second glance, appear noticeably uninhabited. Are
we located in our minds, or in our bodies, or in the façades we
intentionally and unknowingly present to others, or are all these
aspects only apparently connected?

Send-ups also appear in national advertising campaigns, which
is wonderfully ironic in that Magritte himself actually worked for
a while as an advertising artist (Varnedoe and Gopnik, 1990).
One thinks immediately of the ubiquitous Grand Marnier ads
with their slippers, white lace, floating oranges, birds, minutely
detailed overlapping trees—references both formal and iconographic, subtle and blatant, to the oeuvre of Magritte. A Minolta

camera ad (fig. 1.13) blurs the edges of fluffy Magritte clouds; it suspends a camera against a cerulean sky between a bowler hat and a conservatively striped suit and patterned tie, an update of Magritte's emblematic bourgeois haberdashery. This ad plays not only on such paintings as *The Pilgrim*, *The Great War* (*La Grande Guerre*) of 1964 (fig. 1.14), and *The Idea* (*L'Idée*), in which an apple floats just above the head of an empty suit, tie, and jacket, but on *The False Mirror* as well.

Many of Magritte's fellow surrealists were declared aficionados of *Alice's Adventures in Wonderland*, and Magritte would have enjoyed knowing that his art inspired a set of surreal alternatives to the canonical nineteenth-century Sir John Tenniel illustrations drawn by a prominent contemporary children's book author and artist, Anthony Browne (1988). At the spot where Alice, mistaken for Mary Ann, has just been asked to fetch the White Rabbit's fan and gloves, for instance, the reader might expect to see an illustration of the heroine standing before the entrance to Rabbit's house. Instead, what meets our eyes is Browne's take-off on a Magritte painting entitled *The Unexpected Answer* (*La Réponse imprévue*) of 1933 (fig. 1.15)! The line illustrated reads: "She went in without knocking." Browne's illustration presents, in place of the title character, a black Alice-shaped hole cut from the wood of a paneled door—a door that possesses a rabbit-shaped knocker.

Magritte's own image, the source for this eerie rendering, portrays a similar negative black shape, but this one is just vaguely humanoid and appears sinister, a gaping cavity violently carved from an ordinary door, a rapacious opening in what was formerly closed. Yet, as Magritte himself pointed out in a talk he gave in London in 1937, a door is itself a hole—albeit one that can be shut, unlike the irregular orifice he created here. In attempting to describe his method of working, he characterized the project as a problem to be solved; *The Unexpected Answer* thus became the problem of the door (as *Collective Invention* [fig. 1.7] was the problem of the sea and *The Human Condition* of 1933 [plate 7] the problem of the window). Into his reasonable discussion, however, another level of meaning intervened. Magritte continued: "And through this hole we see darkness . . . enhanced yet again if we light up the invisible thing hidden by the darkness, for our gaze always wants to go further and to see at last the object, the reason for our existence" (quoted in Sylvester, 1992, p. 223). The artist, peering into the shadow he has made, both seeks and shuns the source of his being. Like Bluebeard, like Kafka, like Lewis Carroll, he wrestles with the gendered notion of the door as barrier and with the question as to whether aggression is easier to bear than incessant yearning, whether anxiety is a remedy for depression. The original image works on many levels: it recalls the ineffectual locking up of the artist's mother by his father before the suicide, and it reevokes the notion that violent sexuality can lead to death. It links affectively to other works in which Magritte represents woman not as the gaping hole of this image, but, in a related way, as defective, mutilated, cut up or cut into. It reminds us of the inverted mermaid (fig. 1.7) who is too stupid to realize that she cannot survive out of water and of Alice's concern in Wonderland that she might be drowned in her own tears.

More nightmarish the longer we contemplate it, *The Unexpected Answer* also recalls *Titanic Days* (plate 3), which explicitly denotes rape. Formally, it links with *The Smile of the Devil* (fig. 1.1), a painting that establishes its own relationship to the text of *Alice* through its iconography of ill-matched lock and key. From a Freudian viewpoint, the slender metal key in this picture, which cannot possibly work the enormous lock into which the artist has placed it, unmistakably evokes (with irony) the humiliating erotic posture of a little boy vis-à-vis his enormous mother (an idea expressed also in Magritte's painting *The Giantess* [*La Géante*] of 1935). Given such a reading, the smiling devil of the title would be none other than the triumphant, malevolent oedipal father (or even, with a twist, the colossal mother).

In order for Anthony Browne to have quoted Magritte in this context, he must have tapped the anxiety latent in *Alice*, a book that, while beloved of Magritte, other surrealists, and many adults more generally, is often ambivalently received by children. Its little girl protagonist—unmasked in this image as a cipher, an absence, a female-shaped *nothing*—fails in Lewis Carroll's narrative to find her own fantastic adventures amusing; instead, she responds to them with deadpan seriousness. *We* laugh, but Alice herself does not. For most adults, humor serves as a distraction as well as an outlet and a defense; but young children's laughter (Wolfenstein, 1951, 1954; and see below, "Musing on the Absurd: Oysters, Cannons, and Morons") stems largely from gratification in fantasy of recently repressed desires and from the need to master trauma. For children, odd juxtapositions and absurd word play (as in *Alice*) may seem, at times, simply too real to be funny: a response that often seems appropriate to Magritte's paintings as well, but a response that is, in fact, unpredictable (*imprévue*).

39

Young children, however, *do* respond with pleasure to Magritte. On her school lunch bag (fig. 1.16), a seven-year-old girl created a take-off of her own. In this particular case, by so doing, she was clearly trying to participate in her mother's pleasure as well. Working from her memory of *The Great War* (fig. 1.14), she redrew it carefully, but with significant alterations. Interestingly, she "corrects" the apple by turning it upside down so that its stem overlaps the figure's neck, thus creating a more unified, less disjunctive form. She also restores not only both of the figure's occluded eyes but its missing mouth as well! On the reverse side of her bag (fig. 1.17), she re-created another Magritte, *The Pleasure Principle* (*Le Principe du plaisir*) of 1937 (fig. 1.18). A man's exploded head renders his face invisible while robbing him of the power of sight. Here, the child, in her remaking, counterphobically invokes her mother's ability to see, both by commanding her to look and by turning the *O*'s into eyes (or breasts). And we note with fascination the connection here between this child's experience and Magritte's image *The Rape* (fig. 1.6), where eyes and breasts are also equated.

Succumbing to his magnetism, new devotees are drawn into the orbit of Magritte's bold visual analogues for compelling themes in ordinary life as well as for dreams and his heady pronouncements about existence on the rim of the abyss. Given a psychoanalytic spin, his works acquire a velocity that propels them beyond the limits of their frames.

1.11. Flier for *Core Questions in Philosophy: A Text with Readings* by Elliott Sober.

1.12. Magritte, *This Is Not an Apple.*

1.13. Advertisement. Minolta Corporation.

1.14. Magritte, *The Great War.*

1.15. Magritte, *The Unexpected Answer*.

1.16. Rivi Handler-Spitz, Lunch bag drawing in crayon based on *The Great War*.

1.17. Rivi Handler-Spitz, Lunch bag drawing in crayon based on *The Pleasure Principle*.

1.18. Magritte, *The Pleasure Principle*.

1.19. Magritte, *Hegel's Vacation*.

1.20. Pieter Breughel, *Landscape with the Fall of Icarus*.

1.21. Magritte, *The Lost Jockey.*

1.22. Magritte, *The Tomb of the Wrestlers.*

1.23. Magritte, *Discovery*.

Visual Oxymorons

Sophisticated and witty, Magritte's panorama of uncanny images
presents us with a world in which laughter belies anguish. Pleasure merges with horror to form absurd unions, as in *Hegel's
Vacation* (*Les Vacances de Hegel*) of 1959 (fig. 1.19), and metamorphoses, as in *The Red Model* (*Le Modèle rouge*) of 1935—in
which the domains of intellect and affect are eternally isolated in
dazzling displays of defense, dexterity, and repetitive division.

From a psychoanalytic point of view, the manifest aim of these
surreal images—that is, to illustrate existential puzzles, to contest the syntax that unites words and objects, to represent and at
the same time undermine concepts—masks primitive confusions
and early, barely defended anxieties, anxieties that continue to
smoulder in a posttraumatic state of mind. In one particularly
clear example of this project, *Evening Falls* (*Le Soir qui tombe*) of
1964, as the sun sets, the glass window through which we view it
cracks into smithereens; thus, the so-called fall of evening results
in an actual smash. Change of time converges with change in the
material substance of an object, and the double registration of
word and thing is collapsed. Beneath the surface of this humorous convergence we detect echoes of shock and sadness: night
fell, and my mother's body was destroyed. In thus literalizing the
metaphor of its title, the painting reveals that, for a victim, the
moment of trauma transcends any dichotomy between words and
things; as does the humor that serves to defend against it, the
painting prompts and defuses our response.

To upset expected relations of distance, dimensionality, scale,
and inner and outer boundaries is another of Magritte's aims. One

can think perhaps of *The Blood of the World* (*Le Sang du monde*) of 1927, in which bright red (and black) veins, arteries, and corpuscles adorn a forest of limblike forms, and the boundaries of the human body are put in question. The eternal mysteries of gender difference are evoked by a painting called *The Spy* (*L'Espion*) of 1927, which depicts a man peering through a keyhole at an eerily impassive disembodied head of a woman. And living and dead are horrifically combined in *The Spoiler* (*La Gâcheuse*) of 1935: the torso of a full-breasted young woman is surmounted by a grinning death's head. *Personal Values* (*Les Valeurs personnelles*) of 1952 demonstrates how significant objects, such as a double bed, can shrink while trivial ones—a matchstick, comb, wineglass, bar of soap—suddenly expand incongruously to occupy vast space. The unbearable anguish of loss and the ambiguities of reparation are conveyed by *Homesickness* (*Le Mal du pays*) of 1941, in which a winged man leans pensively over the railing of a bridge, as thick fog enshrouds the shore beyond him and a tawny lion calmly rests behind his back. ("Leo" was the name of Magritte's father.)

The splitting of subject and object that pervades this entire body of work seems to evoke in beholders an array of responses ranging from chuckles to grimaces. Magritte himself once said that looking at his own pictures gave him a strange feeling and that "a really vibrant painting has to make the onlooker sick" (Torczyner, 1979). He also said, in a rather classic formulation of projective identification, that he wanted to make the most familiar objects *howl* (Wolfenstein, 1974, p. 11). What intrigues me is the mix of cognitive and emotional dissonances he elicits and the ability of his art to bring genuine laughter to some viewers while others respond with outrage or disgust.

For although, as Foucault (1983) and others (Gablik, 1976; Hammacher, 1985) have pointed out, Magritte's uncanny images debate the project of art as representation and thus challenge its function more globally—a project shared by all serious modernists from Duchamp to the abstract expressionists—there is something unusual at stake here emotionally. In subverting the syntax that unites words, ideas, and objects by mislabeling his images, Magritte underlines the arbitrariness of connections between speech, written language, and ideas (see Saussure, 1916) and in turn their connections with material objects and painted images.

A work like *The Key of Dreams* (*La Clef des songes*) of 1930 thus functions *aggressively*. This painting (which exists in several versions, including a small English-language version made in 1935) is divided into six identical gray squares arranged in three rows of two each. In the squares common objects are realistically depicted and deliberately misnamed. Under a bowler hat, Magritte writes the word *snow* (*la neige*); under a woman's black high-heeled shoe, the word *moon* (*la lune*), and so on. In this manner, the painting attacks our facile assumption of an identification between words and the essence of things. By disrupting connections already in place and substituting new ones, it disorients beholders and recalls the hierarchical alphabet primers of childhood, which function to familiarize strange and unknown written words by matching them with friendly pictures. Magritte, on the other hand, defamiliarizes both words and images and leaves us longing for a recognizable relationship.

By setting things up this way, he re-evokes moments in childhood when the discourse of adults was mysterious to us and we had to make up our own theories to explain what seemed like bizarre juxtapositions of speech, behavior, and feeling—a state obviously far more anxiety-provoking for a child subjected to ongoing trauma, such as parental depression, than for one who has not so suffered.

James Thurber (1945) has recalled this state in his description of his own youthful reaction to hearing about a man who had left town under a cloud: "Sometimes I saw him all wrapped up in the cloud, and invisible, like a cat in a burlap sack. At other times it floated, about the size of a sofa, three or four feet above his head, following him wherever he went. . . . There were many other wonderful creatures in the secret surreal landscapes of my youth: the old lady who was always up in the air, the husband who did not seem to be able to put his foot down, [and] the man who lost his head in a fire but was still able to run out of the house yelling."

In his own more sinister fashion, Magritte, with his visual oxymorons, induces not light-hearted merriment generally but rather queasiness and paroxysms of disorientation, of epistemic disequilibrium.

The (E)vocation of Absence

Because Magritte was wont, teasingly, to join the same title to different images or to yoke versions of one image to different titles, neither a chronological nor a topical approach is ideally suited to the contemplation of his oeuvre. Combining and recombining, his symbols may be best encountered in metaphorical motion—that is, best seen from the shifting viewpoints of one who moves among them as through a maze. But *maze* is a metaphor that brings to mind Crete, Daedalus, Icarus, the Minotaur, and drowning.

In *The Palace of Curtains* (*Le Palais de rideaux*) of 1929, Magritte splits verbal and imagistic versions of the sky, that airy locus for the wildly assorted, ambiguously invested objects he chooses to elevate or resurrect there. Identical irregularly-shaped framed canvases display the word *ciel* ("sky") side by side with its illustration—blue ground daubed with cottony clouds. Again, we detect pathos beneath the manifest puzzle—namely, how pictures, objects, and words are related. One side of the work cannot be transduced from, does not match with, the other: in vain do we say what we see. This problematic equates, moreover, on a deeper level, with another enigma: I *saw* my mother, but *she was not there*. Thus, what was seen (a body, a person) did not match what was actually there (death); neither wish nor will, neither effort nor expectation, nor the name by which she was called could stanch the wound opened by her suicide. Each death, like and unlike every work of art and new love, creates an absence, a fresh potential for separation.

The title of this painting and the words inscribed within it are integral aspects, and this matters even though the titles of Magritte's paintings were occasionally added later, as a result of collaboration and debate among his coterie of friends (Sylvester, 1978; Hammacher, 1985). He was nevertheless their final arbiter and, fussing over their precise aptness, he occasionally altered them, even years later.

Arthur Danto (1980) has pointed out that the titles of art works give us directions for interpreting them. In their seeming irrelevance, Magritte's titles not only fail to give us clear interpretive directions and thus work to subvert convention but also create in their viewers a heightened sense of cognitive dissonance.

For a particular sixteenth-century painting in Brussels by Pieter Breughel, that brilliant artistic ancestor of Magritte, the title is crucial. *Landscape with the Fall of Icarus* (c. 1558, fig. 1.20) portrays the son of Daedalus, the great artificer who conceived the labyrinth by which to imprison the Minotaur and who later made wings of feathers and wax to enable himself and his young son, Icarus, to escape from the Isle of Crete. Icarus, according to the myth, disobeyed his father and flew too near the sun. As the wax melted, his father's warning was fulfilled, and the hapless boy fell headlong into the sea. Breughel paints the moment when Icarus has already reached the water, and all we see of him are two small legs thrashing—two small legs that, without the title of the painting to guide us, we might easily overlook or misconstrue.

Parenthetically, this myth is of psychoanalytic interest because, at some time before the flight, Daedalus, who is always described as cunning, vain, and jealous of his prowess, had apparently feared the growing talents of his young nephew and apprentice and, to be rid of him, had flung him into the sea—after which he went on to perform ever more wondrous deeds and artistic works for Minos and Pasiphaë, the king and queen of Crete. Thus, an oedipal rivalry, thinly disguised by reversal—the unconscious wish of a father to destroy a son in the form of the apprentice—is replicated in the myth. Daedalus, having actively attempted to enact his fantasy by drowning his young apprentice (who, however, managed to escape death) now suffers passively (in the better-known part of the myth) the fulfillment of his wish in the form of the loss of his own son. The themes of drowning, punishment, and artifice (the artist as sorcerer) are, as we have seen, central to the saga of Magritte.

In the same vein as Magritte, though by very different strategems and with a vastly greater conscious range to his emotional palette, Breughel chooses in his painting to obscure the tragedy in the guise of using it to illustrate human indifference to the fate of others. Here, as in Magritte, affect is isolated from event, but intentionally so. In engraved versions of the picture, a Netherlandish proverb is appended: "Not a plow stops when a man dies." As in Magritte's paintings centuries later, the tragedy is seen and not seen; noticed, but not comprehended; comprehended, but willfully ignored. To experience Brueghel's painting fully, then, we must know its title.

In 1960, Magritte painted a picture entitled *The Childhood of Icarus* (*L'Enfance d'Icare*). A small, mounted jockey beats a horse, though they are not apparently moving. The space involves a reversal of scale that suggests the perspective of childhood. We note the presence of an upright, clearly inanimate but humanoid object called a *bilbouquet*, a term that literally means "baluster" but in French slang means a person lacking stability. We can imagine unconscious identificatory feelings predisposing Magritte toward this subject, a boy drowned before reaching maturity, the drowning in Magritte's own life being an event blanketed by massive repression and behavioral constriction (such as a highly routinized daily life maintained for defensive purposes, as Wolfenstein suggests [MS]; see also Whitfield, 1992, p. 42).

The image of small horseman and whip conjoined with baluster reverberates throughout Magritte's work in a series of lost jockeys that runs from 1926 (see fig. 1.21) to 1943. Wolfenstein reads in them a conflicted sexual, possibly masturbatory, theme, a reading that would fit with notions of childhood and punishment that the reference to Icarus implies (death being an equivalent, in dream symbolism, for castration) and with Magritte's own strange comments on the theme of the lost jockey, a motif he used for three decades before producing the version he titled *The Childhood of Icarus*. The lost jockey theme "was conceived," he said, "not with an eye toward aesthetics, but solely as a response to a mysterious feeling, to a 'profound' discontent, to a kind of 'warning' that has occasionally taken over my consciousness and that has guided me since my birth" (Waldberg, 1965). Cryptic as this statement may be, it seems to support Wolfenstein's psychoanalytic reading (MS). Further, the repetition of the lost jockeys and their obsessional, static quality may remind us that, in the case of maternal suicide, disturbances in the mother-child relationship often precede the final event for many years and thus must also be factored in to the reading of images. Here, the frozen stillness, like thin ice on a river in winter, just barely covers the turbulence below.

Returning to *The Palace of Curtains*, I would argue that this title refers both to another favorite image of the artist—namely, his rosy stage or window drapery (as in, among many other examples, *The World Awakened* of 1958 and *The Spirit of Geometry*, plate 2)—thus providing yet another connecting thread in the labyrinth of forms, and to a place where what is within is veiled and what is apparent, though lovely, may screen something sinister. Again, early childhood is evoked: that time when the meaning and context of language and its accompanying affects seem incomprehensible.

Two of Magritte's most famous works are *The Treachery of Imagery* (*La Trahison des images*) of 1929—a pictured pipe which reads "Ceci n'est pas une pipe" (This is not a pipe)—and *This Is Not an Apple* (fig. 1.12). Each image-text exists in several versions. Each refuses to let us take for granted the relations of observing eye, listening ear, and writing or drawing hand (Hammacher, 1985). Again, humor belies the aggression latent in the project (see Freud, 1905b). "Ceci n'est pas une pomme" (This is not an apple) implies that this does not satisfy me emotionally: I cannot bite into it. It fails to give me sensual pleasure. It fails to nourish me. Not only that, but I cannot destroy it! Intellectual, artistic, and visual mastery and possession are only partial. They frustrate, while at the same time they serve defensively against both aggression and regression. With his fund of pictorial exemplars, Magritte in this way challenges the very relation of the painted image to the gratification of desire, of sign to body and of art to life. *Can* he, *how* can he, as artist, sorcerer, magician, undo the trauma and bring his mother back to life?

What kind of pleasure can *we* obtain from pictures? What price are we compelled to pay for substituting eye for mouth, and for sexuality more generally (one thinks again of *The False Mirror*) and also for aggression? At what peril do we ignore taboos against forbidden looking? A painting of 1964, described earlier, depicts a man in a bowler hat with a bright green apple hiding his face—except for one eye, which peeks out. The title of this image, *The Son of Man*, evokes the figure of Christ, who, like the artist, is both son and sacrificial victim, both vulnerable and a survivor, visible and invisible. The very word "survivor" calls up yet another painting by Magritte, a bleeding gun, painted in 1950, and called precisely *The Survivor* (*Le Survivant*).

The Son of Man can be linked with another work produced in the same year, *The Idea*, where a floating apple substitutes for a head. It is also related to *The Great War* (fig. 1.14), in which both of a man's eyes are hidden by a great green apple. Parenthetically, in musing over the title of the latter picture, an inescapable reference to World War I (although Magritte denied this and insisted that it had strictly to do with "the eternal struggle between the gaze and objects" [quoted in Whitfield, 1992, p. 124]), I thought that for Magritte the most compelling agendas are never those of external war and politics but rather the internal battlegrounds of memory, fantasy, and desire, where strife is equally intense but, paradoxically, both more and less possible to control. For Magritte, it is not at Verdun or in the trenches but rather internally, behind the apple, that the "great war" is continually being fought.

Such pictures bespeak deep cultural equations between oral and visual experience—equations that permeate ordinary language in the form of expressions mentioned earlier as well as "we drank in the scenery," "he devoured me with his eyes," "what sharp eyes you have" (the eyes here substituting for teeth). But these images also convey the danger in this equation—that is, the tradition of the artist as a vulnerable interloper in the first garden, of Eden. Furthermore, the apple, as a symbol of forbidden knowledge—knowledge, that is, concerning the mysteries of human sexuality—is here both the object behind which the figure hides and also that which blinds him. Thus the apple not only fails to gratify but actually punishes, and it is, interestingly, in these pictures where it obscures the face, a green (unripe? tart?) rather than a red fruit.

To substitute visual for oral is, nevertheless, to achieve a partial victory over destructive impulses in that, whereas the objects of overtly expressed oral impulses are consumed and destroyed, the eye takes objects in and preserves them in lasting imagery. Speaking of the childhood of artists, Phyllis Greenacre (1955) said, "The eye borrows from the mouth an omnivorous delight in taking in objects." Powerful voyeuristic urges, displaced from incorporative cravings to visual avidity, are ubiquitously evident in Magritte.

Apropos of these equations, Whitfield quotes a story from Mariën about Magritte's going into a grocery store to buy some Dutch cheese. When the shopkeeper reaches into the window to take out a round cheese that has been on display there, the painter tells her that he must have his piece cut from another cheese, located on the shelf next to the counter. The shop-keeper protests that the two cheeses are identical. "No, Madame," Magritte objects. "The one in the window has been looked at all day by the people passing by" (cited by Whitfield, 1992, p. 43).

As we chuckle, we can unpack this joke, psychoanalytically speaking, by recognizing that this artist has been struggling to master oral aggression by transferring that intensity from mouth to eye—a transference that, since it never fully works, recreates the original ambivalence and a subsequent layering of denials of the efficacy of the defensive maneuver.

In *The Postcard* (*La Carte postale*) of 1960, for example, a man apparently hallucinates an apple: it floats out of reach, both too large and too far away to offer satisfaction. But by hallucinating, by conjuring, a visual image that substitutes for a reality which, as Freud points out, inevitably frustrates and disappoints, the artist merely replicates the original state.

When the apple reappears in *The Listening Chamber* (fig. 1.2), normal relations of distance and scale are again suspended. Claustrophobic sen-sations are evoked by the enormous fruit, and the relative scale suggests a tomb, an association strengthened by the title of a related painting, *The Tomb of the Wrestlers* (*Le Tombeau des lutteurs*) of 1960 (fig. 1.22) and only weakly disavowed by the presence of an open window. Here, as always, *the apple fails to gratify*—this time not only because it is too close but because it has preempted all available space; there is simply no room for anyone or anything else. Again, the strangeness of this image betokens a return of the repressed, perhaps in the form of an infantile experience when the breast, the source of oral pleasure, appeared to have such mammoth proportions that it threatened to overwhelm and smother the baby, rather than to gratify. Panic, helpless rage, and the passivity of infancy mingle with the asso-ciations of the tomb—a convergence of beginnings and endings that has special personal meaning for Magritte and also a long tradition of linkage to Eve's tempting but dangerous apple. Here the title, *The Listening Cham-ber*, underscores the enforced passivity of infancy by focusing on hearing—sound being more difficult to avoid than sight—and by adumbrating typi-cal synaesthetic experiences of infancy, when oral, visual, spatial, and auditory sensations, both inner and outer, are conflated (R. Spitz, 1965).

The Tomb of the Wrestlers similarly presents a claustrophobic space and the young child's sense of being excluded, the feeling that "there is simply no room in that place for me." A huge red rose, emblematic of both love and death, has supplanted the green apple of *The Listening Chamber*. In the context of its title, the image suggests a fantasy of parental intercourse— a primal scene in which lovemaking may metamorphose into aggression, a dangerous wrestling match between the parents, so destructive that it might even end in death for one of them. And Magritte made yet another version of this scene (*The Anniversary*, 1959) in which an enormous boulder substitutes for the rose, which takes the place of the apple. Such a conjunction of new aspects (the substitution of rose or rock for apple) with familiar motifs permits us to look back and discover associative connections (mother-sexuality-tomb, perhaps) that enrich our respective experiences with each new pairing. In tracing these thematic recyclings throughout Magritte's oeuvre, we may wonder whether, beneath all the disorientations and disruptions, these recurrences express a certain craving for stability. In other words, the repetition as reparative and affirmative rather than a sign merely of intractable unconscious conflict and pain.

The presence of an open window in these and other Magrittes links the artist to a time-honored Netherlandish painting tradition (as in the art of Vermeer and de Hooch) in which representational schemata were conceived as enclosed spaces with side windows that open to hint of other, broader vistas—a deep cultural metaphor, perhaps, for timeless creative dialogues between inner and outer space. In Magritte as well, the window at times seems to offer a possible way out of the labyrinth of inwardness and obsessionalism.

The most famous of such images, *The Human Condition* (*La Condition humaine*) of 1933 (plate 7), depicts an easel set up before a window in such a way that the scene on the canvas precisely overlaps its counterpart in the world outside the window. What we see is the interior of a room; we look out onto a peaceful, wooded landscape with trees, roadway, and a blue sky filled with Magritte's signature clouds. Only a few slender clues—the legs of the easel, the tacked white edge of the canvas, the clamp, and a slight overlap of the canvas with the window curtain—allow us to read the doubleness of the image.

The window itself is framed by heavy curtains, suggesting, as always, a theatrical motif—play, artifice, the notion that nothing here is actually real. Literally and figuratively, Magritte dramatizes here a set of problems that range from the ultrasophisticated—the Cartesian duality of mind and body—to the more mundane but no less complex technical challenges inherent in solving the contradiction between two-dimensional space (the province of every painted picture) and the third dimension it seeks to capture, to, on the most basic level, a young child's questions about what exists inside and what lies outside the self, what is real and what imaginary, what is me and what not-me. And it is important to realize that Magritte is not just pointing out or underlining these dichotomies. He is actually daring us to question the very notion of dichotomy itself. In the world he creates here there is nothing that is me; therefore everything is me. Hence, the claustrophobic feeling: the experience of no exit.

Incredibly rich and suggestive, this image is one that Magritte works off again and again. In one variation mentioned earlier, he paints a similar curtained window, but there is no easel. The sun, a great orange disk like a copper penny, sinks on the horizon. The window pane has shattered. Pieces of glass overpainted with the scene we are looking at through the window are propped against the wall beneath that window. Titled *Evening Falls*, the image concretizes the idiom: evening literally falls and breaks. So here the artist's questions exert pressure on verbal language, and linguistic puns translate into visual mischief. Our expectations and presuppositions are perpetually contested.

The object before the face and the back turned toward the spectator (as in *Pandora's Box* of 1951) are visual equivalents for Magritte's oft-quoted statement, "I despise my past and that of all others." The immobilization of objects and of human subjects in his pictures and the careful delineation of—almost a clutching at—well-defined forms betoken a warding off, a blocking of, a guarding against the outbreak of some potential violent occurrence and emotion. One senses that when these feelings do flare up, they burn with a heat that scars—as we have seen, for example, in *Titanic Days* (plate 3), where we are made to witness a paralysis of fantasied heterosexual violence, and in the blazing tuba of *The Discovery of Fire*.

When the Hour Will Strike (plate 6) places a nude, decapitated woman before an expanse of water. The body is neither living nor dead, neither stone nor flesh. The title suggests a reversal of the actual time sequence, as though the past event (the death of the mother) has somehow been deferred to the future (where it can then be uncertain). Whereas normally a mother's head and face are exposed and her body hidden, in Magritte's presumed fantasy, as recorded by Scutenaire, these were reversed in death, so that, here, the image is headless. At the same time, the impulse of a

51

pubescent boy to break the commandment and violate the taboo against forbidden looking is defended by turning the body at least partially into stone. A balloon floating out of reach recalls the airborne apple and many other dirigibles, such as the one in *The Thief* (1967, the year of Magritte's own death), a painting which also connects with *The Palace of Curtains* and with numerous painted predatory and vanishing or wounded birds—such as the tombstone bird in *The Fortune Made* (*Fortune faite*) of 1957, an image that weaves together the themes of mother, death, and oral gratification and/or deprivation.

One of Magritte's most remarkable works, *Philosophy in the Boudoir* (see a variant, fig. 1.10), depicts a sleeveless white nightgown trimmed with ruffles suspended on a clothes hanger before a wood-grained wall. Emerging from this garment are two vibrant rosy-nippled breasts, and on a table in front of it rests a pair of high-heeled pumps, the fronts of which are in the process of turning into fleshly feet with toes. The image evokes Magritte's presumed fantasy that his dead mother's nightgown failed to conceal her nakedness, while simultaneously it averts the irrevocability of death by problematizing the difference between what is alive and what is not—a theme addressed elsewhere by *When the Hour Will Strike* and by *Discovery* (*La Découverte*) of 1927 (fig. 1.23), in which the skin of a woman's naked body seems to alternate with a woodgrain that suggests the material of a coffin. The pain and horror of the event and its accompanying sadistic fantasies are heightened by the title in the original French, *La Philosophie dans la boudoir*, which clearly refers to a work by the Marquis de Sade that narrates a series of sexual and mutilating assaults on an aging mother.

In 1951, Magritte repainted Jacques-Louis David's 1799 portrait of Mme Récamier, in which a lovely young moneyed Parisienne, attired in a simple blanched Empire gown not unlike the white garment of Magritte's imagination, reclines on a chaise. What we behold in the surrealist version is an unadorned green-walled room, another claustrophobic interior space (see fig. 1.9). Within it, we encounter not the representation of a living person, as in the David, but a nailed wooden coffin bent in the middle as though containing someone sitting up inside it or as though the person on the chaise had metamorphosed into a casket. Strangely, as the bent attitude of this box calls to mind an infant's cradle, we are brought, as so typically in Magritte's oeuvre, to an eerie equation of birth with death. From beneath the box, a bit of white cloth spills—white cloth charged with dramatic personal resonance for Magritte. To attach this meaning, drawn from his own life, to the period dress of the eighteenth-century portrait is to confront the uncanniness inherent in the image: to behold, suddenly, the beauteous Mme Récamier in her shroud.

Wit barely distracts us from the searching questions implicit in this image and from a lurid uneasiness that erupts through its veneer of cleverness and spills out, like the cloth from beneath the lacquered coffin. For Magritte wants to push us into a new place. He is saying: Aha! you thought you knew all about portraiture. You thought you understood that a portrait is made to preserve a beloved person, the object of one's affections, through time, to keep her alive, as it were. Perhaps it works just the other way around. Perhaps, he says through this image, to paint a portrait or to gaze at one is not to keep the beloved alive but maybe, to the contrary, to kill her again and again. For, in looking at David's original painting from the perspective of Magritte's re-creation, we are inevitably reminded not only that Madame Récamier was once beautiful but that her beauty has now utterly vanished since she is, in fact, dead.

How much of an artificer, how much of a Daedalus, then, is Magritte? What, for him, is the nature of artistic vision and creation? Although he can paint an apple, a pipe, a beautiful woman, he cannot bring them or restore them to life. Questioning the reparative value of art, this image suggests, in a manner that betrays both depression and manic denial, that to depict an object may not be to preserve it but, rather, repetitively, to hurt and even destroy it. And the larger fear here—the fear of doing damage to the person and thing one loves most—is the same fear that causes an averting of the eyes, a turning of the head. Like the drowned corpse itself, this theme continues to surface, to bob and ricochet on the icy waters of Magritte's painted panorama.

I should like to consider just two more of Magritte's paintings. *Girl Eating Bird* (plate 1) is one of his most disturbing works. A young girl dressed in a robe trimmed with the handmade lace for which Brussels is famous calmly devours a live bird, while drops of blood spatter her white collar. This image explodes with a horrifying sadism and condenses many of Magritte's most persistent themes. Oral aggression, usually displaced to the eyes, is here returned to the mouth, and it is *our* eyes, as spectators, that are made, by projective identification, to witness it. Living and dead are again reversed and confused, as Wolfenstein (MS) has pointed out, as are the aesthetic and the gustatory—for the birds in Magritte's picture are colorful, plumed creatures, birds to admire with the eyes, not barnyard fowl to be consumed with the teeth. Most striking of all is the projection of infantile oral aggression onto the woman against whom it is originally directed—woman disguised here as little girl. Thus, the artist is able both to enjoy and to deny his enjoyment of the cannibalistic act. I am reminded of the Medusa who destroys you if you look at her so that, although *you* are the one who looks, the aggression is always *hers*. Grotesque and repugnant, the image constitutes a sight from which I feel impelled to turn away—thus replicating, as Wolfenstein has noted, the presumed fantasied experience of the adolescent boy at the scene of his mother's death. Or, from a Kleinian perspective: the internalized persecutory object, the mother, despite (and because of) her death, continues to feed on the living child. In this profoundly unsettling painting, any intellectual agenda of depicting paradox must wither before a torrent of feeling that erupts to overthrow the hegemony of the sign.

Finally, I want to consider a painting called *The Waterfall (La Cascade)* of 1961. Here, in a paradigmatic image, an easel is set up before a bush. The bush, however, has invaded its own representation on the canvas. Not content to remain behind the easel, it has emerged to a spatial plane in front of the stand. Thus, model invades canvas, life invades art, fantasy overwhelms reality. At risk and threatened with the possibility of being inundated by stimuli from both within and without, the artist, burdened (and blessed) with an extraordinary sensitivity, must struggle with all the ingenuity, craft, wit, and artifice at his command to master and bind anxiety by inscribing it in a maze of images—into which, however, new paths are constantly being etched by the unconscious. For Magritte, the means of so doing was the projection of this anxiety into existential puzzles, representational paradoxes, and witticisms. We, then, as spectators of his paintings, in turn experience his imagery as invading our space—as disturbing, repelling, or seducing *us*.

The task of a psychoanalytic interpreter of the arts is never to reach closure or to solve for x. Observing more narrowly than some but noting the circulation of signs, she may find herself dwelling temporarily within the countertransference or in what Winnicott liked to call that "intermediate space" where critic's eye meets artist's painted product. The rewards of such meandering, moreover, may not always be accessible to words because they occur mainly in terms of the visual medium itself. One pictorial symbol attentively beheld will foreshadow new ones and gesture back to others, which then glide (or pop) into view and into new relations with them—like a mobile jigsaw puzzle or a kaleidoscope. Variations, modifications, combinations of motifs emerge to become focal and then recede. Tuba, bells, women, clouds—a thicket of forms surrounds us.

To wander through this maze of imagery may lead us now or in the future to hitherto unrealized moments with individual works of art, to a more finely tuned sense of the subjective experience of the given artist, above all to insight into our own psyches and into the tortuous means by which each of us constructs a private labyrinth for imprisoning the Minotaur.

> Men make their own history, but they do not make it just as they please. **Karl Marx**

Tension and Intention

Just two years before the maternal suicide around which all our threads have been twisted, Sigmund Freud ventured into the then-uncharted realm of psychoanalytic biography with his vexed study of Leonardo da Vinci (1910). A year later, Béla Bartók composed his mesmerizing, ghostly opera, *Bluebeard's Castle* (1911). I want in this section to take up the latter work as a musical metaphor—not only for the biographical, interpretive project theorized by Freud, but also for my own. In part, I invoke it to problematize the commonsense distinction between living and dead artists, for to suspend this distinction is also to call into question other cherished oppositions—principally those between fiction and fact, fantasy and history. It is to foreground the indeterminacy of our signs and referents. And it is, of course, to mirror in words the visual project of René Magritte. Can it be that, in the discourses of art, the living artist is one whose works are present to consciousness? To assume such a position is to see Magritte himself as very much alive today and those who write and teach about him as contributors to his longevity, prolongers of his existence.

Predictably gendered according to the familiar ideology of its epoch, Bartók's opera depicts a man forced by the irresistible power of a woman to yield to her insatiable desire for absolute possession and forbidden knowledge of him. She urges him to surrender, one by one, the keys to his castle and to reveal to her that which is absolutely private, that which is secreted behind each of his locked doors. As these doors are flung open, they reveal, in succession, instruments of torture, blood-soaked treasures, a bleeding garden, a lake of sighs and tears. Conveyed in the terms of a musical palindrome, the balance of power gradually shifts between the two characters. Repeatedly questioning the woman, Judith, as to whether she is frightened by what she is finding, Bluebeard at last yields up his seventh and final key. From behind this door emerges each of his previous wives, voluptuous and still alive, but *only within the castle of his mind*. Judith trembles and pleads for mercy. Relentlessly, however, Bluebeard closes the door, shutting her up in his castle forever with her knowledge. As the opera ends, he stands alone on a dimmed stage. "Night," he sings, "Nothing but darkness here. Eternal darkness."

This parable exposes the aggression that fuels the biographical quest— the wish to know the secrets of the other—biography as blood-letting, with its seductive intrusiveness, its shifting fears and dangers, and also the harrowing fantasies and disavowed aggressions of creative minds, male and female alike, displaying the prices that must be paid both for privacy and for revelation.

Biographical adventures into the lives of artists feed on awe, envy, idealization, and burning curiosities about the wellsprings of creativity. Neither exclusively fictional nor dispassionately historical, they are fueled by and perpetuate our Western mythologies about art. But to take such myths about artists' minds for granted, to fail to interrogate them, is to perpetuate the ideologies they embody. To redeem writing about art from the grip of nineteenth-century Romanticism, we must, following Bartók (both libretto and score), reconsider the polarities between so-called life and so-called art: we must understand *both* to be fully and deeply implicated in the riddles of representation.

Roland Barthes (1957) has reminded us that biographical details often render the artistic product more, not less, mysterious. Far from bringing the nature of inspiration into sharper focus, such details may actually heighten a sense of awe or, alternatively, drain it away, reversing it into its opposite, namely, contempt. And when complex signifiers, such as the bleeding contents of Bluebeard's castle, are reduced to symptoms, the aesthetics of biography may swell into a buffer that forestalls our confrontation with multiple meanings. In this misuse, biographical data can restrict rather than augment the interpretive process.

In these pages, I have tried to use a quantum of biographical knowledge to foster perception. Perhaps, as James E. B. Breslin (1991) once suggested, this enterprise, when it works, does so by spawning a cluster of

57

narratives and thus empowers us to refuse the dualistic gap that theory tries to open between art and life, process and product. This text has attempted to blend many voices. Inherently interdisciplinary, it betrays hidden motives, countertransferences; the artist's own conflicts over exhibitionism and voyeurism have doubtless been replayed, and some element of aggression, reversed imperceptibly into idealization, may have infiltrated the whole project. Thralldom to reanimated ghosts, as in *Bluebeard's Castle*, has remained a constant threat.

The psychoanalytic author struggles toward an elusive intersubjectivity. She must respect her subject without mystifying it and analyze it without dismembering it. She must reunite the artist with the art without reducing either to the terms of the other. Withall, she must serve the guardians of civilization—memory and truth.

As a visual metaphor for this quest, I would evoke the serene equestrienne Magritte painted in 1965 in a work called *The Blank Signature* (*Le Blanc-seing*, plate 8). Partly hidden as she journeys through a labyrinthine forest, she becomes strangely, intermittently, one with it. Tranquil and contemplative, this female figure seems to inhabit a realm beyond that of the lost jockeys; she seems to have left behind the anguished milieu of *The Childhood of Icarus*. As we glimpse her and her prancing steed emerging and vanishing among the trees, we also glimpse momentarily a different resolution perhaps to the conflicts posed so insistently throughout Magritte's oeuvre. "When someone rides a horse in the forest," the artist once said, "first you see them, then you don't, *but you know that they are there*" (quoted in *Life* magazine, 22 April 1966, p. 117; see also Whitfield, 1992, p. 125; italics mine). If that is indeed the case—or, more important, when that is *felt* to be the case—even if only intermittently, as illustrated by the image of the equestrienne, it may be taken as a sign that we are in a realm of safety, of relative object constancy and mature human relationships—a domain of peace rather than of danger, war, and fragmentation.

Part Two

Writing across the Disciplines

"I weep for you," the Walrus said;
"I deeply sympathize."
With sobs and tears he sorted out
Those of the largest size,
Holding his pocket handkerchief
Before his streaming eyes.
Lewis Carroll
Through the Looking Glass

Musing on the Absurd
Oysters, Cannons, and Morons

An ongoing fascination with the painted puzzles of René Magritte and with children's picture books has led me to ponder the possible interrelationships of our unstable capacities for tolerating epistemological uncertainty, cognitive dissonance, and emotional ambiguity. This chapter records those musings by thematizing the notion of the absurd. In juxtaposing selected contemporary philosophical and psychoanalytic perspectives, my aim is to open questions for future debate; I note with amusement the awkward (and delicious) chance that whatever follows might easily be read as replicating the object of its inquiry.

Let's begin with a glance at etymology. Although the word *absurd* has come in English to mean "ridiculously inconsistent, preposterous, and nonsensical," its original derivation from the Latin, as was pointed out above, has to do with the notion of being offensive to the ear, *surdus* meaning "deaf" or "unwilling to listen." Hence, the absurd connotes that which it is difficult to hear or, by extension, difficult to accept. A related meaning, conveyed by the original Latin, has to do with discordance, harshness, and bad taste. Thus, Cicero uses the expression *absurde canere* ("to sing jarringly, disharmoniously"), and he joins the word *absurde* with *aspere*, meaning rough and grating.

In a brief but thoughtful chapter of his book *Mortal Questions* (1979), the philosopher Thomas Nagel calls attention to the fact that, although people often complain about the absurdity of life, the reasons usually given do not stand up to the simplest sort of reasoning. He points out that if, as people sometimes say, human life is absurd because nothing we do will matter in a million years, it is equally true that nothing that will happen in a million years matters now. Furthermore, he argues, even if what we are doing now *will* matter in a million years, how could that keep our present life from being absurd? For if our life doesn't matter enough now, it is not at all clear how it would help if it were to matter a million years from now.

In this analysis, Nagel indicates that, although people seem to experience life as absurd or, at any rate, to accuse it every now and then of being so, the reasons they give for this accusation are as absurd as the experiences for which they are attempting to account. Considering this conundrum, he comes eventually to the conclusion that the experience of absurdity not only is inevitable in human life but is, curiously, a manifestation of our most advanced and interesting human characteristics (p. 23).

Nagel bases this determination on the notion that, as human beings, we experience the world from different and essentially incompatible viewpoints. It is indeed the irreconcilability of these viewpoints, subjective and objective—or, to put it somewhat differently, our capacity to transcend ourselves in thought—that makes possible our sense of the absurd. He argues cogently for an irreducible polarity between two extremes: one, a point of view that originates with "a particular individual, having a specific constitution, situation, and relation to the rest of the world" and the other, a point of view that moves through various levels of abstraction from an individual's spatial, temporal, and personal position in the world to a position that eventually regards the world as centerless, with the viewer just one of its contents (p. 206). Our experience of the absurd, he claims, derives from precisely this polarity, from our capacity to juxtapose viewpoints, to be simultaneously spectators of and actors in our own lives, to be (my example) caught up in a daily whirl we measure with our wristwatches while concurrently able to locate our lives in historic or even geologic time. Sartre's (1956) most frequently cited examples of subject/object caesura occur in his chapters on "Being-for-Others"—the character in a public park who both sees another and knows he is at the same time the object of that other's gaze, and the man who clandestinely peers through a keyhole while suddenly hearing footsteps behind him. Magritte, of course, typically renders such states pictorially in his vivid canvases. Prime examples would be *The Human Condition* (plate 7) and *The Month of the Grape Harvest* (fig. 1.3; see also the discussion in "Optical Appetites," above), the first of which relates the problematic of the absurd to that of artistic representation. Experiences of the absurd have to do, then, with juxtapositions and gaps that, as far as we can tell, play no role in the lives of nonhuman creatures. We, whose consciousness permits (and condemns) us to awareness of perspectival incompatibilities, encounter these incompatibilities under circumstances that can elicit a wide range of response: we may react to them as comic, tragic, or tragicomic, as awe-inspiring, profoundly unsettling, or even terrifying. Concurring with Nagel, I wish to extend his discussion by asking whether some of it might bear restatement and elaboration in psychoanalytic terms while, *pari passu*, I submit accepted psychoanalytic views of the absurd to the light of his critique.

How can psychoanalysis illuminate the problematic of the absurd as Nagel has defined it? Two relevant perspectives spring to mind: the *dynamic*, explored by Freud most directly in his writings on dreams (1900), jokes (1905b), obsessional neurosis (1895, 1909), phobias (1918), and the uncanny (1919), and the *developmental*, considered with particular brilliance by Martha Wolfenstein in her work on children's humor (1951, 1954) as well as on the paintings of René Magritte (MS).

Rather than starting, like the philosopher, with a concept that seems to require further clarification, the psychoanalyst often begins in the accepted mode of observational science, by locating the object of inquiry in a context: namely, in those domains of human experience where it is most commonly found. This somewhat different *terminus a quo* does not, however, mark a definitive distinction between the disciplines because at least some philosophers tend to begin here too, and in fact Nagel actually commences his own essay by implying he's *noticed* that people on certain occasions seem to find life absurd.

Freud determined that absurdity is experienced with predictable frequency in the realms of both dream and joke, and thus it was in the course of studying these phenomena that he investigated its role. He wrote of absurdity also with respect to obsessions and phobias, and he commented on a related phenomenon *unheimlichkeit* ("the uncanny")—which shares with it experiential elements of the eerie, the discrepant, and the bizarre (see the chapter "Collective Inventions").

In all these cases, Freud, like Nagel, derived the experience of the absurd from a momentary convergence of incompatible points of view. Not entirely unlike Nagel's, Freud's way of describing this incompatible convergence was to consider it an intrapsychic conflict. I say "not entirely unlike Nagel's" because Nagel claims specifically that the absurd derives "not from a collision between our expectations and the world, but from *a collision within ourselves*" (1979, p. 17, my italics). Furthermore, in summing up his argument, Nagel states: "The coexistence of conflicting points of view, varying in detachment from the contingent self, is not just a practically necessary illusion but an irreducible fact of life" (p. 213). I take these two statements to be consistent not only with Freud's views but with much contemporary psychoanalysis as well (see Brenner, 1982): the implication here being that internal conflict is an irreducible factor in human life.

Of course it is possible to argue that, once past the notion of mental conflict, these terms carry quite different meanings for Nagel than for Freud; that, whereas Freud was concerned with incompatible wishes, fears, sanctions, and prohibitions, Nagel's interest is limited to cognitive dissonance— to the irreconcilability of perspectives and ideas. In other words, the philosopher deals with conscious phenomena, the psychoanalyst, with the unconscious. But how are these types of mental conflict related? How does the polarity of which the philosopher speaks bear on the intrapsychic dissonances noted by the psychoanalyst? Are they different but similar and connected species of mental conflict, or divergent descriptions of underlying splits in the human psyche? Do they have different developmental roots? Is it helpful to categorize them in topographic terms, as conscious and unconscious—to state that, with respect to the question of psychic splitting, the psychoanalyst is concerned primarily with the jagged fault between awareness and the subliminal while the gap that intrigues Nagel exists *within* consciousness? This way of framing the problem may prove useful by offering clues to the different developmental origins and roles of the two versions (or two descriptions) of conflict. Further, it may bear on the disparate routes by which such conflicts enter the clinical arena.

As noted above, one avenue of approach has been to examine the milieus where these apparently different kinds of discrepancy occur most frequently in tandem, that is, the realm of jokes and the domain of dreams. A good joke often depends on just such a convergence of wish-defense conflicts *plus* a clash between subjective and objective viewpoints. (I shall illustrate this below.) In dreaming, a similar phenomenon occurs, but here, of course, we accept the merging of incompatible viewpoints and discrepant intentions, and it is only upon awakening that we experience our dreams as absurd: it is only then that we protest and try to link or mitigate nonsensical polarities by recourse to strategems of interpretation and/or disavowal. Jokes, on the other hand, possess verbal structures which call up images that cancel each other out so that mutually opposed ideas, though momentarily joined, are yet kept sufficiently separate that unconscious fantasy can dissolve before anxiety reaches awareness (see Wolfenstein, 1951, p. 341). Thus, a joke, because its own censor is, so to speak, built in—or because, as Freud put it, the censor has been bribed—permits us to take pleasure in its absurdity whereas with dreams we feel compelled, upon awakening, to explain (away) their unreasonableness.

Freud claims that when, upon awakening, we remember dreams as absurd, we do so not merely in response to the jumbling and condensation of elements that have occurred routinely during sleep but also because of our need to criticize and censor the latent dream thoughts. In particular, he claims, we feel constrained to banish those dream thoughts that are at odds with our manifest values and ideals. Yet the jumbling of elements is itself jarring to our ordinary modes of thought: remembered dreams may replace diachronic sequencing with synchronism, contiguity and identity may supplant rational causation, and spatial relations may (as in Magritte's paintings) appear anomalously transformed. Pictorial versions of such transmutations and inversions abound in the painted imagery of Magritte. *Personal Values* (1952), for example, portrays a bedroom in which the walls are sky and a huge comb, goblet, matchstick, and bar of soap dwarf the double bed and transparent wardrobe. The image thus suspends normal relations of scale and opacity so that multiple perspectives may be conjoined. Yet, at the same time, all its disorientations occur safely within expectable spatial conventions, the so-called perspectival cone of vision (see Burgin, 1990), so that beholders' experiences of the absurd are simultaneously contained and heightened. Our reactions in such cases are, it seems to me, determined by cognitive dissonance as importantly as by deep needs for the censorship of unacceptable desires.

During the psychoanalytic process, following the classic Freudian description, details experienced subjectively as absurd (that is, foolish, embarrassing, even shameful) are traced to condensations and displacements from the dreamer's life history, unconscious fantasy, and daily waking experience, including, importantly, transference elements arising in the analytic situation. Via a sophisticated armamentarium of interpretive modalities, psychoanalysis seeks to expand the analysand's awareness so as to include previously disavowed aspects. Thus the range of consciousness, choice, and control is extended. Freud teaches that, by means of this process, the patient may, momentarily and in small increments, gain insight into the discrepancies he or she once experienced as absurd (slips of the tongue, for example). According to this model, then, psychoanalytic process might be seen as aimed at reducing each individual's experience of the absurd. The idea would be that, through interpretation and insight, the patient's range of tolerance is gradually extended so that much of whatever behavior, thought, and fantasy once felt discrepant (and thus was disavowed by being labeled absurd) will gradually gain acceptance.

Curiously, if this description were valid, it might, by Nagel's criteria, warrant an indictment of psychoanalysis, for, as we have seen, Nagel regards our capacity to experience the absurd as a uniquely human characteristic and one, moreover, that implies a high level of evolution and development. To relinquish this for a unity bought at the price of reductive interpretive maneuvers would, his text implies, constitute a major loss— indeed, an intellectual regression. Parenthetically, Orwell's (1949) description of "doublethink" comes to mind: that continuous revision of memory in which what is deliberately forgotten includes not only the content of past experience but all memory of the processes of forgetting as well, so that any conscious objective standpoint is continually being altered. This is a striking example of a system of thought that excludes the experience of the absurd and, by so doing, utterly dehumanizes its practitioners.

If we were to debate the view that psychoanalysis aims at reducing the experience of absurdity by interpreting it away, we might invoke Nagel's notion of irreducible cognitive conflict and add several classic psychoanalytic concepts, such as the negative therapeutic reaction and the repetition compulsion, both of which contributed to Freud's (1937) sense of the interminability of the psychoanalytic process. Freud held that, because of the power of the unconscious and the continual undertow of repression, many therapeutic goals are ephemeral and must be perpetually renewed and reexperienced. As has been noted many times, his verbal images often suggest battlegrounds where conquered hillocks are besieged again and again or where the enemy, turned back on one front, mounts counterattacks from other, less well-defended positions. Given this perspective, the chances for a harmonious inner life, as described by psychoanalysis, do not seem high.

Moreover, if, as indicated above, we consider the split described by Nagel as occurring *within* consciousness and the split focused on in the psychoanalytic situation as occurring between consciousness and the unconscious, or outside of consciousness altogether, it is possible to formulate the situation somewhat differently: namely, that the psychoanalytic process, by extending an individual's range of consciousness, does not interpret *away* discordance but rather, by converting unconscious conflict into conscious contradiction, actually *expands* the individual's capacity for experiencing and tolerating the absurd. On this model, the resolving of deep affective psychic splits can be viewed as serving to free individuals to embrace oddly divergent perspectives more fully and even relish the juxtaposition. On this alternative model, our capacity to experience absurdity constitutes a developmental achievement dependent on the prior resolution of primitive intrapsychic schisms (such as, for example, those described vividly by Melanie Klein in her work on the paranoid/schizoid position).

Rather than choose between these competing views of the relationship between psychoanalysis and the absurd, we can discern in both a convergence with the claims of philosophers such as Nagel that absurdity is endemic to the human condition—a point intuitively obvious the moment we reflect that whatever it is like to be you or me and/or whatever matters to you or me necessarily implies viewpoints incompatible with objective descriptions of us. This insight matches all psychoanalytic models that claim the ubiquity of conflict in human experience. Thus, the philosopher's perspective adds both a caveat and an important missing dimension to the psychoanalyst's conception.

We return now to the topic of jokes. Freud (1905b) showed that the absurd is often used as a way of simultaneously revealing and evading. A perspicacious example concerns the tale of the artilleryman Itzig, who was accepted for service but was utterly intractable and uninterested in the military. A superior officer remarked: "Itzig, you're no use to us. I'll give you a piece of advice: buy yourself a cannon and make yourself independent!" (pp. 56–57). Freud points out that in this case we laugh because the officer's advice is obviously nonsensical. By suggesting to Itzig that he purchase a cannon and set himself up as a military entrepreneur, the officer identifies with Itzig's stupidity in order to show him the foolishness of his own behavior: "I'll give you some advice that's as stupid as you are." In another sense, however, by a twist of irony, he shows himself to be just as stupid as Itzig, for apparently he completely misunderstands Itzig's point of view: that is, he gives advice that is not only nonsensical from a pragmatic (objective) standpoint but also preposterous in light of Itzig's subjectivity. With respect to this aspect of the joke, it is the hearer of the joke who has the last laugh, for he or she can feel superior in the end not only to Itzig but to the officer as well.

Returning to Nagel, there may be a parallel here. In analyzing the statement that human life is absurd because nothing will matter a million years from now, Nagel points out the inherent absurdity of the statement itself. His analysis thus functions like the officer's joke: by offering a corollary that seems nonsensical—namely, that, after all, nothing that will happen in a million years matters to us now anyway—he uncovers and demonstrates the foolishness of the original statement. And the parallel continues in that, from both the philosopher's and the psychoanalyst's viewpoint, what is fascinating is that when incompatible perspectives are brought together, the result is laughter and/or anxiety.

Missing from Nagel's account is precisely what is lacking in the officer's joking remark to Itzig (and perhaps even in Freud's analysis of it): namely, an inquiry into and serious consideration of its emotional resonance. In the case of Itzig, laughter as a defensive reaction to phallic masturbatory associations may also count as an issue. Nagel, however, *does* remind his readers of the pain, nausea, and even suicidal anguish that plagued many existentialist philosophers as they contemplated the absurd. He even quotes Camus's recommendation that the only appropriate attitude toward it is one of defiance and scorn. From a psychoanalytic point of view, such an attitude would be considered a manic defense that, like the joking posture itself, provides a temporary illusion of mastery and control but easily reverses into depression. One cannot joke forever or be perpetually scornful, and, as clinical case histories have documented, one pays dearly for the phobic and obsessive rituals that mask failure to come to terms with life's absurdity.

Without explicitly intending to do so, Martha Wolfenstein (1951), in her classic paper on children's humor, offers a psychoanalytic developmental perspective on the problem we have been considering and thereby sheds light on the possible relations between cognitive dissonance and emotional conflict.

Wolfenstein commences her study with a wealth of examples culled from her own clinical practice to demonstrate that young school-age children do not experience jokes in the same manner as adults. Specifically, children between the ages of six and twelve, though they adore jokes and riddles, may completely miss their absurdity—absurdity defined, that is, as I have done in the previous pages. In other words, children fail to respond to the wordplay that conveys the double meanings or opposed viewpoints upon which the humor of jokes would seem to depend: they avoid or bypass cognitive dissonance. Since this is so, reasons Wolfenstein, we must seek elsewhere to discover what it is that makes jokes so pleasurable to children.

It turns out, according to Wolfenstein, that what makes jokes funny to children is, paradoxically, the children's very capacity to bypass wordplay and react directly to latent content. In contrast to adults, for whom cognitive dissonance serves as a defense and a distraction, the two opposing ideas enabling them to decathect the latent content (as nonsensical) before it becomes conscious, children's pleasure comes precisely from the gratification in fantasy of repressed desires and from a concommitant (counterphobic) sense of mastery over them. Thus, what children experience and enjoy in jokes is more likely their magical solutions to real situations than their comic absurdity. Lewis Carroll's Alice serves as an ideal exemplar of this in that she is portrayed as responding with deadpan seriousness to all the oddities that surround her; only occasionally does she teeter on the verge of experiencing the fantastic absurdity of her situation. An informal survey suggests that at least some children seem to find both *Alice's Adventures in Wonderland* and *Through the Looking Glass* somewhat more scary than funny, although extremely compelling and attractive (presumably because of their engagement with deep psychological issues, among other reasons; see Greenacre, 1955), whereas for adults, clearly, the opposite is the case.

Why is it that children are unable to enjoy the absurdity of jokes? Piaget and Inhelder (1969) offer a plausible schema—the notion of the child's gradual development toward abstract thinking—that is, toward the capacity to transcend the self in thought; however, this is a notion that has come under attack by other child psychologists (see, for example, Donaldson, 1978). Wolfenstein, on the other hand, in the 1951 article proposes purely psychoanalytic hypotheses that strike me as particularly helpful and that intuitively seem to be true. She suggests that, in childhood, an attraction to images and investment in them may be stronger than an investment in words. Thus, wordplay itself may simply dissolve under the pressure of fantasy. Rather than reading double meanings, the child experiences mutually opposed images as fusing on the basis of their emotional connection (as in dreams) and responds to them accordingly. This sort of phenomenon, which

69

Freud called condensation (in chapter 7 of *The Interpretation of Dreams*), is graphically illustrated throughout the oeuvre of Magritte; one thinks, for example, of his painting *The Explanation* (see the chapter, "Optical Appetites"), in which a carrot merges with a glass bottle to form a frustrating (and absurd) object that can be neither eaten nor drunk. Another operative factor may be that children are still learning and struggling to keep sense and nonsense apart—to separate fantasy from reality (see Fraiberg, 1959). Thus, they are resistant to what they must experience as a cognitive regression to the infantile stage through which they have so recently passed—a time when, as it seemed, sound and sense were arbitrarily joined.

Therefore, whereas for the adult the experience of the absurdity of a joke serves defensively to ward off anxiety and facilitate the release of tension in the form of laughter, children cling tenaciously both to their recently acquired mastery over words and to their vivid fantasies. Consequently, they use jokes progressively in the service of development—a factor that explains, as Wolfenstein points out, their love of endlessly repeating the same joke or riddle, a practice rarely encountered among adults, for whom a similar need does not exist. Because the decathexis of latent content is successful for adults, the joke *can* be forgotten. With children, however, where the joke touches on issues that are live and burning, the defense of denial ("It's only a joke; I don't really mean it") cannot operate so successfully.

There is, however, a sense in which children *do* seem aware of divergent viewpoints similar to those described by Nagel. As Wolfenstein points out (1959, pp. 93–157 passim), in versions of the "moron" joke, they do experience themselves in a double sense—as telling the joke and as identifying with its protagonist. In this way, the child can be smarter than the adult whom she stumps with a riddle ("Why did the moron throw the butter out of the window?" "Because he wanted to see the butterfly"). She can turn the tables by knowing in the present what once (the first time she herself heard it) she did not know. At the same time she can both be the moron (who, though seemingly stupid, turns out to be smarter than one who cannot answer the riddle because he actually produces reasons for his preposterous behavior) and feel superior to the moron (because she understands that his reasons make no sense). In this example, a child's emotional needs seem to be convergent with her cognitive functioning, and the pleasure apparently derives from both spheres.

Wolfenstein's work thus lends cogent support to Nagel's view that the capacity to recognize the absurd represents a positive human achievement.

As was pointed out earlier, Nagel likens this ability to the capacity for living with epistemological uncertainty. The psychoanalyst extends his discussion by demonstrating that this capacity is intimately linked with affective components, with feelings, with emotional growth and maturity. The more pressing an individual's emotional conflicts, the closer together her worlds of fantasy and reality, the less likely it is that she will have the capacity to experience with pleasure the divergence between subjective and objective views of self and other.

Philosopher and psychoanalyst, in my present example, concur in maintaining that absurdity, inherent in human existence, arises from conflicts which, given human limitations, are not fully resolvable, and they would agree that absurdity itself becomes a major problem only under special circumstances. One such circumstance is when it is not recognized (as in the obsessions of the Rat Man); another is when it is recognized but taken as a permanent obstacle to action (as in Beckett's *Endgame*, 1957).

Nagel does address briefly the interesting question of why absurdity warrants so much distress, but he spends a great deal more effort in indicating precisely how intellectual stratagems have been devised to alleviate this distress. In attempting to bypass the experience of the absurd by unifying the polarities it entails, the usual tactics have been to allow one of its terms (normally, the objective) to swallow up the other (the subjective) and then to engage in a process of rationalization involving one of three artifices— reduction, elimination, or annexation (1979, pp. 210–11). These have been the usual paths of normative science.

Rather than rehearse these strategies for mitigating the pain of entertaining divergent viewpoints, I want to consider momentarily the question Nagel leaves behind: namely, what is it that makes such strategies necessary? What *is* so disturbing to us about the simultaneous awareness of opposing viewpoints? Whence our yearning for grand syntheses, metanarratives, unified perspectives—for oneness, be it positivistic or idealistic? What precisely is it that makes the absurd *absurd* in the original sense of being hard to hear and to bear?

Again, psychoanalysis offers tentative answers in both dynamic and developmental terms. Freudians (and Kleinians), in trying to account for such yearnings and fears, might turn to the notion of the death instinct. A developmental viewpoint is found perhaps most eloquently expressed in the writings of Margaret S. Mahler (1968), who speaks of a lifelong longing for return to symbiosis with the imaginary all-good, all-nurturing mother of

71

earliest infancy. If indeed such regressive yearnings underpin our wishes for synthesis and our perennial discomfort in its absence, it seems clear that Nagel's argument for creative acceptance of coexisting conflicting points of view is the progressive position. Clinically, this might translate into therapeutic goals that include maximizing an individual's capacity for awareness and tolerance of divergent perspectives—on the part of both self and other. Again, however, a caveat is in order. As Wolfenstein's work on children's humor implies, awareness of ambiguity and absurdity can be used regressively in adults. Beyond the realm of jokes, it is also possible for an acceptance of the absurd to function pathologically: to ward off intimate attachments, to avoid commitments, to rationalize indecisiveness, to ridicule the long-term loyalties and heroism that depend on single-mindedness (as discussed in "Reading *Antigone* Again," below), to condone a narcissistic adaptation, to defend hypocritical behavior, to justify distrust, suspicion, and even brutality.

For both the philosopher and the psychoanalyst, therefore, the chief difficulty in explicating the absurd is that our attitudes toward it are so various. The human potential for transcendence in thought can be accompanied by a spectrum of affects ranging from delight and amusement to aversion and horror. Above all, this potential entails an important *ethical* dimension; the label of *absurd*, for example, can be used to reneg on responsibility and to avoid engagement with the perspectives of others. I have suggested that these varying positions are predicated on the mutual fit of our emotional and intellectual development, awareness, and competence. Psychoanalysis indicates that, whereas emotional conflict can interfere with our awareness of and positive response to cognitive complexity, epistemological uncertainty may likewise give rise to anxiety and emotional distress as well as, occasionally, to a heady sense of living fully at the height of one's powers. Optimally, the absurdity of our human lives can be accepted as a challenge both with respect to our selves and in our encounters with others.

An earlier version of this chapter, under the title "Oysters, Cannons, and Morons: Psychoanalytic and Philosophic Musings on the Absurd," was published in *American Imago* 49, no. 1 (Spring 1992): 81–96. I am grateful to Mary Mothersill for introducing me to the work of Thomas Nagel, to Donald Moss for firing off his devastatingly delightful first reading, and to Nathaniel Geoffrey Lew for persuading me that writing about the absurd is not ipso facto absurd but that, even if it were, that might in itself constitute a powerful incentive to proceed.

Writing across the Disciplines

Surprise Ending
Vodka, Oats, and Pistols

To carry on with the notion of the absurd, let us consider Anton Chekhov's *The Bear*. Dubbed a farce or jest by its author, this charming work was first performed to wildly enthusiastic audiences in Moscow in 1888. Since plays (scripts), like concertos (scores), are written to be performed, and I am persuaded, with Susanne Langer (1953) that any particular performance completes (or possibly foils, in the case of a bad performance) an original creative effort, I shall refer throughout this chapter to a particular incarnation of *The Bear* that took place several years ago at the Juilliard Theater in New York.

I have chosen to discuss this work because it offers an almost continuous barrage of incompatible viewpoints and emotions, contradictions and paradoxes. Three exaggerated characters confront one another in a bizarre but actually quite banal situation exacerbated by the fervor of their reactions. The content is a heady mix of life and death, violence and passion, genuineness and pretense, the sober and the comic. Above all, it offers a final moment of absurdity—a startling, tenuous moment which serves as a brilliant climax to all preceding tensions. The point I hope to make is that no measure of psychological or formal analysis can obviate its quintessential absurdity.

First, to refresh the memory: Chekhov's three characters are Luka, a devoted but peevishly ineffectual old manservant; Popova, a dimple-cheeked young widow in deep mourning for her recently deceased and, as it quickly appears, not entirely faithful husband, Nikolai; and Smirnov, a mercurial, complicated, and oafish middle-aged landowner and creditor—supplier, we learn, of oats to feed the horses of the said Nikolai.

The play begins with an extraordinary speech by Luka, rich in imagery, in which he enjoins Popova to cease her exaggerated mourning, emerge from her seclusion, and begin to enjoy life again. She obstinately refuses, proclaiming resolutely that she will remain faithful to her beloved Nikolai (mean and errant though he was) even unto her death. Suddenly recalling the handsome figure Nikolai used to cut on horseback, she directs Luka to give the deceased's favorite horse, Toby, an extra bag of oats.

A loud ring is heard, and Luka is unable to prevent the entry of Smirnov, who intrudes with a conspicuous lack of ceremony and demands immediate payment of his overdue account. Popova, distracted, agrees to pay him two days hence, when her bailiff will return, and then leaves the room to avoid further contact.

Smirnov, now alone in her drawing room, soliloquizes with a curious mixture of boorishness and self-consciousness on the desperate state of his own finances. He determines to remain there until he gets his money. Shouting for Luka, he commands a glass of vodka. Popova returns and politely entreats him to depart. Smirnov refuses and assaults her with a spirited, venomous, comic, and impassioned tirade on the vices of women both in and out of love. Popova, her rage escalating, responds sarcastically, contrasting her own fidelity with Nikolai's lack thereof, and orders Luka to put Smirnov out. Smirnov hotly refuses to go and abuses the old servant; Popova, in high temper, proclaims him a crude, ill-mannered bear. Stung by this insult, Smirnov impulsively challenges her to a duel, and she, to his astonishment, agrees. Fetching her dead husband's pistols, she asks Smirnov to teach her how to fire. As he does so, his tone and gestures exquisitely convey the intensity of his rapidly shifting feelings. He announces that he intends to fire into the air. Exasperated, Popova goads him, taunting him with his cowardice.

Finally, with hesitation and embarrassment, Smirnov admits the dawning of his admiration, his tender feelings, for her. Laughing angrily, Popova mimics his preposterous words, orders him out, demands the promised fight, and shouts, "I hate you!" Smirnov grabs her hand, sinks to his knees, and proposes to her. Then, ashamed, he gets up and moves quickly to the door. Popova calls to him. She drops her pistol. He approaches her. She protests. Suddenly, they embrace in a sustained kiss. As the curtain falls, Luka returns, bringing with him a motley band of rescuers armed with gar-

2.1. Sketches of costumes for characters in Chekhov's *The Bear*.

den tools. Popova has only time to say, with lowered eyes: "Luka, tell them in the stable not to give Toby any oats today."

Emphasizing visualization and concretization of its humorous, even ridiculous elements, the Juilliard performance interpreted *The Bear* as a ribald farce. One result of this approach was to throw into question the nature of the serious and the comic as well as the relative merits of relying on an author's words to evoke imaginative response versus using the stage as a means of objectifying those words, giving them concrete form, color, and specific action. It suggested the necessary interrelatedness not only of all character interpretations but of all aspects of a theatrical production. By drawing attention to design, costume, and staging, it hinted at the almost infinite nuances of imaginative interpretation to which a work of dramatic art is subject when the intuitions of actor, director, designer, and playwright all merge and emerge in the magic of a live performance (fig. 2.1).

Imagine the stage: Beginning with the tolling of bells and a darkened space, the lights gradually rise on a whimsical set—red, blue, and yellow—with a diminutive suggestion of onion domes and fragile furniture, its bright, simple colors and bold art-nouveau flowers hinting at the light, unstable nature of the dramatic action and the interpretation to come. In this gossamer setting, Luka's opening address to Popova masterfully draws us into an imaginary world. The stage is packed with subtle clues. The speech, spicy with imagery, vivid and visual, ends on a note reminiscent of Campion, Herrick, or Marvell—immediately jarring as advice to a mourning widow. Introducing themes that will continue throughout the play, Luka's speech thrusts us at once into a world of contradiction. This first perplexing picture of Popova forms a template for our subsequent contrapuntal experiences of her.

One thread of imagery introduced by Luka's speech is that of eating. The cook, he says, has gone berry-picking, the cat is catching birdies, the mice have eaten the livery, the officers are like bonbons. To eat is, of course, to live. Luka importunes Popova to cease her preoccupation with death and to imitate the cook, the chambermaid, the cat. By including the regimental officers as "bon-bons—you'll never get your fill of them," he equates the ideas of eating and sexual/social activity, while identifying them as life-enhancing and positive. Eating and prolonging life are featured a few moments later in Popova's own speech when she directs Luka to feed extra oats to her late husband's horse, thus in a sense prolonging Nikolai's "life" for her, perpetuating her involvement with him in the form of the animal so closely associated with him in her imagination.

Eating images and the reference to berry-picking were concretized in the Juilliard performance by a bowl of fruit strategically placed on the table of the set and by actual eating on the part of all three actors during the production. Their eating was noisily aggressive, and they engaged the fruit in slapstick interchange, thus both reinforcing and disclaiming the special significance of these images in Luka's speech and in the drama itself. "Berry-picking" alludes to Luka's view of Popova as a ripe fruit which will rot and decay if she continues to mourn in seclusion and not allow herself to be "picked." She is thus exhorted both to eat and to be eaten.

Animal imagery abounds throughout the play. In part, it functions to enhance our amusement, our experience of the absurd, our sense of it as being more comic than tragic. To characterize human beings or their behavior patterns as animallike simplifies and exaggerates them, so that we can gain perspective on them and laugh. For instance, when Luka mentions the cat catching birdies, he insinuates that Popova herself may be seen as either cat or birdie. As the cat, who expresses enjoyment of life by causing death, Popova has come to live life by dwelling upon death. The birdie, on the other hand, foreshadows the image of the peahen that Luka describes later in his speech, conceiving of Popova as spreading her tailfeathers before the officers; in this marvelous image, Popova is seen as the animal to be caught.

It is important that the animal identified with Popova's late husband is a horse, an ancient symbol of passion. She reminisces: "How wonderfully he rode! How graceful he was when he pulled at the reins with all his strength!" These sensual lines evoke Popova's yearning for, and simultaneous denial of, the sexuality that has been lost from her life. It is Toby, Nikolai's horse, that she wishes to feed and pamper in order to preserve some living symbol of her memories. Smirnov, of course, is not just any creditor but the supplier of horses' oats. To embrace Smirnov and deny oats to the horse is, for Popova, to choose the more exciting yet risky pleasure of present passion over the dubious satisfactions of fantasy, of savoring past love and martyrdom, of preserving the purity of her masochistic ego ideal. Because the horse is so closely linked with Nikolai, she may, by refusing him oats, be at last directing her anger against her dead husband, rather than against herself or Smirnov. We cannot know. Does she, in this moment, begin to free herself from the tyranny of the past?

What about the title of the play, which is, after all, another animal image? The bear clearly refers to a Russian character stereotype—intense and volatile, rapidly shifting from one mood to another—and since the epithet is used by Popova to describe Smirnov, we might take her remark at face value and assume for the moment that he represents this Russian character. I rather like this idea because, from his soliloquies, we learn that there is more to Smirnov than the brutish, clumsy façade which is first perceived.

Smirnov is witty, self-conscious, and introspective as well as emotionally labile. ("Not one of those swine wants to pay me! And all because I'm too

77

nice to them. I'm a sniveling idiot, I'm spineless, I'm an old lady! I'm too delicate with them." "Nobody would say I was looking well! Dusty all over, boots dirty, unwashed, unkempt, straw on my waistcoat." "The dear lady probably took me for a robber. It's not very polite to present myself in a drawing room looking like this.") Self-deprecation, turning inward, sensitivity to the way one is perceived by others: surely this is not the usual conception of a bear! Smirnov is oafish, a *bear*, in his manners, appearance, blunt expressions, but inside he is perhaps fully human—warm, vulnerable, and wracked with all the ambivalence and fragility we recognize. It is this complexity, this absurd contrast between his inner feelings and outer appearance, that renders him comical but at the same time keeps him from collapsing into a thoroughly ridiculous character.

More animal imagery. Smirnov calls Popova a common crocodile and says he will shoot her down like a chicken. He compares a faithful woman to a "horned cat" or a "white woodcock" and declares that "a woman is capable of loving [nothing] besides a lapdog." I agreed with the decision in the Juilliard production to interpret *lapdog* as an oblique reference to Luka. Luka's sash fell between his legs; he crawled on all fours; he was patted and fed by Smirnov's hand. At a certain point Luka, the servant, simply metamorphosed into a faithful, ineffectual canine pet.

Other metaphoric aspects of the play were similarly objectified in the Juilliard production. The furniture in Popova's house, for example, emblematic of the fragility of her exaggerated mourning, her self-deception, literally fell apart on stage several times during the course of the action. Smirnov broke her furniture as he broke through her defenses. (Chekhov wrote this action into his stage directions.) Our sense of the absurd arises here perhaps because of the very concreteness of the interpretation. That which is too obvious can also seem absurd. Eating, as mentioned before, was in this production highly aggressive and rowdy, with both Smirnov and Popova smashing half-eaten pieces of fruit into each other's faces. As they ate and sparred on stage, the mood of mourning (established by the initially darkened stage and tolling bell) gave way to ribaldry.

What was the effect of it all? And can psychoanalysis lend any further insights? Why do we perk up and pay heed precisely when we are confronted with a series of contradictions? (The surrealists played endlessly on this motif.) Chekhov pastes life to death: death in life (Popova mourning) and life in death (Nikolai as Toby). Smirnov, under threat of death himself ("If you don't pay me today, then tomorrow I'll have to hang myself"), offers both death and life to Popova by challenging her to a duel, teaching her how to shoot a pistol, then asking her to marry him. Hatred or rage metamorphoses into love (or lust), passionate feelings are transferred to inappropriate objects, most significant, there is an ending that startles and amazes us while striking us as entirely satisfying and appropriate. This is the crux of the play: the embrace—shocking, valid, and thoroughly absurd.

This embrace, this culminating kiss, so indispensable, confers upon the play its meaning, even if only in terms of the world onstage. It may be that, as Nagel (1979) intimates, meaning exists only within the context of the absurd, much though we often view it otherwise—equating absurdity with lack of meaning. But, putting such notions aside for the moment, can psychoanalysis aid our understanding?

Among the psychoanalytically charged thoughts that occur to me, the most salient have to do with violence and passion, aggression and sexuality. At the fever pitch of emotion, under threat of death and heightened consciousness of mortality, these are readily interchangeable. This fact helps to make believable Popova's stunning transformation from the woman who cries, "I hate you; I . . . challenge you!" to the one who accepts Smirnov's embrace moments later, at the close of the play.

And what about the movement from repression and disguise of emotion to its release and the freedom that follows? As Popova responds more and more heatedly to Smirnov's taunts, she reveals her previously disavowed resentment toward the dead husband for whom she is grieving in such an extravagant manner. We learn that her grief is, like the poorly glued furniture, but a fragile defense, a mask for stored-up anger about Nikolai's betrayals and also, perhaps, for guilt over her own inability to feel sorrow unsullied by ambivalence. Once she has expressed this pent-up anger to Smirnov, she begins to experience renewed vigor, liberation, and the possibility of a new relationship.

First, however, she must negotiate the transference of emotion from one object to another—and then the resolution of that transference. Transference is crucial. Early in the play, when she is explaining and defending her stance of exaggerated mourning both to Luka and to the audience, she acknowledges her husband's ill behavior ("he was often mean to me, cruel . . . and even unfaithful"). At this early point in the drama, however, her admission serves merely to bolster her rigid, self-righteous mask: "But I shall remain true to the grave." Stating the facts serves no deeper emotional purpose. It is only when she says them again later to Smirnov—a man closely

79

identified with her husband—in *anger*, that past and present merge in her consciousness. She can in fact address Smirnov as if he were her dead husband, and at this point the release occurs. Throughout their sparring scene, we sense how much she relishes the combat between them and watch as she prolongs it. Indeed, Smirnov is moved at one point to say: "I don't have the pleasure of being . . . your husband."

Smirnov too experiences a transference and release. His rage at Popova is actually frustration over his own situation—his helpless indebtedness—and it is he who is the first of the couple to recognize that his anger has been misplaced. This happens at the point when Popova accepts his challenge to a duel with pistols. Threat of death serves as a powerful stimulus to altered perception. ("I'll shoot her like a chicken! . . . What a woman! How she blushed, her eyes shone . . . she accepted my challenge!") Gradually the present overcomes the past; Smirnov realizes he is not angry at *her* ("My fury has diminished. Wonderful woman!"), and sexual passion replaces his rage ("I've gone out of my mind. I'm in love like a boy, like an idiot!").

But beyond such thoughts as these, psychoanalysis can do little to explain the meaning of the final embrace. Repeated encounters with *The Bear* leave me struggling with a dangerous wish to stop explaining! A wish, rather, to embrace the final embrace and revel in it as a perfect ending to this feisty play. After all, we do not explain how people turn into rhinoceroses, how feet become shoes, apples replace heads, and noses grow into pipes. We may turn to Sartre's *Nausea* for a description of relevant feelings or to Freud's essay (1919) on E. T. A. Hoffmann's "The Sand-Man" for his grip on the uncanny. A soupçon of that weirdness, a twinge of that existential pain, is foreshadowed in the embrace of Smirnov and Popova, which, however, has less to do with the familiar becoming unintelligible than with the unexpected becoming suddenly, surprisingly, right.

Whatever we say about *The Bear*, the kiss resists analysis. No matter how thoroughly we explain it after the fact or attempt to dismiss it by attribution to a farcical convention, its precise effect could, like life itself (and art), never have been predicted. Though it may lose some of its initial shock after a performance or two, it retains its jarring note, its quintessential mystery.

The idea for this chapter came to me one summer when I attended the Lincoln Center Institute in New York City, a program of aesthetic education in the performing arts of theater, music, and dance. There, at Juilliard, a gifted trio of drama students performed *The Bear* several times and permanently altered my experience of it.

Writing across the Disciplines

Doubling, Disjunction, and Displacement in a Comic Strip

Turning from the absurd to the humorous and from theater to popular culture, we note that contemporary scholarship in the humanities has been questioning the narrow range of cultural objects that traditionally falls under serious interpretive scrutiny and attempting to enlarge our sights. One new focus is the comic strip, a widely circulated and influential medium of popular culture that, highly charged and subtly coded, has a strong impact on adults and children. Combining the two great sign systems of image and text to create humor that is both graphic and linguistic, both self-referential and broadly critical in a social sense, the comic strip provides a locus for the analysis of sign systems and of subjectivity, a laboratory for the study of doubling, displacement, and disjunction. "Calvin and Hobbes" by Bill Watterson (1987, 1988, 1989, 1990, 1991), the example I have chosen here, gives strong priority to psychological, particularly developmental, themes as well.

A recent major exhibition ("High and Low: Modern Art and Popular Culture," mounted at the Museum of Modern Art in New York, 7 October 1990–15 January 1991) featured the comic strip and other modes of popular culture, albeit problematically and with significant acknowledged and unacknowledged omissions. In an instructive essay from the catalogue of that exhibit, bracketing the ancient world (one thinks of Egyptian tomb painting) and the medieval deployment of seriated imagery on altarpieces and in stained glass, illuminated manuscripts, and relief sculpture, Gopnik (1990) traces the comic strip per se to a Romantic dream formulated by Goethe, who in his old age noted with chagrin the passing of what he saw as the unifying culture of folk tales and ballads. Upon seeing the illustrated novels, including humorous sequential drawings, of the Swiss art theorist and educator Rodolphe Töppfer, Goethe speculated that, indeed, *this* medium might become the vehicle for new forms of cultural reconciliation in the future, "a popular form that could make a big, anonymous society feel like a family," as Gopnik puts it (p. 153). The comic strip, in other words, might provide a vehicle for the Romantic dream of a universal language—a dream that extended into modernism in the form of a wish to discover a common vocabulary of form. Further, modernism was preoccupied with fragmentation, anxiety, and alienation, themes equally germane to the comic strip. Thus, in Gopnik's words, "the comic strip is in many ways not a precursor . . . but another kind of modern art" (p. 153).

To this I would add that the particular example featured in these pages, the art of Bill Watterson, occasionally rises to achievements easily comparable to that of major gallery artists of our century. Roy Lichtenstein's work in the early 1960s, for example, derived from comics and dubbed "pop art," demonstrates virtually unmediated the impact of popular culture on what the MOMA exhibit conventionally insisted on calling "high art." Similarly, Maurice Sendak, a premier illustrator of books for young children, admits to having been profoundly influenced by comic strips, particularly by the art of Winsor McCay. One can readily find traces of Sendak's affection for "Little Nemo in Slumberland" (1908) in his widely circulated and somewhat notorious picture book of 1970, *In the Night Kitchen*.

Each individual episode of a syndicated comic strip must introduce itself to new readers while simultaneously continuing its ongoing conversation with habitués. This tandem imperative is redoubled in a strip like "Calvin and Hobbes," which deliberately appeals to sophisticated adults as well as to elementary school children. It also has great appeal for undergraduates, as indicated by a nationwide poll reported in the November 1990 issue of the *Chronicle of Higher Education*. Formal disjunctions between individual strips, moreover (each of which has a separate plot despite continuity of title, character, and general context), mirror the formal disjunctions with which they represent in turn fantasy and reality. What follows here replicates these formal strategems of comic strip art by offering disjunctive takes on "Calvin and Hobbes"—takes unified only by their common subject(s). In so doing, in making discrete sets of comments that resemble the frames of the strip itself, I implicitly critique the myth of absolute division between interpretation and object and/or between artist and critic, in terms very like those inscribed in "Calvin and Hobbes" between the creator and that which is created. One of the most salient features of this art is its lability and spontaneity—its flow of image, word, wish, and dream—which, at its best, co-opts the reader and creates her as co-artist, actor, fantasizer, critic.

The best song in the witty musical *City of Angels* (1989) is sung by a 1940s Hollywood scriptwriter, Stine, and his created character, a private eye named Stone. "You're Nothing Without Me" explodes the presumed hierarchical relations between authors and their characters. It compels the audience to consider that, as in the case of the legendary golem and Rabbi Loew of Prague, a created being, once brought to life, can acquire an impetus no longer subject its creator's will. Indeed, it may reflexively re-create its creator—a notion that applies early on to the relations between children and parents.

In the Watterson strip, little Calvin with baseball bat, for example, and his father with lawnmower engage in a momentary role reversal that also quips on contemporary textual analysis (fig. 2.2). We see another play on shifts of posture in an exchange between Calvin and his mother (fig. 2.3). In this instance, the child gives the sort of obsessively detailed and explicit instructions to the mother (about his jelly sandwich!) that parents and teachers often give to children. Then, true to form, she fails to follow them and thus exasperates him in the same manner that children so often bedevil adults. This strip also spoofs the ritualism that characterizes the developmental landmark when children, in order to conform to social conventions and banish the instinctual (anal) pleasures of messing as well as to shore up bodily and psychic boundaries, produce behavioral reaction-formations that manifest themselves as near-phobias—for example, about different foods touching on the same plate or foods with no distinct color, foods with a formless appearance or a gooey texture.

As a parenthesis here, Watterson also understands the obverse phenomenon, that is, how a child's fantasy life can be organized around and used to justify his or her ongoing pleasure in smearing and in oral aggression. Typically, we find large, vivid, and dramatic dinosaurs of Calvin's imagination who are bitten off by their frames, and the chosen colors often suggest the inside of a mouth. Oral aggression, a theme that recurs in any engagement with childhood, figures prominently if subtly in many "Calvin and Hobbes"

83

2.2. CALVIN AND HOBBES copyright Watterson. Reprinted with permission of
UNIVERSAL PRESS SYNDICATE. All rights reserved.

2.3. CALVIN AND HOBBES copyright Watterson. Reprinted with permission of
UNIVERSAL PRESS SYNDICATE. All rights reserved.

strips. It is featured, for example, in a send-up of nursery rhymes and fairy
tales (fig. 2.4), where the knowing child points out to his "naïve" parent the
oral aggression that is, in fact, *the* underlying, unifying theme among these
texts, the one most anxiously *and* pleasurably attended to by children.

Like much else about the postmodern musical *City of Angels*—a hybrid
in being a stage show *about* a movie and simultaneously representing the
plots *of* that movie and its creation by casting actors and actresses in dual
roles—the duet "You're Nothing Without Me" conveys an aesthetic of displacement and destabilization. Such an aesthetic also informs the comic
strip, which is, like the musical, a hybrid medium of contemporary popular
culture.

Like musicals and movies, syndicated comic strips function as relatively
transparent vehicles for extant social codes while simultaneously serving
as implicit and explicit platforms from which to critique them. The comic

Writing across the Disciplines

84

strip, in particular, by virtue of its humor disguises its subversiveness, its jokes serving as pleasurable vehicles for serious commentary and occasional coy rebelliousness (see Freud, 1905b). In one "Calvin and Hobbes" strip, the widely publicized conflict over the support of the National Endowment for the Arts for an exhibition of the photography of Robert Mapplethorpe, led by Senator Jesse Helms, is subtly alluded to via metaphor: the child Calvin is equated with the artist, and his teacher with the North Carolina senator. This cartoon takes a giant step back from the controversy and reveals the absurdity not only of the diehard reactionary in his or her hotly defended rigidity but also of the posturing marginal artist, who is potentially just as laughable in his or her predictable iconoclasm.

Bill Watterson, the clever animator of Calvin and Hobbes, presents himself to us slyly in a self-portrait-as-cartoon (fig. 2.5). As a highly successful commercial artist, Watterson always implicates himself reflexively in his own critique of art, artists, and the art world. His work demonstrates not only an esprit of experimentation but a continual questioning of reality— hallmarks, as Jean-François Lyotard (1984) has written, of postmodernism.

"Calvin and Hobbes" features a blond, spike-haired six-year-old protagonist usually wearing a striped T-shirt (Calvin) and his toy tiger, also striped and bristly (Hobbes). Their joyful balancing (fig. 2.6) figures the principal agenda of Watterson's art, a light and precarious treading over issues that do, however, often have serious consequences. When no one else is around, Hobbes comes to life for Calvin: Calvin creates Hobbes as his imaginary companion in a florid fantasy life that interpenetrates everyday

2.4. CALVIN AND HOBBES copyright Watterson. Reprinted with permission of UNIVERSAL PRESS SYNDICATE. All rights reserved.

2.5. CALVIN AND HOBBES copyright Watterson. Reprinted with permission of UNIVERSAL PRESS SYNDICATE.

reality and critically appropriates the absurdities and pseudosophistications, the "mythologies," as Barthes (1957) has termed them, of current American culture. There is a fundamental conceptual difference between Calvin and Hobbes and their famous, beloved, far simpler cartoon counterparts, Charlie Brown and Snoopy, drawn by Charles Schulz: for, whereas

2.6. CALVIN AND HOBBES copyright Watterson. Reprinted with permission of UNIVERSAL PRESS SYNDICATE.

Writing across the Disciplines

Snoopy the beagle possesses an independent existence as a willful speaking subject in his own right, Hobbes exists as a sentient being solely in Calvin's fantasy life. He is a projection, an alter-ego, an imaginary companion, and yet, all the same, marvelously *real*. This crucial difference allows Watterson to play with and explore realms closed to Schulz, realms of particular fascination for psychoanalysis.

Strategically imbuing his references to contemporary culture with an *apparently* childlike naïveté and shaping them into wish-fulfilling scenarios, Watterson as author-artist develops playful intertexts and whimsical imagery featuring typically postmodern fluctuations of perspective. The butt of the humor, for example, keeps shifting—not only from character to character but, occasionally, to the reader of the strip, whose expectations are often abruptly thwarted. In this way, this art conveys a sense of mobile subjectivity and casts the reader in serial roles. Moreover, just as the places of creator and created are problematized, so modern culture itself appears not merely as contextualization for, or constituent of, subjectivity, but as *appropriable* by a given subject (in this case, Calvin) for his own unpredictable but psychologically valid ends. The disparity—or serendipitous convergence—between private, wishful, fantastic ends and the public iconography that encodes them produces hilarious moments for the reader— moments that mask anxiety with pleasure.

For example, in a wonderful send-up of cubist painting (fig. 2.7), the child's developmental and cognitive imperative to locate self at the centerpoint, to isolate perspectives and divide up the world unproblematically into right (that's *me*) and wrong (that's *you*), coincides with a cultural critique that flags the tendency of information overload to induce chaos and/or paralysis. It illustrates the bond between multiple perspectives and maddening indecisiveness. It offers, in short, a critique of postmodernism by humanism, but staged ironically in reverse historical sequence as a rebellious gesture by the child toward the parent.

Another strip combines cultural critique with developmental savvy and, like the one previously described, plays on the child's need to maintain dualities. Watterson marvelously illustrates the Kleinian notion of splitting—that is, the maintenance of good internal objects by the projection outward of badness and of the state of being wrong. He accomplishes this by using the literal absence and presence of color in his drawing symbolically. Calvin wakes up in a totally polarized world where everything has

87

suddenly become black and white. Speculating that some strange nuclear reaction has occurred on the sun, so that radiation is prevented from defining itself in terms of a spectrum, or that specific objects are no longer reflecting different wave lengths, Calvin decides it would be pointless to try to discuss this with his dad. In the final frame, however, he does go to his father, who—buried in a colored book that looks suspiciously like a comic book—tells Calvin that his problem is that he sees everything in terms of black and white. To which Calvin retorts that every once in a while this is, in fact, the way things actually are! Thus, again, Watterson renders problematic our acquiescence in simplistic dichotomous thought by implying that what underlies the father's apparent "rationality" is as contaminated by dualistic thinking as is the supposed "irrationality" of the child.

A third strip in this genre (fig. 2.8) also works with a convergence between public and private, outer and inner, reality and fantasy. Here, the child/artist, by testing, by suspending accepted conventions, precipitates an aversive response on the part of his parent/audience. Calvin's mother's ensuing threat thus entails a restoration of boundaries, in particular, punitive boundaries; in addition, by introducing the word *sell*, it interjects a reference to commodification in our culture—both in art and in human relations. In each of these strips, vision is equated with certain kinds of knowing and being and, significantly, with power. Watterson perpetuates, but

Writing across the Disciplines

characteristically reinterprets in his sharp-eyed and unique contemporary idiom, the ancient metaphor of seeing as understanding.

A somewhat different way of instantiating the convergence of internal and external worlds occurs where Calvin, totally absorbed in one of his favorite daydreams as the intrepid "Spaceman Spiff," blurts out in arithmetic

2.8. CALVIN AND HOBBES copyright Watterson. Reprinted with permission of UNIVERSAL PRESS SYNDICATE. All rights reserved.

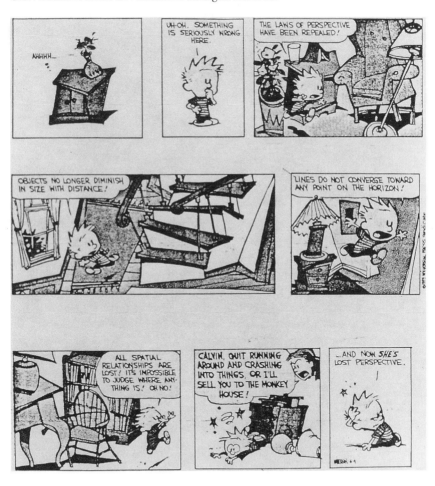

2.9. CALVIN AND HOBBES copyright Watterson. Reprinted with permission of
UNIVERSAL PRESS SYNDICATE. All rights reserved.

class the correct answer to his teacher's question, solely because that precise number happens to be just what his fantasy at that moment requires (fig. 2.9). It is especially delightful here that Watterson allows reality to intrude for only one strategic moment, while fantasy regains its hegemony at the end.

In another example (Watterson, 1988), Calvin is dwarfed in an art museum by what others call "great art" but which he, the quintessential naïve viewer, perceives quite logically as "decapitated naked people." He metamorphoses suddenly into an enormous, devouring Godzilla and swallows a museum guard in one ferocious gulp. Thus, popular culture triumphs over high art, while the genuinely disturbing and stimulating sight of realistically portrayed bodily mutilation is conquered by an act of primitive oral aggression. Little Calvin grows larger than all the adults, both flesh and marble, that surround him. This cartoon sequence, which alludes in passing to film, painting, sculpture, and music, comments also on the relative status of the different arts.

Watterson's schema here recalls Hogarth's graphic parodies of ancient statuary. In a famous plate from his *Analysis of Beauty* (see Paulson, 1974), the eighteenth-century English satirist depicted a sculpture garden in which casts of renowned classical statues are seen indulging in indecorous acts and absurd exchanges with human figures. The Medici Venus, Belvedere torso, Farnese Hercules, Apollo Belvedere, and Laocoön all appear in anomalous poses. Both Hogarth and Watterson ridicule (their) art along with those who revere it and those who know absolutely nothing about it.

Another Watterson strip (1990) portrays Calvin with his feet up on his "desk," his father's hat pulled down rakishly over his eyes. The light coming through the window covers him with tiger stripes (evoking Hobbes, who is absent). He has been transformed into "Tracer Bullet," a tough private eye. In turn, he remakes his mild-mannered Mom, who enters stage-left with potholders and casserole, into a "brunette," a "pushy dame" (she tells him to take his hat off at the dinner table), and "trouble." (She interrupts his daydream with "a case"—in other words, with *food*, in the sense that, in terms of his fantasy, a client who comes to the down-and-out detective with a problem to solve will literally put food on his dinner table.) In this strip, the final frame provides the joke by supplying an image that both completes and contradicts what precedes it: Calvin shrinks back to child proportions,

91

and his "desk" resumes its normal guise as the dining-room table. This sequence plays on the clichés of the so-called film noir of the 1940s and 1950s, especially in its use of venetian blinds to transform Calvin into his double, Hobbes. In typical postmodern fashion, however, this iconography is not only quoted but also parodied.

Watterson manages never to foreclose the relations between fantasy and reality; their priority over one another fluctuates. Strips may begin or even end within the realm of the fantastic; there is no consistent agenda to bring things back to one particular mode of consciousness. Calvin's teacher, Mrs. Wormwood, with her spotted dress, is seen transformed into a hideous, blotchy monster reminiscent of those created by Mathias Grünewald for his *Temptation of St. Anthony* (fig. 2.10). In another instance, Calvin's mother, hoping to advance her cause by corroborating his fantasy of being a dinosaur, produces just the opposite result by giving his daydream license to flourish in a way that (temporarily) outwits her. When she tells Calvin (who is pretending to be a dinosaur) that if he sees Calvin he should send him in for dinner, Calvin metamorphoses into a "real" tyrannosaurus and comes roaring and grimacing to the dining room table!

Thus, visual dialectics and image-text relations encode shifts from Calvin's fantasy life (its iconography drawn from television, film, science fiction, advertising, art, and contemporary culture at large) to the apparently prosaic world of home and school. It is the unexpected convergences and disjunctions between these realms that produce humor and provide moments of parody as well as psychological insight and social commentary.

In a *New York Times* article, John O'Connor (1990) chided television cartoons on many counts, including their failure to educate children regarding the timely issue of environmental pollution. "Calvin and Hobbes," however, gives strong priority to this issue, and not without warmth and sophistication. One strip, for example, takes Hallowe'en as an opportunity to ask philosophically whether the greatest danger to human beings comes from without or from within. When the issue of environmental pollution is at stake, as here, this is shown to be a nonquestion, since the outside danger is in fact caused by human selfishness and neglect: thus, when Calvin and Hobbes discuss what they are going to be for Hallowe'en (the point is to be as scary as possible), Hobbes replies tigerishly that he will go as himself, while Calvin announces that he will masquerade as a barrel of toxic waste.

Another instance of Watterson's concern with the environment is an en-

2.10. CALVIN AND HOBBES copyright Watterson. Reprinted with permission of
UNIVERSAL PRESS SYNDICATE. All rights reserved.

tirely pictorial representation, in which, as they contemplate scattered trash
in a parklike setting, the abject sadness of Calvin's gesture and of Hobbes'
facial expression tell all. Yet another sequence on this topic (fig. 2.11)
parodies the totalizing myth that civilization equals progress. (In its fourth
frame, it refers indirectly to an illustrious forebear, the comic strip *Li'l
Abner*. In a musical based on the strip, its locus, the town of Dogpatch,
narrowly escapes being sacrificed as a nuclear weapons testing site. The
character General Bullmoose bellows a number entitled "Progress is the
root of all evil," the theme of the Calvin strip.) The second frame underscores the postmodern theme of representation, while the final frame wrings
a humorous twist on a parade of images in Western art of the formerly naked
but summarily covered Adam and Eve leaving the Garden of Eden.

In a typically self-conscious postmodern gesture, "Calvin and Hobbes"
every now and then breaks through its own medium to address the reader
directly. Calvin, for example, sticks his head into Hobbes' yawning mouth
and then, emerging, turns and bows to the reader ("TA DAA!"), while
Hobbes' facial features express disgust (his bubble reads: "SHEESH").
Pointing out its own mise en scène, the sequence here flags the theatricality
of its characters' interaction and parallels it with the artificiality that necessarily intervenes between reader and text. Thus, the explicit staginess
of the medium becomes a metaphor for the presence of an implied spec-
tatorship in (all) interactions: the scrims of representation are in this way
foregrounded.

Image and text reinforce each other to heighten the contrast, suspense,
and tension that release laughter. Often, for example, Hobbes, springing to
life when alone with Calvin, engages with him in a round of role reversals—

tackling him, advising him, doing his homework, and so on, so that he, like Calvin himself, is reliably unpredictable. Calvin, in one cartoon, reads while Hobbes swings. As soon as Calvin describes his book as a science-fiction story where machines take control of men and turn them into slaves, a pictorial shift occurs and the book suddenly appears in *Hobbes's* paws. The tiger then points out to Calvin how scary this idea actually is. In the final frame, Calvin agrees, while at the same time checking his watch frantically to be sure he has not missed his TV show. Hobbes remains quizzically holding the book. In this case, the visual twinning of the two characters seems particularly effective: Calvin's striped shirt mirrors Hobbes' fur, and his bristly hair, the tiger's whiskers. The joke, of course, is not only on Calvin but on the reader as well, for he or she, as comic-strip buff, falls willy-nilly into place with Calvin as an addicted consumer of popular culture.

It is significant that Calvin is a child. As such, he serves a number of functions in the context of the strip and can be understood historically in

2.11. CALVIN AND HOBBES copyright Watterson. Reprinted with permission of UNIVERSAL PRESS SYNDICATE. All rights reserved.

Writing across the Disciplines

terms of the traditions for adultomorphic representations of childhood in the texts and images of Western culture. Their vagaries have been traced in the disciplines of both history and psychology (for example, Ariès, 1960; Opie and Opie, 1969; Marcus, 1978). Adults have often seen (and represented) children in a humorous way. Joking enables adults to revel in the subversive, alternative reality of this *other*, bygone stage of life while asserting superiority over it and maintaining a necessary distance from it.

Psychoanalytic discourse makes much of the need for parents to survive the aggression of their children, aggression projected defensively, as it is theorized (particularly by Klein, 1964), onto them. Yet this discourse often fails to note the very real aggression parents may feel toward their children, a topic broached with great courage, sensitivity, and clinical relevance by Winnicott (1965). "Calvin and Hobbes," playing continuously with this motif, never shies away from portraying the counteraggression of Calvin's parents; it permits an eruption of laughter as evasion of normally operative internal prohibitions (see Freud, 1905b). In figs. 2.12 and 2.13, Watterson toys with the problematic philosophical distinction between *is* and *ought* while he tropes on the battle of the generations. In another sequence (fig. 2.14), Calvin's mother tickles him until *she* falls to the ground from exhaustion (a marvelous send-up of the overstimulating parent whose antics relate more to his or her own needs than to those of the child victim!).

Because of the reference to Reformation/rationalist history inscribed by the names of Watterson's title characters, it seems worthwhile to consider a perceptive article (Snow, 1983) that analyzes Pieter Breughel's *Children's Games* (1560, fig. 2.15). Painted just four years before the death of John Calvin, it encodes views of children that continue to have an impact on modern American culture. A visual dialectic in this teeming picture opposes contrasting but mutually dependent views of childhood. We can discern these views by applying different strategies to the reading of the imagery in the painting, strategies dictated by formal and iconographic elements of the imagery itself that involve an "argument" between childhood as a metaphor for *folly* and childhood as an embodiment of *innocence*. To discover the former, one must read for disguised meanings; to experience the latter, one reads surface appearances. These polar but mutually dependent views and the interpretive modes associated with them were deeply implicated in debates during the Protestant Reformation over the nature of mankind, particularly in theological arguments concerning the doctrine of original sin.

95

2.12. CALVIN AND HOBBES copyright Watterson. Reprinted with permission of UNIVERSAL PRESS SYNDICATE. All rights reserved.

2.13. CALVIN AND HOBBES copyright Watterson. Reprinted with permission of UNIVERSAL PRESS SYNDICATE. All rights reserved.

Small children, on the one hand and at a distance, seemed contaminated by evil—impulsive (aggressive) and immodest (sexual). On the other hand, close up, they were cherished as lovable, guileless, and pure.

Such polarities, perpetuated in secular forms, reflect continuing adult ambivalence in contemporary American culture. We relate discordant imagos not only to childhood as an abstraction but to the actual children who surround us, to ourselves as we believe we once were, and to traits and wishes that persist in us despite our apparent so-called maturity. Surviving in updated versions, such contradictory views pervade, for example, the representation of children as aliens or as demonically possessed in both popular science fiction (see Bick, 1989) and the current cinema. Likewise, they infiltrate and perpetuate themselves in popular syndicated comic strips, like "Calvin and Hobbes," that feature a child as protagonist.

Writing across the Disciplines

2.14. CALVIN AND HOBBES copyright Watterson. Reprinted with permission of
UNIVERSAL PRESS SYNDICATE. All rights reserved.

Calvin and Hobbes are title characters, therefore, whose names playfully evoke the general historical context of Breughel's painting, a period that continues to have an impact on the American psyche. Little Calvin himself typifies a modernized incarnation of the incorrigibility, recalcitrance, skepticism, superstition—in short, the "folly"—against which his reforming namesake might have addressed improving sermons. Expectably surprising (both pictorially and textually), often deadpan in his silliness, and sinless in his naughtiness, he spoofs the rigorous Calvinist doctrine of predestination. Meanwhile, the whimsical and commonsensical toy tiger Hobbes figures by indirect representation and reversal his own atheistic namesake, Thomas Hobbes, who was concerned, for example, with the control of "Desires" and "Feares," and with matter in motion. Beyond this, we can read a tease directed at Hobbes' nominalism, for, enticing us with names that suggest a more precise link to their most obvious referents than is warranted, the comic strip refuses one-on-one construal. In a typically postmodern ges-

2.15. Pieter Breughel the Elder, *Children's Games*.

ture, it evades interpretation based on correspondence. Even the dialectic *between* Calvin and Hobbes, because of its playful variety, escapes an emblematic reading. One strip, however, does in fact cast the little boy and his toy tiger in their appropriate theological and philosophical guises. Hobbes asks Calvin whether he thinks there is a God, to which Calvin replies that, well, *some*body is out to get him! Thus, Calvinist predestination is pitted wryly against Hobbesian skepticism/atheism.

Another strip (fig. 2.16) bears on these motifs by depicting the two characters sledding down a hill studded with tall trees. Rather than steer, Calvin prefers to philosophize. Addressing Hobbes as they careen downward (in a possible visual pun on "the Fall"), he poses Breughelian questions concerning the fundamental goodness or evil of human nature. The stuffed tiger, however, cannot respond to this level of abstraction. Unlike Calvin, he is thoroughly preoccupied with appropriately Hobbesian concerns—that is, with the primacy of material reality and the factor of matter in motion: he focuses on the speed and direction of their sled and reacts directly to the perilous proximity of trees, rocks, and ledges. Predictably, in a scene that recalls Edith Wharton's *Ethan Frome* (a text tormented with ethical conundrums), their sled crashes into a tree. With his *body* in the snow, Calvin berates Hobbes for interrupting the discourse; while with his *head* buried under the snow but his body largely visible, Hobbes responds implicitly in the final frame that people are neither bad nor intrinsically good but rather "crazy." Thus, Watterson takes a covert swipe not only at philosophy and theology but at the mental health establishment, where ethics often translates into diagnosis.

One last example of postmodernism at work in the cartoon strip is another sledding sequence (fig. 2.17) that begins with Calvin stating: "Television validates existence." Virtually illustrating the work of Jean Baudrillard (1988), this image-text, despite its sophisticated self-reflexive humor, its opposition of high and mass culture, and its direct address to the reader as consumer, never abandons childhood. Calvin and Hobbes instantiate the delicious egoism of very young children—that appealing bravado and sense of being at the center of things which we adults never dare to acknowledge quite so openly—but cast here in terms of the hype and high-tech of 1990s America.

By stressing the motifs of doubling, disjunction, and displacement, I have been making a claim here for the value of interpreting not only comic strips

99

2.16. CALVIN AND HOBBES copyright Watterson. Reprinted with permission of UNIVERSAL PRESS SYNDICATE. All rights reserved.

such as "Calvin and Hobbes" but popular culture more generally. Its agendas are often complex and mischievously satiric. Its execution can be quite brilliant. Achieving representation by means of analogy, contiguity, and indexicality (Goodman, 1976), the best such work enthralls its devotees by means of dialogues that blend subtle psychological overtones with trenchant social criticism while remaining supremely witty and entertaining.

Versions of this chapter were presented at the annual meeting of the American Society for Aesthetics at the University of Texas at Austin, October 1990; at the University of Tennessee, Knoxville, March 1991; at the William Alanson White Institute, New York, June 1991; at Child Psychiatry Grand Rounds, New York Hospital–Cornell Medical Center (Westchester Division), February 1992; and at the Oregon Psychoanalytic Foundation, Portland, October, 1993. For generously sharing their enthusiasm for and insightful comments on "Calvin and Hobbes" with me, I wish to thank Peter Jelavich, Joan Baudouine, Anton Kaes, Judith Farr Tormey, and, above all, my son and daughter, Nathaniel and Rivi. I also wish to thank Carola Mann for her kindness and, finally, Mary C. Suggett of Universal Press Syndicate for arranging permission for the reproduction of the comic strips. A version of this chapter appeared in *Psychoanalytic Review* 80, no. 1 (Spring 1993): 55–82, under the title "Calvin and Hobbes: Postmodern and Psychoanalytic Perspectives." Permission to reprint it is here gratefully acknowledged.

2.17. CALVIN AND HOBBES copyright Watterson. Reprinted with permission of UNIVERSAL PRESS SYNDICATE. All rights reserved.

Carpe Diem, Carpe Mortem

Like "Calvin and Hobbes" indisputably a vehicle of popular culture, a Hollywood movie rather than an esoteric work of cinematic "high art," *Dead Poets Society* (1989) treats themes of timely and perennial concern to mental health professionals, parents, and educators, as well as to the general public. This film played successfully in theaters throughout the country for two years, won national acclaim, and was nominated for various awards. It was screened by at least one major airline on transcontinental flights and is now available for home viewing. Thus, if only by virtue of the many who have seen it, continue to see it and to be moved by it, *Dead Poets Society* warrants critical attention.

Observers have noted occasional outpourings of affection and enthusiasm from the film's often youthful audiences. One critic who disliked the film remarked that the rest of the audience who saw it with him "all but gave it a standing ovation" (Heilman, 1989, p. 417). Such displays are worth reflection because, notwithstanding its imperfections, *Dead Poets Society* raises questions about the quality versus the length of life, what it costs emotionally to teach and to learn, how verbal acts differ from deeds, how, more generally, symbolic acts connect with the real, and how art relates to both life and death. These are ambitious questions, not the usual fare of films that boast a comparable box office success.

Some colleagues have expressed bewilderment at my fascination with *Dead Poets Society* because it seems retardataire in taking as its subject a white Anglo-Saxon Protestant all-male prep school in the 1950s, thus superficially avoiding the social ills (gender, race, and class) of a later time. Such reservations are seconded by a strong undercurrent of published negative criticism emanating from both the political left (for example, an article by Evan Carton [1989] in *Tikkun*) and the far and moderate right (articles by Heilman [1989] and Bawer [1989] in the *American Scholar* and the *American Spectator*). Different but also strangely similar, these critiques focus, it seems to me, too narrowly on manifest content; they thus miss much of the psychological richness and philosophical depth of the film.

I have, however, taken a certain risk in asking you to consider or reconsider it, since, for all that it offers moments of exquisite cinematic beauty and visual poetry, it *is* a *deadly* (pun intended) straightforward Hollywood picture that reels along inexorably, compelling and manipulating us with near-transparent contrivance. How does it achieve the heady triumph of its unforgettable last scene? Perhaps because it forces tough ongoing themes upon us, jogs our memories, touches our immediate lives, and in so doing ignites a cauldron of latent energy, even if, in the final analysis, its overall artistic verdict must be rendered less than brilliant.

Aesthetic judgment, however, is not my focus here. Rather, my concern is with the forms and messages of popular culture, for it is my conviction that such culture not only reflects but actually helps to shape the inner landscapes of our minds, in a manner graphically illustrated by the two-projector model proposed by Jacob Arlow (1969) in his classic paper on unconscious fantasy. Arlow described two movie projectors focused on a transparent window from different sides and running along simultaneously —one set of images coming from inside the house, the other emanating from a projector outdoors. Thus, he speculated, inner fantasy life runs along in tandem with external events. Yet, I submit, culture—especially perhaps, visual culture—also acts deeply on the psyche, helping to form *both sets of images* that project onto the screen. Thus, the field of imagery currently circulating in a given culture should be of paramount interest to psychoanalysis (although it is often neglected), for it is in terms of this imagery that both conscious and unconscious fantasy and psychobiological data are experienced, by analyst and patient.

Precisely because they are often perceived unreflectively, artifacts of popular culture possess a unique power to stock the intrapsychic storehouse of images built up over time that I have called museums of the mind. Our intellectual defenses are not so readily mobilized against them. Thus, while

I make no brief here for the canonical inclusion of any specific work, including *Dead Poets Society*, I *do* argue implicitly by this choice (and throughout this book) for the expenditure of critical energy and interpretive efforts on works that, however flawed they may be, hit hard in our culture, influencing our children, our colleagues, their patients, and ourselves.

As school opens in the fall of 1959, Welton Academy, a fictional boys' preparatory school in the United States, celebrates its centennial, a fact notable in that landmark years are destined, one hopes, to be blessed with achievement, not besmirched by disgrace and tragedy. A new English teacher (played by Robin Williams) has arrived on the scene. His name, John Keating, is a thinly disguised allusion to the short-lived British Romantic poet John Keats, and, as we discover, the tenure of this teacher at Welton is to be similarly short-lived. By means of unorthodox teaching methods, Keating broaches a philosophy of individualism that contrasts dramatically with that of the more senior teachers in the school and that changes forever the lives of his adolescent students. One critic of the film (Heilman, 1989) claims, however, that Keating never teaches anything, that he is merely a performer. This critic, apparently a former English teacher himself, opines that teaching poetry involves slow, careful reading and *explication de texte*— none of which ever occurs in the film. But it is this very issue—namely, the relative merits of reasoned discourse as against drama, philosophy versus art—that is the central dilemma posed by the film.

If we forsake concreteness and enter the domain of the symbolic, which is, after all, not only the province of art per se but the very subject of this work, Keating's methods become fascinating. They can be read as presupposing and conveying a view of knowledge not as product, not as worthwhile acquisition, but as movement, direction, and process, an engagement of mind and body in spaces both open and closed, outdoors and in, in which the teacher is cast as facilitator, elicitor, provocateur, even seducer, rather than as master, disciplinarian, judge, owner of what must be either given or taken.

What does it mean to teach? Clips of three classroom teachers precede our introduction to Keating. In each case, these foils stand erect and possess freedom of motion while, by contrast, their charges sit immobile. In each case, the teacher speaks, while the students remain silent. In each case, power is flaunted and the hierarchical structure of the system laid bare. Rigid, methodical, and demanding, the lab science teacher strides about his domain, inducing admixtures of terror and boredom. The Latin master, framed by his chalkboard, repeatedly intones the declension of the simple masculine noun *agricola*. The math teacher fixes on precision and punishment. Thus the model is unmistakable: rote learning and conformity to a given norm.

Keating instantly punctures this paradigm. We meet him peeking in at the students, who are already seated and waiting in his classroom. It matters that they precede him in entering the room, or rather in occupying it, for, unlike the other scenes, which indicate that knowledge is something that was there before the boys arrived and must be handed over to them whether they will or no, the presence of the boys in the room from the start suggests a more Socratic vision, in which the student (mind and body) exists prior to the influence of any teacher. And one wants, perhaps, to ponder the relevance of this idea for the domains of therapy and parenting as well.

When Keating appears—with an American flag prominently visible in the frame behind him—his behavior diametrically opposes that of every other adult male we have met up to this moment. He does not rely principally on words. He whistles and beckons to the boys. He gestures with his body, and by eschewing the immediate imposition of power through verbal language, above all by encouraging the students themselves to get up and move, he places himself in an altered relation to them. He makes no threats, imposes no rules. By gesturing, by surprising them, he opens for them an opportunity for interpretation, choice, and response. From the start, he signals that the teacher-student relationship can be one of mutuality rather than mastery.

Changing the space where learning occurs matters as well. Keating asks each boy to recite a line of poetry before kicking a soccer ball on the field and actually to play to Beethoven's Ninth Symphony. In order to move the boys must stand, thus placing themselves on an equal footing with their teacher. In this way, hierarchy is broken down. And Keating's invocation of Whitman's "O Captain! My Captain!" does not, I think, reinstate hierarchy but rather suggests a complex relationship—for the poem is not simply a reference to Lincoln qua president but specifically to Lincoln's *death*, a work of deep sadness and mourning, an elegy—which foreshadows the theme of death that pervades the film. Ironically, a smile spreads over Neil's (the future suicide's) face during this scene as he gradually senses that something new and empowering is beginning to happen.

When Keating ridicules two boys' names (Pitts and Meeks), he reveals to them that what is handed down from the past has power to shape their destinies. Rather than doing this, however, in order to have them accept or repudiate the meaning of the given name, he wants them to note it and transcend it. Thus, he attempts to teach here that identity is chosen by individuals. One decides who one is, in spite of one's paternally derived name, an issue symbolically equivalent to the deadly struggle between Neil and his father.

"Carpe diem," the motto Keating whispers to the boys, relates to the motif of time, time as measured differently by Keating than by the other teachers, for he is interested in quality, not quantity. One may think of Pirsig's *Zen and the Art of Motorcycle Maintenance* (see below), which also wrestles with the problems of time, of teaching, of the relations between a father and son, and of the issue of *quality*. When Keating mentions death—the fact that we are merely food for worms—the camera again focuses on Neil. Keating tells the students that they will one day stop breathing. He shows them photographs of former students at the school, now dead, and urges them to move in close to the photos, to look silently at them and to *listen* to them. In this way, he allows each boy to hear his own inner voice. One boy, Todd, focuses on a young man who might have been, judging from the family resemblance, his grandfather.

Later, we see Todd in his room, writing "Seize the day" and crumpling up the sheet of paper. This new teacher *has* communicated with him, and he writes in response because there is greater distance in this mode than in the spoken word. Desperately shy, he cannot as yet answer back out loud. For him, however, this moment represents the beginning of change—the beginning of the discovery of his own voice. This discovery is dramatized in a later scene when the teacher, by an extraordinary feat of risk-taking, coercion, faith, and empathy, empowers the shy Todd to utter in class as a poem feelings that had been seething inside him and which, as his behavior makes clear, he has been trying to suppress.

Another boy, Knox, invited to the home of his father's friend for dinner, unexpectedly meets the girlfriend of this man's son and falls awkwardly and precipitously in love with her. As he leaves for this major developmental experience, we see once again an American flag flying in the background.

Writing across the Disciplines

Recognizing these natural urges and inclinations as central to adolescence, Keating validates them and attempts to integrate them with literature—to enable the boys to bring together the worlds of symbol, idea, feeling, and external reality.

In resurrecting a defunct secret society, the purpose of which was to meet in the woods at night and recite poetry, the boys show that they have been spurred on by this new teacher to explore and express the full range of their desires. In one striking scene after another, we witness Keating's efforts to teach them that poetry *counts*, that language really *matters*. In so doing, however, he effects an inspiring but insidiously dangerous blurring of the boundaries between symbol and substance, word and deed. As a result, one boy is whipped for staging an aborted rebellion advocating coeducation at the academy, a second is bloodied in his attempt to woo another boy's blonde girlfriend, and a third, the chief protagonist, expressly against the orders of his punitive father, whom he deceives, auditions for and accepts the role of Puck in a local production of *A Midsummer Night's Dream*. This boy, Neil Perry, eventually feels so trapped that he commits suicide.

Thus the film forces us to question the risks and casualties of individualism—an ideology long valorized in our country and perennially subject to reexamination and critique. Additionally, nonconformity, breaking away, "doing one's thing," is, of course, an ideology associated with adolescence, the developmental stage onto which it is here mapped.

By design, much of the poetry and prose quoted throughout the film is nineteenth-century American, by such authors as Walt Whitman, Henry David Thoreau, and Vachel Lindsay, and as noted, the American flag appears at moments when acts of freedom are performed—in key scenes with the teacher, in scenes involving daring acts on the part of the boys, and occasionally in scenes involving the reactionary headmaster—to the end, perhaps, of complicating the notion of precisely what is genuinely "American."

Counterbalanced with this problematized ideology is the old country —Scotland and England, signified by bagpipes, by Keating's return to America from England, by the Latin teacher, MacAllister, whose "realism" and "conservatism" serve as a foil for Keating's approach, and, of course by the other, English, poetry—that of Byron, Shakespeare, Tennyson. These problematic relations between old and new, England/Scotland and America, figure a gamut of hierarchies that involve fathers and sons, adults and children, knowers and learners, the best and the less good. Hierarchy is a theme repeatedly interrogated: what is its place in the project of learning and growing up? For the psychoanalyst, a related question involves the role of hierarchy in treatment, an uneasy question that perhaps must remain uneasy lest danger ensue.

The infrastructure of *Dead Poets Society* is its thoroughgoing ideology of individualism, which is thrown radically into doubt, both by the suicide of its student protagonist and by the dismissal in the end of the teacher who propounds it. "Carpe diem" condenses the values of John Keating: intensity over quantity, passion over reason, individualism over conformity.

An establishing shot at the beginning of the film frames a faded old drawing of several boys. This drawing, a colored mural, hints of art, symbolic representation, youth, and time. The setting of the drawing, in the school, tells us that individual viability in institutional cultures and comparisons between one generation and another may be at stake.

The first scene, Welton's opening ceremony, takes place in the school chapel. Bagpipes play, candles are held aloft, banners emblazoned with *Tradition, Honor, Discipline*, and *Excellence* are displayed. As each student carries his candle (standing concretely for "the light of knowledge"), the camera focuses on single faces, reminding us that all such rituals mask important gaps between any individual and the group and other gaps as well, here, for example, that between the generations. Thus, tensions and juxtapositions involving the themes of time and of individual/group relations are posed visually even before the principal characters are introduced or permitted to speak.

Churchlike, the ceremonial hall evokes religious imagery. It foreshadows the climactic scene of suicide when Neil, framed in silhouette by a frosty windowpane, appears as Christ crowned with thorns, forsaken by his father. It figures proleptically dual aspects of religious behavior: conformity to tradition, unyielding dogmatism, on the one hand, and rebellion at the cost of self-sacrifice, on the other.

Speaking sternly as he claims his school is the best in the country, headmaster Nolan instantiates the notions of hierarchy, power structure, and competition. What does the desire to be "best" mean to human beings and to institutions? We are invited by the film to consider the case of Todd Anderson, whose older brother was apparently "best." He had been class valedictorian, and by comparison the younger boy is made to feel so worthless that he has, at the beginning of school, virtually no voice. Painfully shy, inhibited, he is a cipher compared with his older brother. Comparison erodes the uniqueness of individuals. Similarly, when announcing the appointment of a new teacher, the headmaster cannot resist a reference to Keating's "beloved" predecessor. The new teacher, we are told, has arrived from England, although he attended Welton as a boy. Thus crosscurrents of influence—old country and new—come into play. And comparisons lead, as we know, to extremes of overvaluing and devaluing, a point the film highlights later in what I take to be its key scene—where Byron's poetry is compared invidiously with that of Shakespeare, and Keating, champion of individualism, orders the boys to destroy the pages on which this sort of thinking is prescribed.

Clips of boys and parents saying goodbye invite us to consider whether ceremony and tradition do in fact possess the power to eclipse the wounds of separation. What weight have group and institution over that of individual and of primary relationship? (Again, adolescence foregrounds this contest and tips the scales back and forth as loyalties shift. In the end, however, the boys cling to their relationship with their beloved teacher. As he is forcibly wrenched from them, they stand up victoriously on their desks [in imitation of his behavior] to proclaim that institutions cannot override the ties of personal loyalty).

After the ceremony, Neil meets his new roommate, Todd, and last year's friends appear. Immediately adolescent rebellion is portrayed as taking verbal form. This matters because it indicates the extent to which these boys are already functioning in this mode, to which Keating is later accused of having introduced them. It indicates that he, as teacher, will elicit from them what is already latent, that he will function, in other words, socratically. The boys have converted the school motto of "Tradition, honor, discipline, and excellence" into "Travesty, horror, decadence, and excrement," a crucial point for what comes later in terms of the teaching agendas explored by Keating.

Before we meet Keating and confront the contrast set up between him and other adults, we are privy to an encounter between Neil Perry and his tyrannical father—a dramatization of the conflict that eventually leads to their mutual tragedy. Perry represents, from the perspective of the 1990s, a caricature of rule-bound parenting, the often harsh and punitive paternalism which, as a paradigm, followed the war years of the 1940s and then was abreacted in the decades that followed—decades that saw Haight-Ashbury, Woodstock, and the beginning of the women's movement. Failing to recognize his son as a separate speaking subject, Perry imposes his will without acknowledging even the slightest possibility of any other responsible position. Neil acquiesces in the dynamic—or rather the *stasis*—that will henceforth characterize their relationship. In commanding "Don't dispute me in public," the father betrays the sense in which Neil exists for him merely as a narcissistic projection. Later on, this same narcissism resurfaces when Perry appears unannounced in Neil's room and charges him with insubordination. (Neil has by now begun to rehearse the role of Puck.) The father's line is: "You made a liar out of me." In other words, what is focal to him is not his relationship with his child but the relations between himself and the outside world. Only when Neil's achievement tallies with his own ambition can his tormented narcissism be gratified (see Miller, 1981). Pulling out all stops, he even invokes his absent wife ("You know how much it means to your mother")—who is portrayed as devoid of all independent function with regard to the boy.

Everything that touches Neil must be filtered through the father, whose control is absolute. And the absolutism of paternal power here precisely determines the extremity of the son's act of defiance. He must recapture control over his own life, even if this can be achieved only through death. The suicidal act, therefore, is one not only of resignation but of rebellion— that is, the ultimate removal of his life from external control by paternal authority and the positive reassertion of control, at the terrible price of loss of life itself.

After his father forbids him to continue as editor of the school literary magazine, friends ask Neil why he doesn't stand up to him and add, "Why doesn't he let you do what you want?" Sensitively, Neil responds to these taunts with empathy and a surprisingly mature sense of what his parent's concerns might actually be. (He mentions the family's financial situation, for example.) Thus, we observe an embryonic role reversal that quickly aborts. Neil, still a child, while able to express empathy in his relations with Todd, his agemate and peer, suffers increasing paralysis in the tilted relationship with his father.

A beautifully filmed sequence on time gives us Todd indoors, winding and adjusting his small alarm clock. Then we move outdoors to observe the large clocktower of the school. These visual references to time link with verbal references in the scene of Keating's first class, where he has a student read Robert Herrick's "To the Virgins to Make Much of Time." Thus, image and word conspire to remind us that adolescence connotes transience— an evanescence in life's cycle—figured exquisitely here by the changing seasons. Beginning in autumn, with the falling of leaves and flocks of migrating birds, *Dead Poets Society* ends in winter, with frozen lake and swirls of snow blanketing the landscape. Massed flocks of birds flying in autumn create one of the most memorable visual metaphors of the film. Squawking, hundreds of winged creatures erupt into autumn skies. Immediately a shift of the camera brings us a bevy of boys shouting and wildly massed themselves—a crowd in motion that descends a winding staircase and thus completes the visual sequence initiated by Todd's winding of his clock— a sequence signifying change, inexorability, fate. Hope at the start of the school year ends in winter death.

By their apparently disorderly but in fact preordained flight, the birds symbolize complex relations between freedom and order, a theme that resurfaces in the marvelous moment when Keating asks the boys to march around the school courtyard and forces them, by so doing, to confront the tremendous pull of conformity, so that, even though they begin marching to different inner rhythms, they end up keeping time with one another and clapping in unison, rhythmically. Notions of time and order are thus conjoined.

It is Keating's second English class, however, that stuns us with the central problematic of this film. Neil is asked to read aloud from the preface to a book called *Understanding Poetry.*

Parenthetically, the title of this fictional textbook is also that of a veritable bible of "new criticism" by Cleanth Brooks and Robert Penn Warren, published originally in 1938 and reissued and widely circulated in the 1950s. Since it goes without saying that readers of literary criticism are even fewer in number than readers of poetry, we can reasonably assume that only a tiny fraction of the contemporary filmgoing public would have recognized this coincidence. Thus, insofar as it works as a parodic reference, it does so only for insiders. Taking a curious look at the 1956 edition of the Brooks-Warren textbook, I found myself wondering about the precise nature of the citation here. Perplexities and possible ironies abound, for the rather pathetic Dr. Pritchard, fictional author of the infamous introduction to *Dead Poets Society*'s version of *Understanding Poetry*, seems utterly foreign to the design and intent of the original text, certainly to its eloquent introduc-

111

tion. One wonders whose misconstrual this is and whether or not it is meant ironically. Is it, for example, supposed to be taken as a swipe at the bastardization college books supposedly undergo when brought into secondary education, or as a commentary on the contemporary backlash against the "new critics," or is the reference entirely coincidental?

To return to the film, Keating, with the students conscientiously imitating him, follows the text by drawing a graph on the board that rates "perfection" on its horizontal line and "importance" on the vertical and, as the text directs, pits Byron against Shakespeare. Suddenly, however, he stops writing and exclaims: "Excrement!" This is, of course, one of the very words used by the boys themselves in their private parody of the school's motto; thus, it provides a link between the secret worlds of teacher and students.

Now the question of word and deed is posed in a shocking spectacle. Keating asks the boys to rip out of their books the offending pages where poetry is described in quantitative terms. Their faces in response to this request manifest a gamut of emotions, ranging from horror to glee. To many, the command serves merely as an opportunity for sanctioned destructiveness; Keating's reasons for finding these pages offensive are opaque to them. Others, taught to respect property and above all books, seem incredulous; one boy, Cameron, complies with active distaste, placing his ruler against the pages and ripping them out neatly, as if to demonstrate that his act is solely one of obedience to a teacher's commands, in accordance with the rules.

This scene is observed with horror by another teacher, the Scottish "realist," MacAllister. To rip pages out of a book because the ideas in them are offensive is only one step away from the infamous book burnings of the Nazis in 1933, or from those of the Chinese during the so-called cultural revolution, when large masses of books were destroyed because they were written under a regime that differed ideologically from that of the time. It is to conflate the symbolic and the real, to think that by destroying the pages on which words are written the ideas expressed by those words will likewise disappear. It is to move from the realm of the pen to the realm of the sword. It is to substitute deed for word, to assume that language, thoughts, and ideas can be controlled by violent acts. It is to demonstrate in vivo, but misguidedly, the two notions that Keating articulates immediately after the page-tearing; namely, that one must take one's life into one's own hands (he means: learn to think for oneself) and that words can change the world. These are, in fact, the very principles that lead to Neil's suicide.

Unable in the end to talk to his father, as Keating urges him to do, precluded from the possibility of verbal dialogue and linguistic expression, Neil takes up a gun and acts out his desperation. His turning from the symbolic order of language and communication to the order of the real is prefigured in the page-tearing scene orchestrated here by his teacher. Keating, in an effort to demonstrate to the boys the deep bonds between language, passion, and the world, shortcircuits the gradual step-by-step process by which the complexities of these linkages need to be developed. The scene spotlights a moot and troubling issue for teaching, for clinical work, and for parenting as well.

To dramatize a point is inevitably to distort it. Gestures that make ideas concrete and give them a living presence beyond words alone run the risk of being misinterpreted or, worse, of remaining uninterpreted, being enjoyed merely as spectacle in their raw gratification of impulse and desire. How to titrate this risk is a central problem for both teacher and artist, therapist and patient. And the intimacy between teacher and artist is made explicit in this film by the colored drawing with which it begins.

When, after the page-tearing, Keating has the boys huddle up (a wonderful image in that it transforms the English class momentarily into a football team) and tells them his secret—namely, that we read and write poetry because we are members of the human race, that poetry, passion, and love are what we stay alive for, that we are here and life exists—his approach is frankly seductive. Gathered about him in a group, the boys are told (à la Whitman) that the powerful play goes on and that each of them may contribute a verse. They are asked: "What will your verse be?" Thus the central dynamic of tension between individual will and the necessity of group function is foregrounded again as previously in the film. Addressing the boys en masse, the teacher means to address each in his own uniqueness. How is this possible?

Immediately after this class, ceremony is reinstated. We see the school at mealtime: grace is pronounced in unison. MacAllister, who has observed Keating's radical class, confronts him now and warns him of the risk he is taking by encouraging the boys to be artists. They will hate you, he predicts, when they find out that they are not. Keating counters that he is merely teaching them to be freethinkers. The opposing viewpoints of the two, labeled realism and romanticism, are epitomized by these quotes: "Show me a man unfettered by empty dreams and I'll show you a happy man" (MacAllister) and "Only in their dreams can men be truly free" (Keating).

What matters here is the polarization of positions. *In exaggerating them, the film, as art, replicates the central dynamic it poses as a problem for the teacher.* It restages the Platonic concern over the relative merits of philosophy and tragedy. Reasoned dialogue allows the fullest exploration of any substantive idea, but powerful depiction on stage (like the tearing out of a page or the burning of a flag) may engrave a deeper impression with tools far sharper than the most pointed logic. Keating's method involves, however, a fateful categorical mistake, for in asking his students to destroy a book's pages, what he does in fact is to further polarize the realms he seeks to unite. The students' act is committed blindly and (with dramatic irony) *in extremis*. Yet, as every psychoanalyst knows, to remain only in the world of words is equally fatal. Patients must move on to deeds. How that move should come about is the dilemma posed by this scene and by the film as a whole.

Central here is the issue of quality over quantity. We have already noted the presence of clocks and the thematics of time as a measure. Neil's father will not allow him to assume editorship of the literary magazine because he believes that this will not permit sufficient time for him to pursue his academic study. Later, when he lays out for Neil the course of his life, including Harvard and medical school, the boy protests, But Dad, that's ten years! Keating teaches, on the other hand, that time counts only in terms of its quality. Thus, by implication, it is better to have lived a short but *expressive* life than a long one under *oppression*. In this sense, Neil's suicide can be related directly to the precepts of his teacher, and, in this limited but crucial sense, the school officials are accurate in implicating Keating in the boy's death.

Following Keating outside, in a beautiful autumnal scene, the boys ask him about his own adolescence, in the form of questions about the "Dead Poets Society," which is mentioned in an old yearbook they have unearthed. Significantly for what is to come, the color of this book is red. We note the close identification that Keating's seductiveness has stimulated. The boys want to be like him, to replicate *his* youthful experiences. The notion of a secret (which comes up repeatedly) is a wonderful ploy. Secrets bind their sharers and exclude the outside world. Thus, by calling some of his ideas secrets, Keating ties the boys to him and shuts out the school authorities. Hierarchy crumbles again in the close physical relation depicted between them (in sharp contradistinction to the policy of Headmaster Nolan, who begins every interaction with students by barking: "Sit!").

Yet, despite his rejection of conventional methods of demonstrating leadership, Keating has the students call him "Captain." By whispering, by setting up experiences that compel them to respond to him and to each other and to participate in their own learning, he does manipulate them, though at a deeper level than the more traditional teachers whose externalized methods of maintaining discipline foster a distance that permits resistances to be more easily and effectively mobilized.

The boys' excitement is electric as they plan their first nocturnal meeting in the cave. Plotting in the back of MacAllister's classroom, as he puffs his pipe oblivious to their heightened affect and anxious whispers, they ignore his tired imprecation, "Oh, shut up."

Then, filmed in a surreal bluish light, veiled with mist and haze, and partially in slow motion, the seven conspirators escape from school and run in their hooded jackets with flashlights through darkened woods toward the secluded cave, accompanied by eerie strains that will reoccur in the suicide scene, as in an exquisite dream. Hoods suggest plotters and also monks, and the profusion of tree trunks figure the phallic, all-male world in which the entire drama is being enacted.

Neil convenes the Dead Poets Society, and it is he, in his deep identification with Keating—a new-found good father to replace the bad father of his home—who reads by flashlight in the darkened cave the central passage from *Walden:* "I went to the woods because I wished to live deliberately, to front only the essential facts of life, and see if I could not learn what it had to teach, and not, when I came to die, discover that I had not lived."

The scenes of both the first and subsequent meetings of the society wonderfully depict the confluence of major adolescent themes. Shortly after lines from Tennyson are juxtaposed with a glossy pinup poster of a large-breasted woman, Meeks begins to recite lines from Vachel Lindsay:

> Then I saw the Congo, creeping through the black,
> Cutting through the forest with a golden track.

At this point, the boys begin to chant and move and gradually empty out of the cave into the night, dancing, high-stepping, marching through the trees and back to the sanctuary of the school. Their physical movement and gradual reconforming of individual to group recall the earlier image of squawking migrating birds and prefigure the scene of marching in the courtyard. It is significant, too, that a clock chimes at the end of this scene. Measured time, rather than Thoreau's quality time ("Time is but the stream

I go a-fishing in"), is reintroduced as a feature of the world to which the boys must inevitably return.

In thematizing time, it is worth reemphasizing that Keating does not always conduct his classes within school walls. Again and again, he leads the students outside into the fresh air and tells them that each one must find not only his own voice but also a new ground. This, too, is an aspect of the American dream (and, parenthetically, an aspect tragically lacking for urban adolescents today, whose territorial strivings in the form of graffiti mark American cityscapes from Los Angeles to East Harlem [see E. H. Spitz, 1991]).

A final impression: Keating, at one point, asks the boys the purpose of language. Neil's response, "communication," is, of course, profoundly ironic. When he and his father meet in their last confrontation before the suicide, the latter—having withdrawn Neil from school, enrolled him in a military academy, fixed the entire course of his life for the next decade—asks him, from a position of total control, to say what he thinks. Neil can only mutter, "Nothing." Language thus fails at this fateful juncture to convey what must be conveyed. Whatever this son had wanted to communicate to his father had already been uttered in the previous scene when, from centerstage, becostumed, he had passionately recited Puck's farewell speech at the end of *A Midsummer Night's Dream*. There, in the words of the greatest dead poet of the English language, was the real message which, if his father had been able to hear it, could have forestalled tragedy. By the last scene between them, however, the realm of the symbolic—of measured time, of rhythm, of art, of teaching and of learning—had ceased to be available to either Neil or his father. All that was left was the real: one act, filmed in slow motion, an act to stop time forever.

Early versions of this chapter were presented to members of the San Francisco Society at the John W. Mudd Memorial Clinical Psychoanalytic Meeting in San Diego in October, 1991, and to members of the Cincinnati Psychoanalytic Society in March, 1992. For their unflagging (pun intended) encouragement, I wish to express my appreciation to Sylvia Hoffberg Franklin, Jennifer Beulah and Nathaniel Geoffrey Lew, Joanna Burnstine Strauss, Angela Clark, Mark Levy, and James Tichener. A version of the chapter, under the title "'Carpe Diem, Carpe Mortem': Reflections on *Dead Poets Society*," was published in *Post Script: Essays in Film and the Humanities* 11, no. 3 (Summer 1992): 19–31. Permission to reprint it is here gratefully acknowledged.

Some time afterward, God put Abraham to the test.
Genesis 22:1

The physical distance between people has nothing
to do with loneliness. It's psychic distance.
**Robert M. Pirsig, *Zen and the Art of
Motorcycle Maintenance***

Recycling

Extravagantly praised and much beloved—an emblematic text of
its era—Robert M. Pirsig's *Zen and the Art of Motorcycle Maintenance* (1974) went through twenty-three printings in its first
five years. It captured the rapt attention of a generation that had
weathered the radicalism of the 1960s but was still caught up
in its issues and attempting to redefine and restructure lives in
accordance with its ruptures. As a New Yorker sojourning recently for a year on the West Coast, I thought to revisit this text
about a westward journey which, on my first reading, had elicited
passionate feelings, both positive and negative.

I am interested here in exploring notions of distance: both those
figured and implied in the text itself and those I as critic have encountered between my own previous and current readings. One
noteworthy change, for example, has been my intensified perception of irony—a perspective that depends precisely on distance.
It seems intriguing to reconsider years later a work that stirred
me so much at the time of its appearance and to reexamine its
impact at a different point, personally and publicly.

I remembered the book as recounting in the first person the
often confusing thoughts and fantasies of a man in motion, physically and intellectually. Engaged on a cross-country motorcycle
trip with his eleven-year-old son, the narrator is unnamed in the
text, so that, inevitably, readers tend to conflate his voice with
that of the author. In what follows here, as a way of acknowledging that elision without surrendering fully to it, I shall refer to the
protagonist as "Pirsig." As "Pirsig" then attempts to recapitulate
moments in his past in order to reintegrate a divided personality

and thus move out of that past and into the future, the text sets up as its principal signifying structure a spatiotemporal axis with deep psychological overtones.

In addition (and in contradiction), it interpolates a philosophical monologue that spans the book, a discourse that works both to establish and finally to deconstruct its own scaffolding of rationalism and rationality. In light of contemporary critical theory, such contradictions—which formerly seemed bewildering and unaccountable, though exhilarating—gain legitimacy now as a brilliant anticipation of postmodernism. Today, *Zen* can be read as an avant-garde work that, in questioning the relations between figure and ground, relinquishes fixity for an animating lability.

In retrospect, the choice of significant dyad here merits comment. Why a father and son rather than, say, a husband and wife, a pair of heterosexual or homosexual lovers, same- or opposite-sexed friends, or an intergenerational cross-gendered pair? Glancing back at the early 1970s as a paradigmatic moment for the refusal of patriarchy, the rapid increase of divorce, the so-called liberation of women, and the erosion of previously hallowed family constellations, the choice of father and son as *the* relation that must be put to the test seems both awkward and masterful. From this perspective, the distance, misprision, and pain of that relationship as portrayed in this text can be read as a programmatic refusal on the part of the father-protagonist to assume his traditional role in the hierarchy—that is, to address his son from a position that assumes superior knowledge and power. Through his deliberate refusals to dominate and manipulate his son, he attempts heroically to bypass the emblematic biblical drama of Abraham and Isaac, where unquestioning obedience to paternal authority leads to the near-sacrifice of the beloved child. Yet, ironically, the alternative strategies of the protagonist turn him, too, into a father who comes within a hair's breadth of destroying his son. Thus, despite efforts to resist it, the predestined patriarchal narrative relentlessly surfaces: its agony and narrowly averted tragedy are here replayed.

Zen seemed, on my first reading, to fail in the end to cohere in a satisfying, comprehensible whole, either philosophically, psychologically, or aesthetically. Today, that critical judgment seems harsh, predicated on principles not necessarily applicable to a hybrid text that openly resists classification as *either* philosophy *or* psychology *or* literature *or* autobiography. *Zen*, in fact, explicitly disclaims a place in any of these categories and even straddles the border between fiction and nonfiction. Prematurely postmodern in its willful defiance of preconceived boundaries, it formats philosophical discourse in codes imbricated with narrative and framed by mise en scène, a blend that captures, at its finest moments, the very conditions of thought—not of free association quite, but of the reasoning process. And the content of that thought is often a sustained effort to dramatize, problematize, suspend, and/or nullify the distances that open between self and self, between self and other, and between subject and object.

Inhospitable, therefore, on formal and substantial counts, to any holistic reading, the text of *Zen* consciously thematizes (or unconsciously collapses into) repetitive splits. Paramount among these is the severing of cognition from affect. Whereas in the past I tended to count such ruptures as deep flaws scored by unresolved crescendoes of pain, today I read them as masterfully ironic and integral to the design of the work. Between such poles of response falls a long shadow that undoubtedly owes its shape to personal as well as to public history.

Now, as in the past, I am captivated principally by the tormented psychic distance that separates father from son, a stubborn *méconnaissance* that sparks ongoing drama and plays against the grain of continuing soliloquy. An undertow of missed cues and unrequited desire flows from, breaks into, and obstructs both the tenor and the substance of Pirsig's philosophical discourse. Paternal-filial relations recall not only the paradigm offered by Socrates' liaison with Phaedrus but also the implied text of Goethe's poem *Erlkönig*, which Pirsig refers to and paraphrases but never names. Finally, "Pirsig's" highly intellectualized monologue now seems all the more transparent as a filter and mask for his own desire—his psychological quest—from which it emerges, with which it alternatively merges and diverges, and by which at the end it is totally submerged.

When the reader meets "Pirsig" and his son, Chris, they are already embarked on their adventure, an archetypal trek through the northwestern United States that parallels and figures a journey of the mind, a journey toward understanding. Just as it is unclear precisely when learning begins in a human being and how one might construct an endpoint to knowing or becoming, so this motorcycle trip has no beginning and no end. We meet father and son moving along a highway at sixty miles per hour and leave them on a widening freeway, still traveling.

This metaphor simultaneously grounds and destabilizes both Pirsig's philosophy and his psychology, for just as travel skews our orderly perceptions of space, time, and human relations, so Pirsig's philosophy likewise seems uncanny, paradoxical, inchoate.

The journey, both spatially and temporally, is an oxymoron. Heading westward in the venerable tradition of all American pioneers—in the direction, that is, of mythically new territory—"Pirsig" at the same time returns to old ground, revisiting his haunts before the mental breakdown he suffered years ago, which continues to vex him with recurrent imagery of ghosts. Thus new and old conflate, as do inside and outside. The motorcycle trip instantiates Plato's dictum that all learning is a form of relearning. Geographic space, in its public and private doubling, mirrors diachronic time, which is called into question by the opening lines of the text, as follows: "Pirsig" raises his hand from the left grip of the motorcycle to consult his watch. Immediately, cognitive awareness of early morning evokes physical sensations of speed and wind and their impact on his body—his skin and nostrils. While checking the present clock time, he fantasizes about the future ("I'm wondering what it's going to be like in the afternoon") and takes pleasure in the pull of the personal past ("I'm happy to be riding back into this country"). Thus, a mobile consciousness ranges over space-time, constituting and reconstituting its own fluctuating reality.

The motorcycle itself, as focal image, begins as a signifier for the rational, scientific, technological society "Pirsig" seeks to valorize. Its operation and maintenance serve to exemplify the ways in which we are asked to fuse ourselves with the tasks we perform in order to achieve what is here called "Quality." Yet, although Quality is juxtaposed with notions of "caring," a motorcycle as a means of travel uniquely isolates its driver (by its noise) from all other human beings, even from traveling companions. Thus, a distance opens up between the recommended treatment of machines (cycles) and of people (the protagonist's son). Having read these gaps years ago as a discovery of my own, I see them now as built craftily into the design of the work in order to create a binding tension, an irony that works simultaneously to subtend and undercut the philosophical theses explored on a manifest level.

Early on, "Pirsig" makes a distinction between journeying by car and by motorcycle. The former, he avers, forces the passenger or driver into passive observation as he or she peers through a (window) frame at the world. By contrast, the motorcyclist is "completely in contact with it all. You're *in* the scene, not just watching it anymore, and the sense of presence is overwhelming. That concrete whizzing by five inches below your feet is the real thing . . . and the whole thing, the whole experience, is never removed from immediate consciousness" (p. 4).

Yet, of course, this is *not* the whole story, for to be in motion, to be on the road (in whatever vehicle), is in fact to be detached in important ways from the surrounding scene and to experience freedom from it as well as presence in it. "Pirsig" attends to *just* those elements of the landscape that corroborate his inner experience and simultaneously allows the passing plains, storms, mountains, and ocean to resonate with his thought processes—to stir up memories and ghosts, to affect his intrapsychic momentum. To move along is, therefore, to place oneself in a more problematic relation to the environment than the text here manifestly acknowledges: it is to sever oneself from responsibility, to unshackle oneself from goal-oriented behavior. As the narrator says, "Plans are deliberately indefinite, [the aim is] more to travel than to arrive anywhere" (p. 4). Space, both external and internal, is experienced as kaleidoscopic, aberrant, idiosyncratic. Boundaries between self and other blur. Yet here as elsewhere, the textual surface can be read as laced with irony.

Just as traveling through space one may reflect upon it but take no direct responsibility for it, enjoy it but feel no commitment to it, so, also, time takes on a different aspect. As "Pirsig" travels literally forward in space, he travels backward in time, reconstructing the intellectual search for "Quality" which, the reader is asked to believe, led him once to insanity. So intent on his reconstructions of that past, he is jolted into the present only by a darkening sky, concern for his motorcycle, or, occasionally, Chris's hunger. Time to him feels infinite, continuous, reversible.

In tandem with these skewed perceptions of space and time, frames for lengthy meditations on quality and truth, Pirsig portrays wrenching distortions in the relationship between this father and son. Although constantly together in the closest physical proximity, jointly straddling their motorcycle, "Pirsig" and young Chris inhabit worlds emotionally and intellectually apart. Pirsig portrays the child as age-appropriate with his petulant questioning, impatience, and, above all, longing for his father's attention and affection and, at the same time, as almost perversely incomprehensible to his father, who at one point opines: "I don't know what he needs or what's sought" (p. 56). Thus, the text presents an ironic contrast between the alleged *knowability* of machines (the beloved motorcycle) and the egregious *unknowability* of men (the human child).

121

Repeatedly, "Pirsig" frustrates his son's plea for direct answers, a plea that transparently veils the boy's need for parental affirmation and psychic intimacy. Again, narrative contradicts thesis: attitudes of "caring" and sympathy, persuasively advocated vis-à-vis the vehicle, are misprized when the context turns human. Contrast Abraham's answer to Isaac's only question in the story of the *Akedah:* Accompanying his father to the scene of potential sacrifice, the boy asks: "Here are the firestone and the wood; but where is the sheep for the burnt offering?" To which Abraham replies, "God will see to the sheep for His burnt offering," a response that works to reassure the child while leaving meaning indeterminate (Genesis 22.7–8). "Pirsig," on the other hand, a father of the early 1970s, produces, in his zeal to avoid foreclosing meaning on the cognitive level, a mounting level of frustration, anxiety, and desperation in his child. He allows the moment of hope to wither (see Winnicott, 1956).

Just as the voyage into new territory overlaps a return to the once familiar, so "Pirsig's" soliloquy muses on contemporary American society at large while attempting to recapitulate private thought processes. Theses of selected philosophers parade by as, meandering through the landscape on his cycle, "Pirsig" roves mentally through a maze of philosophical conundrums. Like the landscape outside, however, these inner vistas are explored without subtlety. Each polarized pair—classicism and romanticism, technology and art, reason and intuition, objectivity and subjectivity—is invoked in order to be dismissed. And just as the reality and continuity of self as well as of time and space are altered by travel, so "Pirsig" blurs distinctions between what he currently accepts and rejects, what he formerly believed and repudiated, and all relations among these sets of variables. His past and present ideas are enmeshed so as to render impossible an attempt to isolate a current claim and subject it to critique. Thus the motorcycling never ends, and the philosophizing leads to no conclusions.

The closest "Pirsig" approaches to an original contribution in the domain of philosophy proper is in his discussion of "Quality," which he identifies as "that which causes us to invent the analogues" (p. 225) with which we respond to our environment: "Quality is the continuing stimulus which our environment puts upon us to create the world in which we live. All of it. Every last bit of it" (p. 225). Although, a few lines later, he pulls back and demurs, "Madness there," he never revises this description. According to "Pirsig," the way a person attains Quality is through "caring." Care and Quality are internal and external aspects of the same thing: "A person who sees Quality and feels it as he works is a person who cares. A person who cares about what he sees and does is a person who's bound to have some characteristics of Quality" (p. 247).

However, "Pirsig," detached as he is from daily life in the countryside through which he cycles, is equally unfamiliar with the ordinary language usage of his chosen terms. He fails to relate his private notions to the complicated network of overlapping similarities and criss-crossings that characterize such terms in common parlance (see Wittgenstein, 1953). Not bothering to relate his versions of Quality and care to the speech and usage of others, he, not surprisingly, fails to bring them to bear on his relations with his flesh-and-blood child.

Normally, when we speak of quality, we associate it with ideas of the good, the worthwhile. "Pirsig," however, makes no provision for this. Nor does he offer guidelines for making choices among greater or lesser goods. Since it is obvious that we are unable to care about everything, we are bound to inquire which of life's endeavors deserve to be invested with Quality. What about, for instance, the problem of Quality in endeavors commonly deemed unethical? Can one speak of it in the doing of a murder? Suppose Pirsig's caring welder (pp. 320–21) were to apply himself not to motorcycles but to instruments of torture and human destruction. Is "Pirsig's" sense of Quality, like his sense of space, time, and human relations, fundamentally amoral and irresponsible, or, like the journey itself, is it merely incomplete? Are we justified in perceiving an ironic twist to the absence of an explicit ethical quest in a work subtitled "An Inquiry into Values"?

Now I wish to take "Pirsig's" choice of the pseudonym "Phaedrus" as an occasion for pointing out certain links between Plato's beautiful dialogue of that name and the text at hand. Like *Zen*, the *Phaedrus* is a work of imagination as well as philosophy, in so far as these genres are separable— which is, of course, one of the questions broached by both texts. Each offers a scene with plot and characters whose relationships to one another and to their creators mirror aspects of the abstract ideas with which they are attempting manifestly to deal.

Socrates and Phaedrus are ever aware of their external world—the river, plane tree, and midday sun—even as they explore the internal domain of thoughts and ideas. Likewise, "Pirsig" and Chris, from their motorcycle, note and respond to the terrain as it appears variously arid, fertile, or mountainous. Thus both the *Phaedrus* and *Zen* create a world in which philosophy appears not as disembodied conceptualization but as the evolving thought processes of personae grounded in an imagery of time and place.

What is the function of this setting in Plato? Whereas, in the modern text our focus shifts kaleidoscopically from foreground to background, Plato takes the dialogue form more strictly as shape for philosophical content. Believing ideas to be independent of their loci in person, culture, time, and place, his characters are animated by raisons d'être other than Pirsig's, whose motivation is manifestly (auto)biographical. At one point in the dialogue, Socrates chides Phaedrus, who has accused him of inventing a tale and then imputing it to the Egyptians. Socrates says reprovingly: "You seem to consider not whether a thing is or is not true, but who the speaker is and from what country the tale comes" (sec. 275). Whereupon, lest there be any doubt that this is error, Plato has Phaedrus acknowledge the justice of Socrates' rebuke.

In light of this devaluation of the identity of speakers, however, Plato's very choice of the dialogue form (rather than, say, the treatise) seems odd. Why bother at all with dramatis personae and mise en scène? An important aspect of the choice, however, and one paralleled in the modern text, seems to have to do with the desire to come as close as possible in writing to what Phaedrus calls "the living word of knowledge which has a soul and of which the written word is properly no more than an image" (sec. 276). Socrates explains that even the best writing is inferior to living speech, for that which is written down cannot reply when it is questioned and is therefore subject to misinterpretation and abuse. By creating characters and constructing their interchange as a formal dialogue, Plato approximates the condition of live speech, which represents for him the ideal. Setting, as in *Zen*, facilitates the imitation of process. In the *Phaedrus*, this is perhaps nowhere more beautifully expressed than in the closing lines, when Socrates prays: "Beloved Pan, and all ye other gods who haunt this place, give me beauty in the inward soul; and may the outward and the inward man be at one"—an ideal of unity echoed at the end of *Zen* by the moment when, for the narrator, all seems to come together (p. 369).

Plato's thought is linear and at least nominally conclusive. For example, Socrates addresses Phaedrus: "And now, Phaedrus, having agreed about the premises, we decide about the conclusion" (sec. 277). The dialogue form thus serves to clarify, to amplify, and to coopt us in its process. "Pirsig's" thought, on the other hand, rendered as monologue rather than dialogue, comes across as cyclical and inconclusive. Painfully won emotional insights at the conclusion of *Zen* never recombine with the philosophizing that precedes them. Openness in the modern text leaves integration as an optional task for the reader.

The one human relationship portrayed in any depth in *Zen* is "Pirsig's" with his son. And as the motorcycle trip counts doubly as a saga of retrogression and progression, so the child serves as a figure for both the past and the possible. Like Plato's Phaedrus, he is portrayed as questing and eager for his father-mentor's answers. The following are typical exchanges between them:

> "When are we going to get going?" Chris says.
> "What's your hurry?" I ask.
> "I just want to get going."
> "There's nothing up ahead that's any better than it is right here."
> He looks down silently with a frown. "Are we going to go camping tonight?" he asks. . . . "Are we?" he repeats.
> "We'll see later," I say.
> "Why later?"
> "Because I don't know now."
> "Why don't you know now?"
> "Well, I just don't know now why I just don't know." (P. 43)

And further on:

> "Dad?"
> "What?"
> "What was it like when you were a kid?"
> "Go to *sleep*, Chris!" (P. 43)

After this exchange, "Pirsig" hears the boy sobbing and speculates that "a few words of consolation might have helped" but notes that he does not believe in the application of "emotional Bandaids" (p. 56).

One more exchange:

> "Dad?"
> "What?" A small bird rises from a tree in front of us.
> "What should I be when I grow up?"
> The bird disappears over a far ridge. I don't know what to say.
> "Honest," I finally say.

125

"I mean what kind of job?"

"Any kind."

"Why do you get mad when I ask that?"

"I'm not mad . . . I just think . . . It doesn't matter what you do." (P. 244)

Over and over again, the boy's questions are frustrated in this manner by a father who never permits himself to intuit the needs and longings that prompt them. Persistently, defensively, "Pirsig" answers on a cognitive level and addresses only manifest content, a ploy he rationalizes by claiming the so-called limits of his own knowledge. Defending the appropriateness of his "honest" answers to the child, he erects an elaborate epistemological folly and ends by doubting the possibility of ever knowing the mind of another (p. 269). Unlike Socrates, he avoids dialogue and keeps his mental processes protectively separate. Preoccupied with his own quest, "Pirsig" fails to assume the parental responsibility of mediating between his child and the outside world. He fails to protect his child—not in a physical sense (although there are episodes of this kind too) but in an emotional sense. He fails to provide what Winnicott (1965) would have called a "holding environment."

In a poignant episode at a campsite, Chris, having been rebuked, feels hurt, misunderstood, and angry. He walks off alone into the night. Typically, his father chooses *not* to follow him: "Chris is off somewhere in the darkness but I'm not going to shag after him" (p. 55). Into "Pirsig's" mind at this moment, however, drift a few lines of a poem he had learned years ago, Goethe's *Erlkönig*. Quoting two lines (but refraining from giving its title), he fails to understand why he remembers it at this precise moment. To readers, however, the irony burns. For Goethe's *Erlkönig*, like *Zen*, features a father, his little boy, and a journey. In *Erlkönig*, however, it is not the father who inhabits a ghost-haunted world but the child, who, ill and in fear, imagines a ghost. He sees a phantasm, crowned and sceptered, who beckons lewdly to him and entices him to come away into the night. The father, however, on horseback, holds the child "safe and warm" in his arms: a second reversal of the configuration in *Zen*, where it is the boy who must hold tightly to his motorcycling father (though we are left to imagine this, for nowhere in the text is physical warmth between father and son described).

As Goethe's poem continues, the little boy imagines first the apparition of the Erlkönig and then the persuasive words of the specter. The father, fully understanding that fear and fever are the causes of the child's delusion and identifying with him, *pretends that he does not understand*. He reassures the child that what he thinks he sees is only a cloud-like shape and the voice he hears merely leaves rustling in the wind. "Be still, be calm," he soothes, while pressing the child tightly to his heart. The Erlkönig continues to stalk them as they ride and in the end claims the child. The poignancy of this magnificent poem comes from its representation of mutuality between father and child, trust in a parent's ability to shelter, to provide a psychic "holding" that complements physical embrace, a "meeting and matching" (see Winnicott, 1956) of each moment of terror (and hope), and then, in the last line, the reader's shock and grief that even this good, this kind, this most loving of fathers cannot protect against Death.

To quote *Erlkönig* is thus to dramatize its antithesis in *Zen*, where "Pirsig" can never pretend to Chris. Displacing to the world of technology definitions of "care" and "Quality," he misses every cue to play his part as protector, mediator, and interpreter. He literally rides roughshod over the needs and secret fears of his young son. Characterized by duality, "the duality between me and him," their paternal-filial relationship both accounts for and gives the lie to his endeavors to eliminate subject-object duality in the realm of ideas, as "Pirsig" comes finally to realize.

In the closing pages of the book, Pirsig gives his protagonist a flash of insight: "In all this Chautauqua talk there's been more than a touch of hypocrisy. Advice is given again and again to eliminate subject-object duality, when the biggest duality of all, the duality between me and him, remains unfaced" (p. 363). Carrying at least a triple valence, the "duality" referred to in this passage is that between the author, Pirsig, and his character, "Pirsig"; between "Pirsig" and his former self, Phaedrus; and, above all, between the father, "Pirsig," and his son, Chris.

The climactic moments of the book come in these final pages with the manifesto that Chris and Phaedrus are one—with the knowledge that one's child is in some way both one's former and one's future self. "Pirsig" attempts here to clarify his reasons for taking the child along on the journey: "What comes to me now is the realization that he's another Phaedrus . . . thinking the way he used to and acting the same way he used to" (p. 364). Thus, "Pirsig's" acceptance of his former self becomes the precondition for negotiating the duality between this self and the other/self who is his son.

Momentary resolution as figured in the text comes now not from philo-

127

sophic thought, nor from the passing landscape, nor from the motorcycle. Resolution, such as it is, comes, rather, on a foggy cliff at the very end of the work with the witnessing by "Pirsig" of a terrible scene: his son decomposes into rocking, wailing solipsism, into behavior verging on insanity. This terrifying sight finally jolts the father into an integration of his own personality. Speaking the words "I am Phaedrus," he, in overcoming the duality within himself, is empowered at long last to turn to the child and genuinely comfort him.

Now, when Chris asks him in desperation, "Were you really insane?" "Pirsig" can at last get it right. His resounding "No!" is precisely what the child at this moment *needs* to hear. It represents knowledge, truth, and caring on a level altogether absent from the foregoing narrative: it instantiates precisely Winnicott's "meeting and matching the moment of hope." A new honesty replaces the old, and, although or because the scene has apocalyptic overtones, it continues to move me deeply. It resonates with and recalls that other scene, on the mount in Moriah, where that other son and father were almost rent asunder and where, as here, they experienced fear, awe, vision, and at least a temporary moment of resolution.

By the end of *Zen*, therefore, "Pirsig" has been transformed, in Plato's terms, from a "non-lover" into a "lover" (as have I, perhaps, by this revised reading). True dialogue, as opposed to monologue, can now begin.

Perhaps the principal psychoanalytic thinker whose work has influenced these pages and has felt exquisitely relevant throughout my readings and rereadings of this text is D. W. Winnicott. His own tenacious refusal of subject-object dichotomies, his sensitivity to nuanced situatedness and to process, his continuing preoccupation with the structuring of parent-child relations, and, above all, his way of interweaving psychology, philosophy, aesthetics, and autobiography have resonated with and deeply informed my own engagement with *Zen*. The debt I owe him, though largely implicit, is nonetheless substantial.

An early version of this chapter was written while I was in residence at the Getty Center for the History of Art and the Humanities in Santa Monica, California. I wish to express my appreciation to the Center and also to Andrew Lewis of San Diego, whose abiding affection for *Zen* kept me moving on it this time around. The earlier version was published as "Recycling" in *Psychoanalytic Review* 79, no. 2 (Summer 1992): 209–22. Permission to reprint it is here gratefully acknowledged.

Reading *Antigone* Again

How different is returning to a work of art from revisiting a street you once skipped and slipped on as a child, or from drinking coffee with a friend who has been absent from your life for years but with whom you once shared intimacies, or from poring over a dusty box of scarves and gloves your mother once wore? First, there is that sense of the uncanny—the distance, the gulf, the strangeness; then, gradually, a succumbing to the irresistible magnetism of the past as it glows vividly once more; finally, the coming into focus of the present. At some point, perhaps, you try to put the experience together and grasp what has changed inside as well as out and what seems to be new, meaningful, useful, for today . . .

We read tragedy according to our own situatedness at a particular moment in time, and I do not mean here principally historic time in the ordinary sense of the term, although this is obviously important. Rather, I want to draw attention to the point that Greek tragedy affects us as individuals throughout the course of our personal development—emotional, intellectual, and professional. It may move us to tears, for example, at a time when death comes close, as happens to the chorus of male Theban elders in *Antigone* when the title character is being led off to the chamber where "all men sleep." With its eloquence of language and grandeur of conception, classical tragedy may embody events that resonate with our own immediate life experiences—our losses perhaps, our wishes, or our fears. And this occurs despite centuries of elapsed time, vast cultural differences, and the ravages of textual modification and translation. Although to utter this is to enlarge only slightly on a point made by Aristotle in the *Poetics*, as a psychoanalytic critic of the late twentieth century, I would reach beyond Aristotle's claim to insist that our tragic loyalties and identifications probably have interesting histories of their own, ramifications induced by alternating fits and misfits between life and art.

To intuit deeply the feelings of this character or to side protectively with that one, to attend to one or another aspect of the mise en scène, depends, as reader-response critics have noted, on latent matches between such details and the changing scenes in which we play out our own lives. Richly layered and thickly textured, the tragic texts of ancient Greece offer virtually inexhaustible possibilities for projection and identification.

To sound a personal note, Antigone appeared to me, when first I encountered her in my adolescence, as a noble heroine, courageous and true. Caught up in the passion of the Sophoclean drama by the skeins of our own fervent rebelliousness, my friends and I sided unwaveringly with her against Creon. Yet, at a later juncture in my life, I found myself overcome with a deep pity as the play draws to a close. Creon emerges for me now in clearer focus, and I can feel the poignancy of this stern antagonist who, by his middle age, has lost everything he ever held dear. Cruelly, he has finally come to understand the magnitude of his loss. When his decree has been disobeyed and the guard informs him that, against his express orders, Polyneices *has* been buried, he is asked whether this unwelcome news hurts his hearing or his mind. Creon cannot fathom the meaning of this question and asks "Why are you out to allocate my pain?" He cannot see the point of distinguishing between reacting to a deed and reacting to a representation of that deed. By the end of the tragedy, however, when grief overwhelms him, the point of such a difference becomes clear. He learns that some deeds, some events, some traumas (as we would put it) exceed any possible representation.

This theme of the relation between word and act resurfaces later in the play when Antigone asks her sister, Ismene, to denounce her since Ismene has refused to cooperate in the defiant act of burying their brother Polyneices. (Just to recapitulate the story, the situation is that Polyneices had been promised the right, after the banishment of their father, Oedipus, to take turns with his brother, Eteocles, in ruling Thebes. When his time came, however, Eteocles had refused to relinquish the power to him peacefully, and Polyneices then had taken up arms against his brother and his native city. In the skirmish that ensued, both brothers were killed, and, while Eteocles was given a proper burial, Polyneices—branded a traitor by the new ruler, their uncle Creon—was abandoned in the dust, uninterred and unmourned.) Defying Creon's decree of death to anyone who would disturb the body, Antigone audaciously prepares to give the last rites to her brother. In her outrage at her sister's refusal to join her, she too (like Creon) collapses the complex separations between deeds and spoken words; spitefully, she dares the gentle Ismene to inform against her and thus speak words that would sharpen definitively the cleft between them.

By the end of the play, even beyond the horror of the knowledge of his terrible losses (including the suicides of his wife and son), Creon must come to accept responsibility for these losses, to acknowledge that it is he himself who has brought them about. As he speaks his last lines, his pain is now as keen to me as Antigone's alone once was. Mad with fear, soaked in sorrow to the bone, he pleads to be taken away. He cannot rest. "My life," he says, "is warped past cure. My fate has struck me down."

I begin here in order to insist that Greek tragedy has to do with the strongest feelings of which each of us is capable at a given moment and with some of the most extreme situations into which human beings, as individuals and in groups, can fall. These points need accenting because, as critics, scholars, mental health professionals, general readers, we tend all too readily to objectify the entities under our scrutiny. We investigate, interpolate, evaluate. Yet it is the power of these ancient texts to amaze, terrify, delight, and inspire us *in the present* that gives them claims upon our attention.

It is their staying power, their genius for reawakening in us the pity and fear of which Aristotle spoke twenty-three hundred years ago that draws us. And this power likewise drew Freud, in his time and for his own very personal as well as cultural reasons (see Gamwell and Wells, 1989), to address them. To paraphrase the Latin maxim concerning time, "Tragediae mutantur et nos mutamur in illis." [The tragedies change and we change with them.]

Greek tragedy, as we behold it through our modern lenses and the particularity of our own scripts, invites us to consider the gaps between our notions of mental health and of a justly lived life. As they deal with the wars that arise between desire and prohibition, fear and defense, psychoanalysts attempt to trace the wreckage brought about by these inner hostilities, which unsettle our fragile equilibria and infiltrate our mental life and behavior. What, however, about conflicts among competing values, duties, and loyalties? Although ego psychologists might want to label these as intrasystemic—locatable within the province of the superego—this attribution, I would argue, can be only partial. The old plays keep pulling us toward questions too large for the discursive boundaries of any single discipline. They pull us beyond the reaches of psychoanalysis. *Antigone*, for example, challenges us to look hard at the relations between mental health and ethics, both ancient and contemporary, and thus surely impels us toward an interdisciplinary approach.

In considering the ethical context of *Antigone*, the philosopher Martha Nussbaum (1986) has suggested that the avoidance of conflict is often taken as a criterion of rationality. We attempt, she claims, to structure our lives so as to live, insofar as possible, in a conflict-free state of mind. Our capacity to do this and our success at it are widely accepted as signs of mental health. Given these assumptions, tragedy, which depicts irreconcilable conflict, might well be taken as representing a primitive stage of moral-psychological development. Nussbaum argues, to the contrary, that when avoidance of conflict is a goal, this very goal paradoxically will produce conflict. This is because, to the degree that an inner world is preserved intact and harmonious, strife must inevitably erupt externally. Moreover, the preservation of peaceful relations in the world at large requires a continual struggle against warring elements within—a grappling that may generate anxiety, psychic pain, and even paralysis, though it falls short of resulting in physical annihilation (as in the case of external combat).

How are attempts made to avoid conflict in *Antigone?* Consider the protagonists: both Creon and Antigone arrive at and sustain their respective positions by espousing an internally consistent point of view that they implement and defend vehemently. Each adopts the strategy of a simplified, reductive redescription of the world. Each narrows the focus of his or her gaze so that it draws them ineluctably toward death. Both players, once having made a decision to act a certain way, avoid anything that would shake their resolve. To achieve this, they must refuse to acknowledge the implications of the radically different perspectives on events that they have generated while moving, as it were, on the same Theban stage. If they could admit this fact, they would see clearly an inherent measure of complexity in their mutual situation, but they cannot. Any recognition of complexity would incur a risk of loss of confidence in the course of action already determined. Thus, each manages to fasten single-mindedly on one perspective and to dismiss values that might exert competing claims. By restricting their sights in this manner, each character ensures his or her capacity to act decisively and with confidence. Neither Creon nor Antigone is derailed by doubts, hesitations, or inner turmoil.

Antigone's treatment of Ismene illustrates this defensive orientation to the world. Horrified by Antigone's intention to disobey Creon, defy the ruling powers, and risk her life to bury their brother, Ismene shrinks from the project. Antigone, however, refuses to attend seriously to the objections offered by her sister. She does not debate with Ismene. Rather, she separates herself. She cuts her sister off emotionally. Redefining a complex psychological and ethical situation, Antigone polarizes it into simple, clear opposites. Implicitly, she defines herself as active, defiant, and noble; she characterizes Ismene as passive, submissive, and venal.

Twice Antigone proclaims that she hates her sister, first, when Ismene does not join her in actually performing the burial rite, and, second, when she fails to share in the agonistic spirit that might spur her on to proclaim the deed and thus participate verbally. Antigone's rejection and devaluation of Ismene here serve an important function with respect to her own psychic economy. They protect her as agent from facing any ambiguities that might impair her ability to commit the dangerous act. Evading an ethical dilemma by fiat, she escapes experiencing conflict by recourse to ruthless dichotomy and aversion.

Later on, after Antigone's fate has been publicly decreed, Ismene asks whether there is any help she might still be able to offer. Coldly, Antigone tells her sister to save herself, and Ismene responds: "Alas for me. Am I outside your fate?" Antigone unhesitatingly replies in the affirmative. The choice she offers her sister is patent: Be entirely of my persuasion or else totally foreign to me. Strife within her own heart is kept at bay. Revealingly, when Creon accuses her of what he takes to be her crime, she answers, "Nothing you say fits with my thought. I pray it never will." Thus, Creon is similarly located outside her recognizable universe.

Creon himself is equally intransigent. All the reasons one character after another advances in favor of Creon's reconsideration of his position—including, most poignantly, compassion for and identification with the desires of his own son—fail to move him. Hardening his heart against the pathos of Polyneices, Antigone, Ismene, his dead sister Jocasta, his wife Eurydice, and his son Haemon, he too avoids painful tension and paralysis by redefining reality so that the good seems unitary and harmonious. His inner object world is temporarily split off. Surely, for the psychoanalytically minded reader, associations to the work of Melanie Klein are unavoidable: this ethical posturing evokes her notion of the *paranoid/schizoid position*, in which good and bad are dissociated and respectively locatable fully within and outside the subject.

When, in the last moments of the drama, however, Creon suffers extreme loss, he moves, perhaps in reaction to his son's suicide, into what Klein would call the *depressive position*. Taking badness unto himself now rather than, as before, projecting it outward and attributing it to Antigone, he utters the words "O crimes of *my* wicked heart" (italics mine). Apostrophizing his son, he admits: "Oh, you have gone away / through my fault, not your own." Shortly thereafter, when he learns of his wife's suicide, he cries out, doubly bereft: "This is my guilt, all mine." From the grandiosity of total righteousness, his position reverses into the ignominy of complete malfeasance and nullity: "I who am nothing," he says, "more than nothing now."

But does Creon's agony represent a greater acceptance of moral complexity? Is the emotional response linked to ethical understanding? Is there any recognition on Creon's part that good is plural, that there may be various ethical desiderata, that genuine ethical dilemmas occur not between the good and the bad but between competing goods? Devastated by the deaths of his nearest kin, is he any clearer about Antigone's moral claims, any closer to an identification with her in the particularity of her own grief and sense of justice?

Antigone, for her part tragically forced into the cave from which she will never emerge, clings to her own moral position. The last words we hear from her reaffirm the conviction of her choice: "Look what I suffer, at whose command, / because I respected the right." Until the end, she remains convinced that she is justified, that Creon is eternally wrong.

What we see here, then, is an avoidance of ethical complexity—an aggressively revisionist strategy, a narrowing of vistas, a constricted conception of justice, an inability to feel what another is feeling and to face up to the challenge this raises for one's own point of view. We learn that such stratagems may indeed work effectively in the short run to allay inner tension and pave the way for decisive action—even, as here, for heroic action. Ultimately, however, these ploys produce tragic consequences. Conflict held at bay and not allowed into the mind erupts externally and doubles back to plague the mind that excludes it.

If conflict-free living is indeed an ideal goal imagined by mental health professionals in late twentieth-century America, *Antigone* compels us to reconsider it. Sophocles' play teaches by implication that such harmony comes only at great cost and is in any case either temporary or illusory. Even more important, it reveals that ethical responsibility consists precisely in *not* avoiding conflict. To restate Nussbaum's digest of Heraclitus, *justice is actually strife.*

Although Creon chooses to ignore it, Polyneices is, in relation to him, not only a traitor to the city of Thebes but also kin—a nephew and grand-nephew. Likewise, to Antigone, though she refuses to see it, he is a violent brother who has borne arms against her native city. To dismiss these facts, to fail to deliberate concerning them, to be incapable of thinking and feeling on both sides (as the chorus, by contrast, does in its ever-mediating role), to forgo exploring alternative possibilities, is to curtail life (both literally and figuratively). In the irrationality of absolute certainty lies the way to tragedy.

If we, as modern readers and spectators of tragedy, attend to episodic shifts in our own partialities and identifications, we stand to enrich our aesthetic experience and to gain in moral insight. Likewise, such a process of reading ourselves into and alongside the works may enable us to peer more keenly into our own psyches and actually to examine those spiders of which Heraclitus speaks, that sit in the middle of their webs, "able to feel and respond to any tug in any part of the complicated structure" (as quoted in Nussbaum, 1986, p. 69).

Both heroism and archvillainy, as we have learned through the atrocities of our era, arise from a hooded vision, a tunneling of sightlines, a failure of memory. *Antigone* disturbs us into a continuing meditation on this twinship by presenting a structure that parallels the doubling of Prometheus and Zeus in Aeschylus' *Prometheus Bound* (see E. H. Spitz, 1993). In so doing, it raises questions that, while yielding in part to psychoanalytic wisdom, cry out for interpretive schemata drawn from other sources.

Nietzsche (1874), for one, by way of contrast, speculates in one of his untimely meditations, "On the uses and disadvantages of history for life," that no deeds could be performed at all without a certain "blindness and injustice in the soul of him who acts" (p. 65). *Contra* remembering, he argues that "the capacity to feel to a certain degree unhistorically [is] vital and . . . fundamental, inasmuch as it constitutes the foundation upon which anything sound, healthy and great, anything truly human, can grow" (p. 63). For Nietzsche, to act well is in fact to forget, whereas to recollect may be to find oneself enslaved and disempowered. As I ponder this radical, profoundly antipsychoanalytic thought in the context of reading *Antigone*, I feel startled and brought up short. For Nietzsche's brazen words compel the realization that to understand the psychodynamic roots of a conflict and even to be able to predict its behavioral outcome within reasonable perimeters is not the same as to assess its value, to judge its ethical weight.

To read *Antigone* at different stages of my life has been to learn to love (and hate) the play in unforeseeable ways. Like an actual human person, it has grown and continues to grow with me. In eluding my desire to encompass it fully, the play has taught me the folly of that desire. It has attracted and infuriated me; always, it forces me to return. While terrifying me, it reassures me patiently that anxiety, passion, and single-minded persistence are the lot of all who love and imagine and fail.

Imbricated with fragments from the shattered moral rebus of *Oedipus Tyrannus* and stained with the sombre varnishes of *Oedipus at Colonus*, overpainted with washes of interpretation, adaptation, and performance, *Antigone* still glistens with a radiance all its own. The beautiful eyes of its heroine are not blinded but dimmed. She stares unflinching into the future. Brave, loyal, unforgiving, heroic perhaps, extremist even possibly to the verge of madness, quintessentially feminine (see Loraux, 1987), the daughter of Jocasta and Oedipus continues to inspire me in battles with intractable foes. She stands beside me in a shrinking world where everyone rushes to escape in the coming century the terrible fates of this last.

A version of this chapter was presented to the Discussion Group on Psychoanalysis and Greek Tragedy at the American Psychoanalytic Association meeting in New York, 18 December 1991. The translation cited is by Elizabeth Wyckoff in *Sophocles, I*, The Complete Greek Tragedies, 9 vols., edited by David Grene and Richmond Lattimore (Chicago: University of Chicago Press, 1954). I wish to thank Bennett Simon and the other members of our study group for their insightful conversations with me on the topic of this chapter.

Sonnet Winnowed
Send My Roots Rain

This chapter and the two to follow are the least psychoanalytic and the least touched with irony. This one is both the oldest and the youngest. It represents the kindling of first love, when all was serious, intense, and dramatic. It brings back the way my own education in the arts began, with a passionate kind of "new criticism," a burrowing into works and losing myself in them—wrapping them tightly around me, breathing only the air they let in, dreaming their imagery, waking up and stretching in their space. With Hopkins' "terrible sonnets," there is still, for me, no other way. Social, psychological, political theories may apply, but from the first to the last line, darkness envelops me and pulls me in.

Justus quidem tu es, Domine, si disputem tecum; verumtamen justa loquar ad te: Quare via impiorum prosperatur? Ec.

Thou art indeed just, Lord, if I contend
With thee; but, sir, so what I plead is just.
Why do sinners' ways prosper? and why must
Disappointment all I endeavor end?
    Wert thou my enemy, O thou my friend,
How wouldst thou worse, I wonder, than thou dost
Defeat, thwart me? Oh, the sots and thralls of lust
Do in spare hours more thrive than I that spend,
Sir, life upon thy cause. See, banks and brakes
Now, leaved how thick! laced they are again
With fretty chervil, look, and fresh wind shakes
Them; birds build—but not I build; no, but strain,
Time's eunuch, and not breed one work that wakes.
Mine, O thou lord of life, send my roots rain.

It never fails me. I have cherished this sonnet since the days when, bent over our scratched wooden desks, pushing the long hair out of our solemn eyes, identifying ourselves as a secret suffering sect, my schoolmates and I passed agonized notes back and forth in French, even Latin—questioning, always questioning, with profound sincerity, never a touch of irony, the eternal verities.

My plan is to move through the sonnet line by line, treading slowly and softly so as to note its riches, both thematic and stylistic, so as to point out its formal paradoxes and its web of interrelated, animating elements. Before beginning, however, a word will suffice to explain that my reading of Gerard Manley Hopkins always has meant entering as fully as I could manage into the religious domain he creates and accepting it as a world which, in the magical moment of reading, becomes mine.

"Thou art indeed just, Lord" (1889) compacts a wealth of emotional and intellectual complexity into the rigid, fourteen-line, decasyllabic Petrarchan sonnet form. It treats a number of intertwined themes of special poignancy to a speaker whom we have no good reason to assume to be other than the poet himself. The first theme, the nature of a human being's relationship to God, is portrayed as a bond fraught with ambivalent dependency and longing. The speaker, while believing in God's goodness, must nonetheless challenge and struggle against him—much as a child, trusting in the beneficence of her parents, must nevertheless enter into battle against them. Closely related to this is the paradox of theodicy: the problem of the continuing presence of evil in a world ruled by a just God. The poet takes up the theme of the passage of time in relation to these paradoxes in order to show that it is the transiency of human life that causes us to experience our existence in these terms. Finally, Hopkins depicts the paradox of the artist who seeks to merge his creative efforts with the forces of nature but who, in his human separateness and self-consciousness, feels he can create nothing but that which is in some sense apart from, in conflict with, God.

Formed as a dramatic monologue, the work begins in a calm, reflective, dispassionately forensic tone. Gradually, it builds through a series of questions to a crescendo of exclamations and imperatives, from the word *plead* used conversationally, even quasi-legally, in line 2 to an ardent plea in the final moments. Words seem expressly chosen for their several meanings and for their linkage with other words in terms of both sense and sound. If one were reading the poem aloud (as all Hopkins' poems are meant to be read), one might begin softly, slowly, contemplatively, and gradually become more emphatic, insistent, and intense. Moving from the initial quotation through the last line, I sense a progression—temporal, emotional, intellectual—a sequence of images, thoughts, and moods that must be lived through with the poetic speaker.

The sonnet is preceded by a quotation in Latin from Jeremiah, xi.i. Since Hopkins gives us a verbatim translation of this verse in the first three lines, we may ask why the original Latin of the Vulgate is included. Also, since the source is not expressly stated, we must suppose either that knowledge of the reference is presumed or that the purpose of the quotation is not to remind us specifically of Jeremiah. I believe the quotation's function is twofold. It does, first of all, establish continuity between the poet and the biblical prophet, but in a general rather than a specific sense—that is, as a reminder, an invocation, of the long tradition of questioning and challenging God. It also establishes a precedent for the specific question the poet is asking about the existence of evil: why evildoers flourish, when God is good. Second, the quotation functions not only as a historical link to biblical times but also as a link to the tradition which, via the Latin language, has become absorbed over the years into the ritual life of the Church. Thus the quotation, followed by its translation, serves to place both the poet's interrogative posture and his particular theme into a historical and a ritual perspective. It sets the poem in a framework in which the passage of time is emphasized; we must hear the poet's question as one that has been asked before and that must continue to be asked.

As we move into the lines of the sonnet itself, we progress from quotation in the public, ritual language of the Church (Latin) to translation—that is, a calm restatement of an age-old theological dilemma—to, finally, the new language, in the poet's own voice, the private, personal question, deeply felt and posed in tones charged with unfulfilled longing. The preceding Latin words had given us a historical locus, but now we can hear the poet himself speaking directly to the Lord as did Jeremiah in ancient days, not merely as linked superficially with the past, but as locked into a historical sequence in a way that confers great moment upon his self-epithet later on as "Time's eunuch."

Hopkins' translation in these first three lines of the sonnet, though apparently straightforward and transparent, involves significant choices. The language is unadorned, but, like any translation, it constitutes an interpretation. It leads us by its form both to feel and to ponder the major theme of the sonnet: the ambiguous nature of the relationship between the human and the divine.

In Latin, there is only one form of the second person singular pronoun and verb, no distinction being made between familiar and formal address. But in translating *tu* and *te*, Hopkins chooses the familiar forms in English, the now-archaic *thou* and *thee*. Although it is true these forms have been traditional for addressing God in English since the time of King James, they also carry important connotations of intimacy, familiarity, and equality which are relevant to the sense of these lines—where the poet is pleading a justice for his words equal to the justice of the Lord's.

Throughout the poem, intimate pronouns continue to refer to God, whom the poet calls "my friend." Twice, however, this effort to achieve a tone of confidential conversation is sharply interrupted by an abrupt switch to formal address, "Sir" (lines 2 and 9). It is as if the poet, talking familiarly with God, pleading his own view of justice, is suddenly wrenched, sensing that in this relationship, hierarchy must supersede intimacy. Thus does his choice of language, the shifting forms of address, reveal an ambivalence of feeling.

Hopkins' manner of translating "Justus quidem tu es, Domine, si disputem tecum" sets up for us the essential paradox and theme of the poem. The translated line has a strangeness about it, a disturbing quality. It seems to imply something conditional about the justice of the Lord, which, within the given context, is clearly preposterous. "Thou art indeed just, Lord, if I contend / With thee" can be restated as "If I contend with thee, thou art indeed just, Lord." Translated as Hopkins has chosen, the statement suggests that the justice of the Lord depends somehow, is contingent upon, the poet's struggle with him, and this is, of course, counter to the ethos of the entire poem, which is founded on devout faith.

In Latin, *si* is unambiguously a conditional conjunction requiring the subjunctive (*disputem*), but, though it is often translated "if," it can also be construed "when" or "even if." *Quidem* also has the force of an emphatic; it might be rendered "still," "even," "certainly," as well as "indeed." Thus, had Hopkins chosen to translate the passage differently, he could have been perfectly correct while obscuring the difficulty inherent in it and avoiding any enigmatic or disturbing quality. He could have said perhaps (barring metrical problems): "Thou art still just, Lord, even if I contend with thee"—

a perfectly clear statement affirming the eternal preeminence of the Lord's justice. What he has done instead is to bear us directly into the heart of the paradox that plagues him. His translation emphasizes the conditional, and, by doing it this way, he forces us to hear his burning question: What is the nature of the relationship between God and man? If God is just, why must man contend with him? It makes sense to contend with an unjust adversary, not with one acknowledged to be just; why should one acknowledged to be just be an adversary at all? Latent here perhaps are deep psychological questions concerning the role of codependency in all relationships.

This problem is given to us in the plainest language, language utterly unadorned so that it can function as a transparent vehicle for the crucial paradox, a paradox seen initially as intellectual. As the poet moves on from lines 3 and 4 to speak in his own voice, the language changes: "and why must / Disappointment all I endeavor end?" Here the problem becomes not an inherited concern, a venerable theological matter, but a personal agony.

The power of line 4 comes partly against its background of quotation and translation as the first words truly uttered by the poet in his own voice. And this idea introduces a secondary theme, that of the poetic speaker as artist. The poignant words of line 4 reflect the artist's struggle to find his voice, his repeated experience of inadequacy and failure. This line contains the longest word in the entire poem—*disappointment*—and the compelling alliteration of the consonants *m*, *n*, and *d*. Impact comes above all from the brilliant juxtaposition of *endeavor end*, which gives us a sense of double ending, of *dead end*, as we take in both the alliterative and the almost anagrammatic structure of these wonderful words.

In the next lines the poet accuses God, his "friend," of treating him like an enemy, thus developing the paradox and the ambiguity of their relationship in increasingly emotion-laden terms. The words *enemy* and *defeat* and the earlier *contend* imply an image of man in battle with God, a theme Hopkins develops in other sonnets. They portray him as engaged in a "war within," as he says, "wrestling with (my God!) my God" ("Carrion Comfort," 1885). This metaphor lends added anguish to the last line of the poem in which he cries out, for it suggests that in his dependent relation to the "lord of life," he must ask the very enemy he is condemned to fight for help in battle. These lines flow musically, with their repeated *w*'s and with the multisyllabic *enemy* and *wonder*. Abruptly, however, we are brought up short with the staccato *Defeat* and the monosyllabic *thwart* of line 7.

141

In that line, the poet conjures up the first important word-picture of the poem: "the sots and thralls of lust." In addition to the suggestively sensual quality of these words themselves, the image is remarkable because again it embodies a paradox. The poet seeks here, as he has done earlier in lines 3 and 4, to contrast himself with sinners. Now he characterizes those from whom he wishes to be distinguished as "sots and thralls of lust"; yet the image links them inextricably to himself.

To examine the image, we must look ahead as well as backward. Sots are drunkards; the word suggests a sodden wallowing in liquid; we imagine sinners who imbibe to such excess that they stagger and the world swims about them. This image connects with the final moments of the sonnet, with the poet's cry for rain to water his "roots," to quench his (spiritual) thirst. In both images, of sots and rain, there is further the association of weeping, of tears. Thralls are slaves—here, slaves to lust. Yet, the poetic speaker is also in thrall, imprisoned in his struggle, "strain[ing]," as he says, "spend[ing]" life "upon thy cause." And *lust* may be construed not solely as carnal appetite but as any passionate or overmastering desire. Surely we have felt the poet's passion throughout, leashed though it is by the constraints of the sonnet form. His own passion explodes in questions, exclamations, repetitions; it is a passion different from that of the sinner, even holy perhaps, but not unrelated to lust.

Among the words in lines 7 and 8, all sorts of interconnections abound that enrich the poem in meaning and/or music. Examples are *thwart*, *thralls*, and *thrive*, all linked by sound, as are *spare* and *spend*, both of which also have multiple meanings relevant to their context. *Spare* applied to time, to hours, may mean meager and lean as well as extra; *spend*, applied to life, to time, to energy, can mean to pay out as well as to exhaust or consume. These linkages all serve to thicken the texture of the work by creating a structure of latent continuity beneath apparent contrast.

In the ninth line, we enter the sestet of the sonnet; here, we encounter a caesura, a shift of perspective. Suddenly the poet turns away from self-consciousness, away from contemplating his plight, away from his relations with God and with other men. He turns outward to consider nature. We can almost see him lift his head as we read the imperative *See*, and then again in line 11, *look*. Turning outward with him, we also move beyond the past and into the present with the word *Now* (line 10). Hopkins gives us in these next three lines a word-picture remarkable because it produces sensations of color and smell without using words that denote either. We actually see green and breathe aromatic garden scents in these lines: "See, banks and brakes / Now, leaved how thick! laced they are again / With fretty chervil." We are given exclamations now, not questions. We and the poet are actively looking around, experiencing the motion of air and the energy of growing plants, moving from the fettered to the free. The human being stagnates, is defeated or enthralled, whereas "nature," asserted Hopkins in an earlier sonnet, "is never spent; / There lives the dearest freshness deep down things" ("God's Grandeur," 1877).

Then in line 12, the ease and innocence of nest-building birds are contrasted with the efforts of the poet, the artist, who must "strain" to create his works. The word *strain* suggests continual exertion, constipation, and impotence, but also, by contrast, the *music* of the poet and the music of the bird as well. Thus again a current of continuity flows beneath the breakers of apparent contradiction.

In line 13, the poet turns back to himself and to his problem with the self-deprecating epithet "Time's eunuch." Again he feels self-conscious, trapped both by his knowledge of good and evil and by the insufficiency of that knowledge, trapped in himself and his internal struggle, rendered sterile. He is not like nature, but something apart from it. Birds build nests for their young, but the poet can "breed" nothing. The word *wakes* is important here for it indicates arousal from inactivity, a coming alive. The poet seems to be pleading here for his works to take on some of the quality of the Lord's works, pleading somehow to link his own creativity with the forces manifest in nature. But this involves a paradox as well, for to create the poet must set himself up as a kind of god, must compete with his maker; thus, all artistic creation involves the sin of hubris.

Finally, in the closing moments of the sonnet, the poet appeals to the Lord in an outcry rendered unforgettable by its insistent repetition, *Mine* and *my*, and by its resonant alliteration. For me this line is reminiscent of spirituals in which the singer asks God to remember him ("Do, Lord, oh do Lord, oh do remember me") and of Dido importuning Aeneas, as he departs forever, to remember her, to not forget her fate. It is an appeal against indifference, an exquisitely powerful line, embodying all the resonance of the dependent love relations between the human and the divine, child and parent, lover and beloved, as well as the paradox that we are condemned to contend with those to whom we are most deeply attached. Hopkins' line returns us to Jeremiah and, at the same time, to Job and to the great English poets Donne, Milton, and Blake. It ends, I believe, on a note of desperate hope. Hopkins accepts the agony of eternal confrontation as he asks the Lord for help in this unending endeavor: "Mine, O thou lord of life, send my roots rain."

Part of what the poem has accomplished by these last words is a heightened sense of the passage of time, a sense of our own groundedness in time, which is central to my understanding of the poem. Hopkins believes that any human view of justice, passionately though he may advance it, is necessarily limited by history, by the process of birth and death to which we have been condemned since the first sin of disobedience ("the earth's sweet being in the beginning in Eden garden," he calls it in "Spring," 1877), whereas the justice of the Lord is formed *sub specie aeternitatis*. This contrast between the eternal and the ephemeral is a major motif of the sonnet: the contrast between that which "prosper[s]," "thrive[s]," "build[s]," "breed[s]," and "wakes," and that which "end[s]," is "defeat[ed]," "thwart[ed]," "spen[t]," "strain[ed]," in need of "rain." The paradox here is that the speaker knows that his own sense of justice is partial and cannot be equal to the Lord's and that he acknowledges his dependence on the Lord and trusts in Him, yet is indignant at what his own senses cause him to perceive as *injustitia*. It is as though, knowing that he cannot know, separate from God, he must nonetheless continually seek union with God, seek to understand that which he believes it is not given to man to understand.

This dilemma, dramatized by Hopkins in the form of a sonnet, seems not unrelated to Kant's discursively formulated notion in the transcendental dialectic that although everyone desires universal knowledge, we are led inevitably, if we pursue it, into contradiction. That we are so constituted, however, does not prevent us from desiring what we may not possess.

Hopkins' anguish here evokes for me also a concept introduced by the theologian Rudolf Otto (1979), the "mysterium tremendum et fascinans." His thesis is that the holy, the numinous, exerts a powerful sway over human beings and that we feel in its presence a helplessness, awe, and dread, the *tremendum* ("Wert thou my enemy, O thou my friend, / How wouldst thou worse, I wonder, than thou dost / Defeat, thwart me?"), a sense of the incomprehensible and mysterious, the *mysterium* ("Why do sinners' ways prosper? and why must / Disappointment all I endeavor end?"), and the element of attraction or *fascinans*, which can be seen as motivating the form of Hopkins' sonnet, in which he addresses God in familiar language as though conversing with a "friend." The glory of the work of art, however, as opposed to philosophical or theological formulations, is that it expresses all this in ways that empower us to experience it intellectually, emotionally, sensually, and, ultimately, personally.

This particular sonnet offers many paths of entry into its pattern of meanings in addition to the religious perspective. By picturing the intimacy, ambivalence, inequality, longing, and struggle that characterize any human love relationship, it transcends its particular theology. As we listen to the poet speaking to God, we can at the same time hear ourselves questioning and contending with those we cherish who have disappointed us, temporarily failed or hurt us, have taken hold of a viewpoint different from our own and seem, even momentarily, unintelligible to us. The poet's voice evokes that of a child who, love and trust for the parent notwithstanding, must assert his or her own position and advocate for its validity. It evokes the lover who longs for union with the beloved but feels equally a need for independence, freedom, and self-determination.

Entering into the aesthetic realm of Hopkins' sonnet, we may choose to imagine the poet's interlocutor in whatever sense is most meaningful to us as individual readers—perhaps, even, psychoanalytically speaking, as a split-off aspect of an inner self, an inner object world. What matters is that we read the poem as an appeal to someone crucially important to the speaker and to whom the speaker is, as the sonnet is to me, forever bound.

When art is made new, we are made new with it.
John Russell

Welcoming the Unexpected
Aesthetics for Children

Themes explored in earlier chapters—our tolerance for the absurd, our conflicted views of childhood, teaching in the arts, and our evolving relationships over time with works of art—lead to the question of how aesthetics might be incorporated into the daily lives and schoolwork of children. In presenting a partial answer to that question, this chapter has an empirical, practical cast that differs from the other sections of the book. However, although it may prove of most immediate use to individuals who work directly in the field, it raises questions of a wider scope. I shall describe a child-centered educational approach that might be considered a variation on what the philosophers Margaret Battin, John Fisher, Ronald Moore, and Anita Silvers (1989) have persuasively advocated in their work with college undergraduates—namely, a "case-driven" method that confronts students with "puzzles about art." The examples presented here, however, stretch that approach beyond cognition to engage other focal aspects of children's functioning and accord a role to psychosocial needs, developmental imperatives, and emotional requirements. These variables, recognized as ever-present and significant, are not viewed as restrictive or censorious. Instead they are factors to be kept in tacit awareness, providing a context that is never to be dismissed.

Work with young children in the arts has, for me, always involved a tension between my desire to allow charged material to challenge and stimulate—to churn still waters—and the sober realization that young minds must be protected from what they may not be ready to negotiate, that children must be able (emotionally and intellectually) to swim before being given the signal to jump in. Titrating these two legitimate aims matters most, of course, with the very youngest children. Older ones, preadolescents, vary considerably in their capacity to handle experiences in the arts and culture, and a reliable study of the relevant variables would constitute a valuable contribution to the literature. Actually, concern with and debate over this issue arises periodically in the press. A recent article in the *Washington Post*, for example, quoted the director Steven Spielberg as saying that he would not take his own young children to see his film *Jurassic Park* (Achenbach, 1993). A few days later the *New York Times* published a front-page story on attempts by Congress to impose controls on television violence, presumably in large part because of its effects on children (Andrews, 1993). Thus, to introduce children to the realm of the aesthetic is to engage with issues that often grow more complex than might be anticipated at the start.

This chapter highlights two experimental programs undertaken with children at the William B. Ward Elementary School in New Rochelle, New York. The "Seminar" program ran during 1979–1980; "Museum/Child/Interact," during 1980–1981. Neither is offered as a paradigm to be replicated, nor are they delineated in full detail; rather, they are meant to demonstrate a general approach. Occasional theoretical comments aim at broader issues, namely, the growing aesthetic awareness of children and the role of aesthetic education for development more generally. The underlying premise in both examples is that the developmental imperatives of children cannot be ignored, but that, within the limits of any given situation, supreme priority should be given to welcoming the unexpected and allowing wonderful ideas (see Duckworth, 1972) to emerge from the needs, competencies, and predilections of individuals. Curriculum was conceived as a bolt of cloth to be jointly chalked, cut, and fashioned by teacher and students rather than as a pattern ready-made.

Seminar

Seminar was a program in aesthetic education targeted for "gifted" fifth- and sixth-grade children who had been selected on the basis of test scores, classroom teachers' impressions, interviews, and writing samples. It was apparent, nevertheless, to the consultants (myself and my colleague Edith

147

Kleiner) that the resulting group was remarkably heterogeneous. We believe that any randomly selected group of children could have fared equally well given similar opportunities. And despite the great variety of talents and abilities displayed by individuals (see Gardner, 1983), we observed widespread adaptive strategies, as well as emotional and social vulnerabilities.

These particular ten- and eleven-year-old girls and boys seemed unusually full of energy. Many possessed an irrepressible and sophisticated sense of humor, and all had the ability to concentrate intensely. On the less positive side, we noted instances of the following: (1) feelings of social isolation—that is to say, loneliness, shyness, a sense of being different from others; (2) excessive competitiveness that occasionally led to feelings of unworthiness and even to bitterness rather than pride when other children excelled; (3) occasional underachievement that seemed to stem from past experiences of having won praise after only minimal expenditures of effort; (4) a prematurely narrowed focus of interest that was often encouraged by parents, who had a tendency to typecast their talented child, as, for example, a musical prodigy; (5) a diffuseness or inability to pay attention manifested now and then by a child who seemed to be marching internally to a different drummer and thus was unable to conform to the pace and direction of the group; (6) rapid oscillations between independent and dependent behavior, a trait we noted primarily in certain very bright girls, who seemed ambivalent about success, distrustful of their capacity to make decisions, and wont to bid petulantly for peer validation and teacher approval (on the topic of girls' differential concerns with relatedness and affirmation, see Gilligan, 1982; Chodorow, 1989; Brown and Gilligan, 1992); and lastly, (7) overachievement, a straining for perfection brought on perhaps by the close binding of a particular child's self-esteem to his or her performance level. All these traits, nascent and ebbing, might be subsumed under the heading of an imbalance, or a lack of integration, among the intellectual, emotional, and social spheres of development. However, it is worth emphasizing that while such imbalances may afflict bright children with particular intensity, they are a part of every young person's journey from infancy to adulthood.

Through aesthetic education, we sought to ameliorate these aporias by providing a milieu that would engage children in a holistic way and thus forge links between their different spheres of competence. We saw the realm of the aesthetic as an opportunity for risk-taking, pattern-making, and dreaming up as well as solving problems. We saw it as an arena for the integration of past and present, and a chance to experiment with enactment, elaboration, variation, interpretation, and critical evaluation. We saw the arts also as a source of powerful models for the children's future selves. Taking the aesthetic as a site of new ways of ordering human experiences and perceptions, we sought to evolve a flexible, integrative curriculum in aesthetic education that would not *cover* but *discover* its own subject matter. To engage the children in many dimensions, we planned to introduce and integrate work in the visual and language arts and the performing arts of drama and dance.

About thirty children culled from the total fifth- and sixth-grade population of this elementary school participated in the year-long venture. They were divided into two groups that met weekly in separate sessions with the two participating consultants. At first we worked independently, while maintaining close communication; toward the end of the year, joint sessions were held, and for the culminating event the groups came together, as will be described.

Our initial task, we felt, was to forge group esprit and foster a basic sense of trust among the children (who at first did not all know one another) and between the children and ourselves. This trust was vital, we knew, to a climate in which mutual self-discovery and creative risk-taking could flourish. To promote it, we hit on the broad theme of *identity*. Not knowing quite where that would lead, we saw as one possible objective the relative distancing of each child from his or her own egocentricity and the gaining of insight through projection onto an imaginary character. We supposed that imaginary characters might concretize wishful aspirations on the part of individual children as well as instantiate partial opposites and/or doubles. Taking up, then, the notion of character portrayal in theater, we thought first to consider its visual aspects and devised exercises on this theme. The children chose and modeled costumes for each other and then wrote about their responses to these newly formed characters.

Surprisingly, the elements that sparked their interest and elicited their most telling responses were not, as we had expected, the obvious aesthetic properties of the garments—their colors, textures, or symbolic associations—but rather their fellow classmates' poses and facial expressions, and their awkward or studied manners as they wore the unaccustomed regalia. Interpreted along the lines of psychoanalytic psychology, this phenomenon made perfect sense. Human response to the external world invariably begins with projections of a rudimentary bodily self (see Ferenczi, 1912; Freud, 1923). The other children's faces and bodies were, in this exercise, at just one remove from the children's own faces and bodies, but now strangely defamiliarized. Thus, the children took note of the postures and contortions of their peers and found them fascinating: they evoked the first authentic identifications and projections. The costumes, on the other hand, to which we had expected them to react with gusto, may have seemed initially just too remote to elicit comment. To grasp this and to understand the children's reactions in light of it is to acknowledge the role primitive projection plays in the process of aesthetic development, as well as in the growth of knowledge more broadly conceived.

Starting at this point, we then wondered how we might urge our group of children to go beyond their first response. How could we get them to notice more, extend their perceptual and imaginative range, refine their first impressions? We did not want to *tell* them or to *direct* their gaze. This posed the next educational challenge. We thought up some new exercises in which yards of fabric of varied texture, color, and pattern could be used to motivate a scene or drama. Several children chose a filmy white chiffon and dramatized a story that took place in a dressmaker's shop. Others selected a large swath of bright crimson heavy-woven cotton and enacted scenes involving horsemen in a chase with a mad dog. A third group chose pink grosgrain silk to drape around themselves in a scene of nasty conflict between two wealthy sisters. In each of these instances, we saw with interest that it was now clearly the visual and tactile aspects of the material to which the children were able to respond imaginatively. Thus, a different level of aesthetic response was called into play.

Movement and mime seemed a natural follow-up, and the children readily transformed themselves into clowns, robots, rockstars, thieves, sports champs, a prisoner, and a tightrope walker. As they created these characters through movement alone, they expressed a dawning awareness of our culture's extreme reliance on the spoken word. Many children expressed frustration at not being permitted to speak while performing, and we explored these feelings in group discussions afterwards. Since our goal was to keep each activity as open as possible, we encouraged verbalization only after an activity had been tried. Our theory was that experimentation in the realm of the aesthetic should follow the path of human development itself and the basic meaning of aesthetic education, as reflected in the *Oxford English Dictionary*, which defines *aesthetic* as "things perceptible by the senses, things material (as opposed to things thinkable or immaterial)." We believed that to talk first would foreclose empiricism but that to talk afterwards would forge important links between deed and word, the concrete and the abstract—links children often need help in forming.

Mime exercises sharpened the children's perception of the expressive possibilities of gesture and walk and gave insight into the specific types of movement that can be used consciously or unconsciously to express a personality or a mood. We discussed different acting techniques. They began to discover they were able to tell a great deal when a character or two appeared onstage, even before any words were spoken. Just by noting posture, gait, and bodily mannerisms, they could predict something about possible relationships and even have a premonition of plot.

Characterization through mime led to exercises in which the children mirrored each other's actions. These proved excellent for inducing intense concentration, as well as frequent outbursts of uncontrollable giggles. The children worked in pairs, one as the initiator of an agreed-upon character's action, the second as a precise mirror. The children were asked, at some point while performing for the rest of the group, to reverse these roles almost imperceptibly, so that the audience could no longer distinguish the initiator from the imitator of the action. The challenge of this work was highly pleasurable to the children. Any ice between individual members of the group had by now thawed, although undercurrents of competitiveness were still occasionally in evidence. We also felt that the children gained much from serving as audience to each other's efforts. Aesthetic education involves learning how to function as a member of an audience; and although this is a complex role in our culture, with both private and public aspects, it is one we tend to take for granted.

During our discussions, several children spoke about trust—their need for confidence in the leader of an activity, the person in control, and their even greater need for trust when the possibility of verbal language has been foreclosed. This theme continued during sessions devoted to "silent group conducting," in which one child would lead the rest of the class in movement by indicating only through his or her own motions what they were to do. Experimenting with the power of nonverbal communication, each conductor learned how to guide the other children in taking on whatever direction, tempo, degree of tension or release he or she wished to achieve and how to produce the general mood he or she sought to elicit. Later, children evinced their greater understanding of the need for theater and movie directors, choreographers, and orchestra and band conductors to win the trust of their respective companies and to communicate clearly in order to achieve integrated performances.

Emotion as a motivation for movement was the emphasis of another exercise and one that elicited a great variety of response. Having asked the group to come up with an emotion and then act it out, we found that, whereas some children could respond freely to the cue of an abstract word, others needed to be primed with a concrete situation. An example was *joy*. Some children were able to take off from the mere idea and jump, or clap, or spin, or leap, or hug another, and so on. Others felt they had to be provided with a concrete instance of a joyous situation—for example, winning a contest or a race, receiving a longed-for present, finally arriving at a place they had always wanted to visit. In discussing the differences they felt between responding to an abstract concept such as fear, grief, or anger and responding to a specific situation, the children taught us that the ability to function on an abstract plane cannot be correlated in any simple way with a more or less sophisticated level of aesthetic response.

A special bonus for the Seminar project was its link with the Lincoln Center Institute, a well-known program in aesthetic education that has been ongoing in the New York metropolitan area since the 1970s. During the course of our work, a modern dancer, Andrew Quinlan-Krichels, came on three occasions to prepare our children for viewing specially repeated performances of Anthony Tudor's ballet *Little Improvisations*. His approach to space and movement complemented and extended the children's ongoing mime and improvisation work, so that their eventual pleasure in the winter performances was greatly enriched.

Concurrently with the work I have been describing, the children were engaged in individual long-term projects, elaborating characters of their own imagining in the medium of collage. These personae emerged gradually on a backing of heavy brown paper as life-sized figures executed in a variety of materials, including fabric, ribbon, buttons, tinfoil, paint, ink, chalk, lace, and yarn. Each character was given a name (which in a few cases changed more than once), and then a dramatic monologue was composed for him or her. By tape-recording the monologues, the children were able to experiment with the problem of refining their texts and vocalizations in order to fit ever more closely the characters' visual representations. Some went further and teamed up in small groups to experiment with inventing plots, dialogues, and scenes involving several characters. They read short stories to each other in preparation for this work, and I read to them as well—principally poetry chosen for its masterful portrayal of character (among the works selected were Edwin Arlington Robinson's "Richard Cory," Edgar Lee Masters' "Lucinda Matlock," and Gwendolyn Brooks' "A Song in the Front Yard"). In conjunction with our exploration of the role of character in literature, I read them Edgar Allan Poe's "The Telltale Heart" and excerpts from Alan Sillitoe's *The Loneliness of the Long Distance Runner.* The children all had a chance to tape-record their monologues or plays and to view sight-and-sound presentations in which 35mm color slides of their characters were screened in synchrony with the tapes.

By this time it became apparent that our collage-character project had begun to overlap ongoing work initiated by the second Seminar consultant, Edith Kleiner, on Shakespeare's *Julius Caesar.* Engaged in close reading of the play with a special focus on character revelation and interaction, the children began to generate an endless stream of questions about life and culture in ancient Rome. As we listened and tried valiantly to answer their earnest queries, we sensed the possibility of an element of aesthetic education we had failed to consider. Thanks to our bright young students, we began to see the inescapable need for research. Not having anticipated this in our initial plans, we now saw that the cloth was truly being cut to the pattern of the children's own needs and desires. What evolved next was a meshing of the work on dramatic character with their fascination with the culture of ancient Rome.

Each child at this point assumed a Latin name and became a character of that ancient society—a particular general, statesman, poet, doctor, architect, cook. We amassed a wealth of materials—books, reproductions, slides of ancient Rome and its arts. Roles were researched, and we read Livy's account of the founding of Rome. At their prompting, I began to teach them Latin by encouraging them to request the vocabulary they wished to learn. Whereas much of our previous work had emphasized the nondiscursive arts, verbal language now came into sharp focus. Treating Latin as a living tongue, the children began to use it orally as well as in writing and to frame simple phrases concerning family, home, school life, and friends.

After several months, many children could translate a stanza or paragraph and were becoming increasingly sensitive to the derivation of English words and to grammatical structures in English. Their joy at this mastery was contagious, and eventually parents and siblings reported being addressed in Latin! We composed short plays based on favorite myths, *Androcles et Leo*, *Arca Pandorae*, and *Midas Rex*.

Individually and in small groups, the children experimented with Roman art media. Depicting themes drawn from their research or from *Julius Caesar*, or taking up simple decorative motifs, they worked in mosaic tiles, painted large murals "in a Pompeian manner," created columns in the different orders, sculpted miniature scenes in plasticene, and even insisted, after hearing Pliny's account of the eruption of Vesuvius, on devising a way of building a mini-volcano capable of being detonated. The psychological spin-off from this flurry of activity was beyond our most extravagant expectations. Group esprit flourished. Cooperation was at a height. Each person's interests broadened, and concentration and focus were observable wherever one cast one's eye. Children also began to point out references to ancient culture in the world around them—in advertising, on television—and to note discontinuities between ancient and modern practice, with respect, for example, to gender. We were amused by how well their naïve intoxication with discovery preserved them from the self-conscious scruples of postmodern scholars who suffer tormenting doubts that they will ever truly understand the past and permitted the children the full range of their aesthetic inebriation, leaving such worries to be conferred upon them by future educators.

The end of the year seemed to approach precipitously, and we suddenly realized that, although our emphasis all along had been on process rather than product, a culminating event could not be avoided. The children wanted at this point to do something spectacular and together. They came up with the idea of a gala Roman banquet to which they could invite family and other guests. Organizing activity by themselves, they prepared authentic foods, built an altar for the requisite libation to the gods, made elaborate decorations and costumes, and practiced for hours both in and out of school a variety of entertainments designed to utilize their own special artistic gifts in myriad ways. Two young trumpeters, for example, provided a fanfare; a budding gymnast performed in the guise of a slave girl; a small troup offered a hilarious original mime version of the Romulus and Remus story;

and our three short plays were performed in Latin along with scenes from *Julius Caesar*.

Evaluating the experiment as a venture in aesthetic education, we felt pleased. Although we had clung tenaciously to our mission of following wherever the children themselves led, or at least of sharing the compass with them, we had not—except temporarily—actually lost anyone. Awareness and sensitivity to the arts had surely increased and intensified during the year for most children in the program, and many had emerged more relaxed and companionable than they had appeared at the outset. Along with a fresh enthusiasm for live drama and dance, for poetry and visual arts, we noted new close friendships, increased self-confidence, and a sense of community, fostered, we believed, by shared experiences in so many modalities. The goal of aesthetic education in children, as I gleaned it from this experiment, should not be conceived as the transmitting of any preordained content; rather, it might be taken as, first and foremost, the nurturing of curiosity, wonder, and an ongoing impetus to become more alive to one's own perceptions as well as to the perceptions of others and to the infinitely expanding and nuanced world of sense and feeling.

Our experiment was limited; it yielded no formulas. It did not include in any important sense, for example, the art of music, nor were theoretical problems addressed as such, that is to say, philosophically. It followed an unpredictable trajectory emanating from its own peculiar combination of teachers, students, and setting. Others can and indeed must find alternative approaches to their own agreed-upon agendas, whether multidisciplinary (like ours) or more narrowly conceived. In each instance, I believe that despite rough spots, failures of nerve, and myriad frustrations, the energy, ebullience, knowledge, and growth that ensue will prove abiding in value for the children (and adults) involved.

Museum/Child/Interact

This program, unlike Seminar, involved several hundred children, virtually an entire school population minus the kindergarten classes, for six weeks. Our goal here—given strictures of limited time and resources, the pressure of numbers, and the usual resistances to contemporary art—was to enable young people to forge meaningful links of their own with the emerging art of our epoch and to foster a sense of continuity between their creative efforts and the work of exhibiting artists.

The challenge of the program was to prepare children of different ages and backgrounds for viewing a particular exhibit but to do so in age-appropriate experiential terms rather than, as is usual, by imparting (verbal) information. We did not want, for example, to name any of the artists in the exhibit in advance or give out any external data (biographical, historical, technical). We wanted the children to enter the museum with whatever preparation they might have gained through the hands-on experiences we devised for and with them and then to be surprised. For practical reasons, Museum/Child/Interact had to be more controlled than the year-long Seminar project. We wanted the children to puzzle over *why* an artist creates and *how* a visual artist talks to us without using words. We actively set up and encouraged (1) moments of slow, careful gazing unfettered by ordinary utilitarian concerns, (2) dialogues, including struggles, with materials, and (3) deep immersion in the related processes of making and seeing art. Our overriding credo was strict avoidance of advance information about the exhibition. The exhibition was to appear to the children after a month of work that, according to our hunch, might prepare them more authentically than any lecture.

The educational challenges were manifold. We wanted to put across several notions: that visual art is made for the *eye* and yet not just for the eye but also for the entire body and sense of self through the medium of *space* (both measurable and imaginary); that an artist's work can fill and transform whatever space it happens to be sharing with us; that visual art communicates with us through a sensuous language of its own; that art has to do with revelation and the shifting limits of the possible, that it exposes much that is weird and wonderful, terrible and beautiful, in the most ordinary aspects of life; that the making of things counts just as much as the things finally made, because making things is actually making oneself; that to play with materials and put something together out in the real world—something new, something that was never there before—is to function like an artist.

After researching forthcoming shows at local museums, I had selected promising exhibits at the Neuberger Museum in Purchase, New York. Located on the grounds of the branch of the state university which was designated specifically as an arts campus, housing departments of theater, dance, and music as well as visual arts, this site allowed us to introduce an interdisciplinary component into what was essentially a visual arts–oriented program. In fact, eventually each trip to the museum did include observation of dance classes, tours of the campus theaters (including a blackbox), and university student–led visits to working art studios.

The exhibit we selected for the younger children (first through third grades), "Seven Artists," included two- and three-dimensional and installation work by the American artists Gregory Amenoff, Eleanor Hubbard, Bill Jensen, Donald Lipski, Bruce Robbins, Judith Shea, and Lynn Umlauf, all born in the decade of the 1940s (see the exhibition catalogue, *Seven Artists*, 1980). Although the group was extremely diverse in terms of style and subject matter, each of these artists manifested a commitment to process—to openly intuitive approaches, to improvisation, and to manifest pleasure in spontaneity. A second exhibit was chosen for viewing by fourth- and fifth-graders: the work of Nancy Graves, including her camels, bones, maps, and camouflage paintings (see the exhibition catalogue, *Nancy Graves: A Survey, 1969–1980*, 1980).

The program design provided for an intensive six weeks with each group of children. First, the consultant was to observe each participating class in session and chat with teacher and students. The goals of this low-key encounter were psychological and practical: to establish basic contact, to gain some initial feel for the style and mood of each milieu (more or less formal or informal, warm or distant, rigid or relaxed), to introduce the general aims of the program, to request materials, and to answer questions. Three subsequent sessions were to be devoted to participatory work on the part of students, consultant, and, an important step, classroom teachers.

To transform ordinary classroom space temporarily into an artspace, each teacher and group of students was asked to clear areas on the wall and within the room. Our rationale was that this would afford an experiential convergence between the realm of the aesthetic and that of the children's ongoing daily life and curriculum; in addition, we felt it would help both teachers and students to feel at home in the presence of new sights, ideas, and objects. Thus, as the program progressed, each group found itself increasingly surrounded by a visual, material environment that reflected its own artistic efforts. Many participating classrooms retained these special artspaces long afterwards as an ongoing part of their educational ambience.

Simple materials were requested, the theory being that lack of technique should not restrict expression or impede experimentation. The fifth week was to be a culmination of the previous month's work: a full-day's trip to the Neuberger Museum to view the "Seven Artists" exhibit (in the case of the younger children), as well as to observe live arts activities on campus. Finally, the sixth week was planned as a follow-up session, a reprise, with 35mm color slides of works from the exhibition and discussion (evaluation) in the school auditorium.

As in the Seminar program, participatory exercises were devised, and these proved of varying value; highly significant variables seemed to be the developmental stage of the children involved and the general tenor of their particular classroom setting. One early activity required the children to close their eyes while sequential and incremental small changes were made in their environment. Gradually, they grew more adept at identifying these changes. In a subsequent exercise, they were asked to imagine that they had just landed in a spaceship from another planet and that everything in their surrounds was therefore utterly foreign to them. They walked slowly around their room—noticing, touching, examining familiar objects that had suddenly become incomprehensible. Selecting one that seemed special for whatever reason, they each made a detailed drawing of it to take back on the spaceship. The goal was to make such a well-observed drawing that the families back in outer space would feel that they too had actually seen the foreign object.

After talking briefly about this exercise, we set up a game reminiscent of the surrealists' "corps exquis." Each child contributed to a joint mural—a long paper taped to the wall, to which each in turn added a line or a shape in response to all that had previously been done by others. This furthered the notion of visual communication, and a follow-up to this proved highly pleasurable for many groups. Choosing partners, the children held silent conversations (and arguments) on paper entirely in terms of visual language (line, color, and so on). Although no explicit correlation was made in advance with "Seven Artists," one special connection we were hoping would emerge was with the biomorphic abstract paintings of Gregory Amenoff.

Donald Lipski, a gestural artist with roots in Dada, had contributed an installation to "Seven Artists," a work called *Passing Time 1980* (fig. 2.18). It consisted of nearly two hundred sculptures made by binding, braiding, folding, wrapping, and winding an assortment of discarded materials, including old mismatched boots, ledgers, skates, paintbrush handles, tubing, and obsolete keys to gallery walls and floors. Lipski had transported his finished sculptures to the gallery in shoeboxes and then did his own installation—on ceiling and floor, in addition to the canonical walls. To

2.18. Donald Lipski, *Passing Time 1980*.

prepare the children for his work (without saying that was the purpose), we asked each child to find a shoebox and to collect assorted small objects that were being discarded but that appealed to them in some way. After amassing worn building blocks, wire, ribbons, used film, batteries, matchbox covers, and the like, they discussed the difficulty of classifying these objects into categories such as rough/smooth, round/sharp, soft/hard, shiny/dull. We talked about how their looks, shapes, and sizes might be altered and how some objects might be joined with others. Employing glue, string, tape, scissors, pliers, and wirecutters, they busily tinkered and at length arranged their newly created objects in space, cooperating in the formation of a joint installation of their own and experiencing the way in which their self-fashioned sculptures, debris rescued from the trashheap, revitalized the classroom and reorganized their space. Eventually, some of the children asked to bring their own sculptures to the museum, and the responses of those students to Lipski were among the most gratifying of all.

Each of the seven artists was approached in a similar manner. The children's responses to the show when they encountered it in the museum seemed to reflect a level of connectedness we believed unattainable otherwise. We observed an unusual degree of comfort, ease, sense of familiarity, and "friendliness" between these children and the exhibited objects. In the follow-up sessions, we asked them to consider the difference between really being there with the art and just seeing the slides back at school. Rather than address this question, however, most of the children preferred to take the occasion as an opportunity to remember—to treat it as a pleasurable return, a reprise of what had been a thoroughly enjoyable experience for them, to talk about what they had especially liked (and disliked) in the museum. With several classes, we experimented with group poems. "*Make us know how you feel,*" we said.

In a lecture sponsored jointly by the Harvard Graduate School of Education and the Harvard Divinity School, the psychiatrist Robert Coles summed up his attitude to the education of children in words that ideally suit the approach to aesthetic education I have been advocating here. "Education," said Coles, "is being shaken up, derailed from those tracks we get onto, with all the certainties, sometimes the false certainties, they offer us—the stages, phases, cycles, categories, definitions, mandates, rules—marching us through anything so that we tame uncertainty, ambiguity, and contradiction—the very stuff of life" (quoted by T. Gardner, 1993, p. 24).

The children in both experiments described here brought with them a rich mix of natural curiosity and inventiveness, along with naïveté, boisterousness, and, in some cases, blasé attitudes like "Show me" and "So what!" The approach taken was to avoid imposing predetermined problems, tasks, or even specific works and instead to provide an atmosphere conducive to discovery. This guiding principle led to projects veering off in unexpected directions and to group dynamics that occasionally took on the semblance of those red, blue, green, yellow, rowdy, confusing, but energetic bumpercar rides at amusement parks. The risks proved worth taking. A quantum of chaos is probably endemic to authentic encounters with the unfamiliar, with art in particular, whenever it collides with curious children of any age.

In thinking about aesthetics and children, I have benefited from contacts with many extraordinary people. Three individuals in particular taught me that one can dive down critically to deep levels of psychological truth while keeping in play the rippling surfaces of art and human perception. To them I owe a special debt of gratitude: Rika Burnham (dance), Randy Williams (visual art), and Ruth Alperson (music). I also wish to acknowledge my gracious colleague Edith Kleiner; Catherine T. Theoharides, the principal of the William B. Ward Elementary School at the time; and, above all, the children who made reality out of fantasy with us.

The Seminar section was summarized in "An Interdisciplinary Approach for a City System: Aesthetic Education for the Intellectually Gifted Child," *The Gifted and Talented in Art*, ed. A. Hurwitz (Worcester, Mass.: Davis, 1983). The Museum/Child/Interact section was outlined in "Museums and Children: A Natural Connection," *Journal of the New York School Boards Association* (May 1981), and in a *New York Times* article entitled "Museum Modernizes Tours for Children" by Judith Wershil Hasan (2 November 1980).

I've lived in the ghetto here more than a year,
In Terezín, in the black town now,
And when I remember my old home so dear,
I can love it more than I did, somehow.

Ah, home, home,
Why did they tear me away?
Here the weak die easy as a feather
And when they die, they die forever.
. . .
Yet we all hope the time will come
When we'll go home again.
Anonymous child, "Homesick,"
in Volaková, 1993

Music of Hope
Brundibár

My subject in this final chapter is the power of art to shape the
mind as well as to be shaped by it. The focal point is *Brundibár*,
a children's opera written by the Czech composer Hans Krása in
1938 and performed many times by inmates of Terezín, a concentration camp outside of Prague, between the years 1942 and 1944.
My reflections are framed by references to the *Haggadah*, the
book of observance, ritual, history, and prayer that is read aloud
each year at Passover by Jews seated around the seder table.

Central to the text of the *Haggadah* is the story of the four sons,
or, as it is now often called, with gender bias corrected, the four
children. This story, not insignificantly, is retold annually toward
the beginning of the seder service when even the youngest members of the family are not yet too tired or hungry to pay attention.
Each of the four characters (often "played" by children at the
table) asks about the Exodus in a different way and thus must be
answered by the leader according to the child's own special requirements. There are, traditionally, a wise child, a wicked child,
a simple child, and a child who cannot ask any question at all.

I would like to focus on the so-called wicked child, the one who asks, "What does this service mean to *you?*" By choosing the exclusionary "you" rather than the communal "us," the *rasha*, or bad child, removes him- or herself from the community. Thus, the choice of a distancing pronoun brings on a condemnatory epithet. And this is a notion that recurs implicitly throughout the text of the *Haggadah* and the course of the seder. It is emphasized in narrative songs like "Dayenu" ("It would have been enough"), where "we" are fed with manna in the wilderness, and in responsive songs like "Echad mi yodeah" ("Who knows one?"), where each person at the seder table participates directly in the action by singing a repeated, specially designated part, and through ritual practice, for example, by tasting the acerbic raw horseradish, the bitter herb, symbolic of *our* harsh treatment as slaves in Egypt. In this way, Jewish children are taught, year after year, that the story of the Exodus is *their* story. As it is written in the *Haggadah:* "In every generation, each of us should feel as though we ourselves had gone forth out of Egypt. . . . It was we who were slaves . . . we who were strangers."

For Jews, history is a reenacting as well as a recounting. It is always, furthermore, a collective experience. To remember this as I write my reflections on *Brundibár* matters deeply to me because I am not a survivor of the Holocaust. While thousands of my contemporaries starved and perished in Europe, I was a healthy baby growing up in New York. Yet an inescapable sense of urgency pervaded my preparation for this project. The *Haggadah*, I am suggesting, offers a way of grasping that sense of urgency and of understanding the problems that I encountered in attaining scholarly distance from my work on this chapter.

The very themes of *Brundibár*, its libretto and its music, have to do with the power of collective experience. (fig. 2.19) The opera illustrates, moreover, as it is performed, the power of enactment. This work, written for, performed by, and witnessed by children, resonates deeply with Judaic themes. They are not explicit or musically inscribed, nor can they be discerned in the manifest text. The composer, Krása, and the librettist, Adolf Hoffmeister, came from assimilated Czech- and German-Jewish families, respectively. Nonetheless, echoes of Judaic observance and practice pervade their work and cannot escape the notice of those familiar with these traditions, as well as with the special circumstances of the performances in the camp at Terezín.

My reflections on *Brundibár* focus on psychological aspects of the work.

163

2.19. *Brundibár* poster.

In addition to contextualizing it with reference to contemporary and related musical works for children and to interpreting elements of its content, I draw on the recollections of Ella Weissberger, who, as a little girl interned at Terezín, played the role of the cat. She graciously granted me many hours of personal reminiscence in her home. Guided by her insightful memories,

I shall speculate on the import of the opera for the children who performed in it and also for those who heard it at Terezín. To consider the powerful role art has played and can play in the lives of all children at risk, whether physically or psychically, children exposed to conditions of extreme oppression, in the past and in our own time, I have drawn on the writings of such psychologists and psychoanalysts as Joan Erikson (see Kivnick and Erikson, 1983) and Judith Kestenberg (1990). This latter theme ties the Terezín performances of *Brundibár* to educational and clinical concerns in communities throughout the United States today.

The opera is in two parts. In act 1 a little boy, Pepíček, and his sister, Aninka, have lost their father, and their mother is very ill. A doctor tells them they must find milk for her if she is to recover. Having no money, they wander into the streets, where they meet assorted vendors—an ice-cream man, a baker, and a milkman—whom they importune in vain. At length, a policeman warns them that nothing in the world is obtainable without money, and they grow discouraged.

Suddenly, the organ-grinder, Brundibár, appears on the scene playing his music, and the children watch with fascination as people throw coins into his hat. It occurs to Aninka that perhaps she and her brother might do something similar, might, like Brundibár, sing for money. They try, but their soft voices do not carry; nobody pays attention. Brundibár, however, becomes angry and threatens them. The street is his empire, he sings, his territory; he is the only one who can make music there.

After he leaves the street, night begins to fall. Pepíček and Aninka, dispirited, weary, and frightened, fall asleep. As they do so, three neighborhood animals appear onstage—a sparrow, a cat, and a dog. Each sings sympathetically about the children's plight, and in a trio they devise a scheme to help. Rather than try to sing alone, the animals suggest, the children should aim for solidarity: Aninka and Pepíček should band together with all three hundred other children in the neighborhood. As an ensemble they will be able to create enough volume to outsing and thus to defeat Brundibár.

Act 2 opens as morning dawns and the brother and sister gradually awake. The street, bustling with life, is thronged with vendors, adults hurrying off to work, and children with schoolbags. Appearing among them, the sparrow, cat, and dog explain to these children the plight of Aninka and Pepíček. All the children agree to help when signaled. Just then Brundibár reappears to preempt the stage. He reasserts his dominance and renders his theme song, which ends: "Mightier than any czar / I, organ-grinder Brundibár."

As he plays his music, however, the cat begins to meow and the dog to howl. Brundibár is enraged by their insolence, but the adults who are watching laugh at him. As he is pushed to the edge of the stage, a large group of children join forces, take over the space, and begin to sing an exquisite lullaby. Although the organ-grinder tries to drown them out, by-standers turn away from him and toss their coins instead to Pepíček. In a final effort to recoup his power, Brundibár grabs Pepíček's cap and runs off with the money. But the children chase and catch him. Returning the coins and cap to Pepíček, they gather once more on stage and together sing a triumphant finale. This chorus, as performed in Terezín to rousing cheers on the part of audiences who crowded in night after night to hear it, was given special words:

> "He who loves justice and will
> abide by it, and who is not afraid,
> is our friend and can play with us."

On both sides of the Atlantic the 1930s saw the composition of a number of operatic works for children that featured themes related to those addressed in *Brundibár*. Hoffmeister conceived of his story, however, as a parable, in the spirit of the contemporary leftist agitprop theater (see Jelavich, 1993) as well as of the *Lehrstücke* of Bertolt Brecht. These related genres were developed to promote solidarity and urge community action against (capitalist) oppression, and clearly the story, with its emphasis on the greedy and callous tradesmen and the overriding importance of money, encourages this reading. However, because of the subjugation of Czechoslovakia by Hitler in 1939, *Brundibár*, except for a premiere and two repeat performances in the Jewish orphanage for boys in Vinohrady, Prague, in 1941, had to wait until the winter of 1942–43 to reach a wider audience. By then, under conditions of war, terror, and displacement, its performances took place not in Prague but at Terezín, where Krása was interned. In the German camp the slender work took on a tremendous urgency and an infusion of new meaning. By this time, thousands of children had been imprisoned in Terezín, and to them, as they watched and listened to the opera, the character of the wicked Brundibár was quickly associated with the figure of Hitler. The opera's message of cooperation and mutual help resounded among them as a clarion call to life and hope.

Among related works composed in this general period was the Bertolt Brecht–Kurt Weill *Der Jasager* of 1930, with a plot in which, as in *Brundibár*, a child seeks aid for an ailing mother. Its ending is grim, for the child is made to die as punishment for not fully grasping the import of solidarity. There was also Hindemith's *Wir bauen eine Stadt* of that same year; Prokofiev's symphonic tale for children *Peter and the Wolf* (1936), in which a child, in collaboration with animals, triumphs over evil; and Aaron Copland's *The Second Hurricane* (1936). The Copland work is an opera composed explicitly to be performed by children. Its story concerns six youngsters who volunteer to help with flood relief, then gradually drift apart, but, in the face of extreme danger (in this case, a natural disaster, a hurricane), rediscover one another and regroup in order to survive.

Janáček's *Cunning Little Vixen* (1924) and Ravel's *L'Enfant et les sortilèges* (1925), like *Brundibár* and *Peter and the Wolf*, allot prominent roles to animal characters. The apparently cross-cultural affinity of children for animals and the replacement of children by animals or the motif of animals assisting children (as in *Brundibár*) boast a long tradition not only in music, art, and literature designed for the young but also in the canons of high art, in allegory, and, especially, in folklore. One thinks, for example, of "The Town Musicians of Bremen," in which a band of neglected farm animals join forces to "sing" loudly and thus to overcome the evil adults who appear in their midst. In *Brundibár*, interestingly, there is a reversal of that situation, for, whereas the evildoers in the old folktale are robbers, in the modern opera they are sellers.

Thus, retrospectively *Brundibár* can be located in a rich musical and extramusical tradition. For a direct debt, however, we must go to Engelbert Humperdinck's paradigmatic children's opera *Hansel and Gretel*, which premiered in Weimar in 1893 and was known, we may assume, to Krása and Hoffmeister. As in *Brundibár*, the protagonists are a brother and sister whose dialogues, duets, and mutual assistance are central to the action. Aninka and Pepíček go forth to seek milk for their incapacitated mother. Hansel and Gretel, on the other hand, go forth to seek nourishment when their angry (and incapacitated) mother breaks a pitcher and spills the milk. Thus, with quite different emotional resonances, both operas stage a reversal of the normal hierarchy in infancy, where it is the mother who provides milk for her children, not the other way around.

Developmental imperatives, however, impel children of both sexes to move beyond infantile dependence on the mother and on milk to establish their own capacities for self-reliance and for the nurturance of others, including those by whom they were once nurtured. *Hansel and Gretel* projects the negative aspects of this effort to outgrow dependency—namely, the fear, anxiety, and counterphobic aggression that accompany it—back onto the mother, in the form of the wicked witch. *Brundibár*, however, maintains the mother, and mothers in general, as benign (never appearing onstage, they are referred to only in song, especially—lovingly—in the lullaby of act 2), and it is an evil male figure, the organ-grinder, who impedes the children's progress.

In Terezín, Hanush Treidinger, the boy who sang the role of the wicked organ-grinder, was a short and slender orphan from Pilsen who had begged the director, Rudy Freudenfeld, to give him the part. He was the only child in the camp who ever played Brundibár, and he became famous there for his characterization. According to Ella Weissberger, who performed with him, he was a superb actor who could twitch his false moustachios with bravado. Delighting the audiences, he gave them opportunities to vent their hostility toward the Nazi oppressor by displacement and at the same time to triumph over Hitler in fantasy by reveling in their secret identification with an aggressor. In *Brundibár*, all the enemy adults (vendors, passersby, and policeman) are male—a gendering of evil that may have matched the children's reality in the camp.

The emotional resonances of all these themes must have acquired an urgency in Terezín that far exceeded the bounds of what we would consider normal in child development. It is poignant to speculate how ordinary childhood issues must have needed to be psychically reworked in each individual according to the extremity of that context. In Terezín, as we know, many parents were in fact removed from their children and forcibly rendered impotent to nourish or protect them. In consequence, the young who survived were pressed to become adults prematurely, to supply food and solace for themselves, for each other, and often for the adults in their midst as well. Coerced by deprivation and brutality to develop adaptive precocities (rather than retain, as in *Brundibár*, the naturally softer voices of children), they learned painfully that when the family circle could no longer provide security for them, their sole hope for survival lay in solidarity with one another. *Brundibár* thus dramatized for these children not an age-appropriate developmental fantasy or a platform for the promulgation of socialist ideology but aspects of a grim and inescapable reality. Yet, by organizing it, by giving it form and substance—musically, visually, and choreographically—by displacing it to an imaginary space where it could be shared with others and safely acted out, the opera, I suggest, represented that reality in ways that may have led, at least for some of the children, and at least temporarily, toward greater inner and outer mastery, competence, and growth.

The child protagonists in both *Brundibár* and *Hansel and Gretel* are made to experience periods of sleep in the middle of the action of each work. From a developmental perspective, the passive state of sleep and rest is often seen as an occasion for consolidation and growth, for restitution— a time out of time, when psychic and physical resources are replenished. On the other hand, for children, falling asleep subjectively means separation from loved ones and thus vulnerability, unprotectedness. As night falls, Aninka articulates her fears, especially of the threatening Brundibár, whom she guiltily feels she has offended. Similarly, as darkness envelops the children in *Hansel and Gretel*, they realize they are lost in the forest and begin to hallucinate ghosts. Significantly, both operas represent the young brother-and-sister protagonists as protected while sleeping. The Sandman and fourteen angels serve as reassuring guardians in the one case and the sparrow, cat, and dog in the other.

In *Brundibár*, the solution to the children's problem arises during sleep, when the three animals appear on stage in sequence, emanating as if from a dream. The scene culminates in a serenade that arguably represents the musical high point of Krása's score. Both dramatically and musically, this piece bears comparison with the beautiful orchestral setting of the "Children's Prayer" in *Hansel and Gretel*.

But how must night, sleep, and darkness have felt for the children of Terezín—children beset with hunger, cold, repeated losses, bewildering uncertainties and often having only a fragile grip on any fragment of a sense of identity? Under such conditions, the inactivity and lethargy of sleep may have been associated first with terror and then gradually with resignation, with loss of the will to live. For the mythic equation of death and sleep was, in this situation, under Nazi rule, an imminent reality.

In talking with me and trying to answer my questions about what *Brundibár* meant to her as a child and to the other children who performed in it and witnessed it, Ella Weissberger proclaimed that the opera meant more to her and to her friends than any type of physical comfort. She put it that, whereas the lack of food obviously played a major role in their lives (thus the depriving figures in the opera of the milkman, ice-cream man, and baker took on added dimensions of hostility and yearning vis-à-vis the children of Terezín), food and physical comfort did not much matter psychically. What mattered, Ella told me with passion, was "nourishment through culture and the hope to survive." There was a wish "to go back between children." By this she meant, I realized, a fervent desire to go back to a normal life with others of her age, a life that meant attending school. (Schools in the camp had been prohibited by the Germans.) She longed to sit down with other children in a classroom setting and be granted once again the right to participate in organized learning. It is fascinating to note that in the original stage design for *Brundibár* by František Zelenka, the only building explicitly identified on stage is labeled in bold letters SKOLA.

As Ella implied throughout our conversations, *Brundibár*, by virtue of both its psychological content and the repeated opportunities for performance it offered, revived in the children of Terezín a will to live, a refusal to give up. It rekindled motivation. It pledged that one *could* lie down to sleep in safety and awaken to hope and to plans for a purposeful (and even successful) action. Although, as we well know, that promise of triumph over evil was not fulfilled for most of the children, the opera—its story, its music, its enactment, and its spectacle—nevertheless worked continually to fuel hope. This is what the children who made it through to liberation remember.

What about the value of music itself as a theme? In particular, the power of music to tame aggression? This is an idea we can trace back through the centuries to the ancient Greek myth of Orpheus and to the biblical story of David, an idea that resurfaces in modern popular culture—for example, in the Beatles' still-beloved song "Yellow Submarine," from the late 1960s. In *Brundibár* the song the children sing together, which finally turns the trick and vanquishes the enemy, is a lullaby, the very sort of song mothers traditionally sing to soothe and calm the fears of children before they fall asleep. And, again notably, it is a song about growing up.

Beginning with the image of a mother who is rocking her baby and imagining what he or she will be like in the future, the lyrics turn to nature and evoke a little bird who flies away from its nest to see the world. The refrain goes: "The tree grows, the stream flows by, time passes, the clouds drift by, year by year, step by step." Then the children sing:

> "Mother, if you could see us today
> How big we are, perhaps you would be ashamed
> That you bathed us naked in a tiny wooden tub,
> And that you called us little girl and little boy."

These words, rendered by enthusiastic young voices a half century ago in Terezín, have a terrible irony when we hear them today. For the children who sang them were kept locked behind walls. They were not permitted to see the trees change with the seasons. They, unlike the bird about whom they were singing, were unable to fly away. In a horrible mockery of their beautiful song, most of them were never allowed to live long enough to grow up. This song, with its hope, confidence, and sensitivity to the passage of time—above all, its projection into the future—was as close as they were ever permitted to come to real adult experience.

Taken as a whole, the musical tone of *Brundibár* is light and tuneful, so that it is easy to catch and carry with childish voices. It parlays its motifs in a modernist idiom, in terms we have come to recognize as the early twentieth-century reaction to Romanticism. Synthesizing many influences, Krása's score draws stylistically on Central European dance music; polkas like those of Johann Strauss; Czech folk melodies; smooth, popular, cabaret-like tunes of the period; and especially the inspiration of Poulenc and *Les Six*. While generally eschewing overt musical characterizations, Krása makes an exception in the case of Brundibár, whose theme is dramatized in part by striking interruptions (bars of rest), and also, one might argue, in the cases of the sparrow (pizzicato), the cat (string chords), and the dog (cello and bass). Nonetheless Krása clearly avoids a musical engagement with the climactic moment of the drama (that is, the organ-grinder's theft of the children's money, which occurs outside the musical score). *Brundibár*, by interpolating songs into its narrative, functions more like an operetta than like classic opera, where plot itself is frequently musically represented. This choice on Krása's part makes excellent psychological sense; having not mastered and internalized the conventions of grand opera, young children often find its representation of dramatic life and death through music unintelligible and alien.

Ella Weissberger spoke to me glowingly of the children's pleasure in their singing. She emphasized their talent, their trembling voices as they auditioned for the solo parts. She also stressed the quality of the dancing in the original production and the charisma of the choreographer, Camilla Rosenbaum, who "made everyone feel like a ballerina." Everything, as she put it, all the energy and drive, had to come from within the children, since they had virtually no costumes and only the simplest of props.

Brundibár as performed in the Nazi camp differed, needless to say, from later performances, including one filmed in Prague in 1965 and directed by Rudy Freudenfeld himself. Because of the prevalence of lice in the camp, Ella reminisced, all the girls had their hair cut short. She alone was allowed the privilege of growing hers a little longer, so that it could be parted in the middle and bunched up on either side to simulate a cat's ears. Her costume consisted of her sister's ski pants and a black sweater that belonged to her mother, who was in mourning for her father. Ella further recalled being intrigued by a thick stick of make-up that was used by all the children. As the Zelenka drawing shows, posters were pasted up against the fence, and later these apparently were changed to represent the dog, bird, and cat, so that, when it was her turn to sing, Ella would poke her face through the appropriate hole and be spotlighted.

Rehearsals, she related, were fraught with anxiety. They took place in a hot, cramped attic at the end of each day. The cast would gather there to wait for Rudy, who also worked with adult prisoners in the stone mines. Each time he finally arrived in his dirty clothing, exhausted, he was greeted with immense relief and joy, for the children knew all too well that people had died in the mines from dynamite explosions, and they feared that one day they would be left waiting for him in vain.

Enthusiasm for the little opera spread rapidly, and although the first room in which performances were held had the capacity to hold only fifty people, it was not unusual for more than one hundred adults and children to squeeze in. Audiences did not want the half-hour-long opera to end, and the finale was sung again and again with everyone joining in. Eventually the "victory march" of *Brundibár* became the emblematic music of Terezín, cherished and whistled daily throughout the camp. As Ella and the other performers returned to their stark barracks, they could hear their friends who were not in the cast continuing to hum its melodies.

The Nazis evidently never quite grasped the power in all this. Ella remembers the late summer of 1944, when the Germans, to whitewash their crimes, made a notorious propaganda film of life in Terezín cynically entitled *Der Führer schenkt den Juden eine Stadt* (The Führer presents a city to the Jews). Under the threat of instant death, the inmates of the camp, including the film's director, Kurt Gerron, were forced to cooperate with the duplicitous image of contentment and well-being the Nazis sought to portray. Cultural life in the camp was to be highlighted in the film, and the Germans rewarded the cast of *Brundibár* for their rousing vocalization by giving each child a small piece of cake with black pudding. Never did they suspect the defiance behind those clarion young voices (fig. 2.20)!

Brundibár gave the children of Terezín an opportunity to feel and to *be* effective in an environment that induced abject helplessness. It gave them chances to transcend, concretely and metaphorically, their artificially restricted boundaries, to develop new skills, to experiment with social issues, to engage in competition and collaboration. It empowered them to integrate reality and fantasy, seriousness and playfulness, verbal and non-verbal forms of symbolic function. Rehearsing and repeatedly performing in *Brundibár* meant, as Ella said, that one could *"forget everything."* One could concentrate totally; one could reinstate the notion that something still really mattered. The art, the music, required a measure of discipline

2.20. Still from Nazi propaganda film *Der Führer schenkt den Juden eine Stadt.*

and a capacity to trust in the future enough to plan for it and work toward it. Through communal experience—not just solidarity with others onstage but with others in the audiences, offstage—*Brundibár* gave the children of Terezín a much-needed sense of active membership in the human race. It thus formed a powerful counterweight to the dehumanization promulgated by Nazi words and deeds. Most important, the little opera sustained these children in hope. It offered them a safe arena, a unique vehicle for dramatizing conflict, for expressing personal joy, fear, longing, and the unquenchable desire of each one of them to live.

Yet, in reflecting on the relationship between art and life, we must never forget that, of the fifteen thousand children under the age of fifteen who passed through the Terezín camp between 1942 and 1944, fewer than one hundred survived.

My reflections on *Brundibár* grew out of research initially supported by the Getty Center for the History of Art and the Humanities in Santa Monica. From its inception, the project was a collaboration with the cultural historian Peter Jelavich of the University of Texas, who drew me into this deeply troubling area of study and also shared with me his encyclopedic knowledge of twentieth-century Eastern European cultural history. Research was undertaken in the archives at Yad va'Shem in Jerusalem, at the Jewish Museum in Prague, and at the Terezín Memorial Archives in Terezín, as well as at the YIVO Institute for Jewish Research in New York. In addition, interviews were conducted with several survivors of the Terezín camp, including Ella Weissberger. Alena Marten at the Getty Center translated the lines quoted from *Brundibár*.

A version of this chapter was presented in conjunction with a historical and political talk by Peter Jelavich at the Massachusetts College of Art, Boston, on 18 April 1991 to help provide context for an exhibition entitled "Seeing through 'Paradise': Artists and the Terezín Concentration Camp." It was also presented, again accompanying a talk by Professor Jelavich, at a Scholar-in-Residence seminar on Yom ha Shoah at the Larchmont Temple, Larchmont, New York, 18 April 1993. I wish to express my appreciation to Peter Jelavich, to the archivists and librarians at the various research centers I visited, and, above all, to Ella Weissberger. I also wish to thank my son, Nathaniel Geoffrey Lew, for discussing some of the specifically musical aspects of the opera with me.

Brundibár has been released on compact disc by Channel Classics Records B.V. as recording CCS 5193 in the series Composers from Theresienstadt (1941–1945). It was recorded in Prague in June 1992 by the Disman Children's Ensemble (Zdena and Václav Flegl, directors; Eva Bošková, musical director; Joža Karas, conductor).

Writing across the Disciplines

Afterword

Not infrequently, at the end of scholarly conferences, I experience a momentary sadness, an unmet need for some convention of closure or farewell. Rarely do such events provide for this; colleagues simply drift away and disappear individually or in small groups. No time or place is specifically set aside for saying goodbye. I want in this afterword to say these words to the unknown reader of this book, lest he or she feel a pang at coming to the end of the last chapter and seeing the back cover with nothing interjacent. Having patiently accompanied me on this tour through the museum of a mind, having thought and felt and silently disputed with me, my reader may now anticipate a warm and proper farewell rather than an abrupt cessation.

This thought, however, returns us to the beginning where the paintings of René Magritte serve to remind us that children who suddenly lose a parent get no such opportunity. For them, words may remain forever unspoken, hopes unformulated, tenderness unexpressed, atonement unachieved. Gaps in memory, as we have seen, may dilate with the passage of time, and fantasies, both grandiose and malevolent, sprout to animate the darkness. And what sort of good-byes were vouchsafed the children of Terezín?

Wisely, I believe, the Hebrew Bible makes much of boundaries and separations; it teaches the good of knowing and observing clear divisions. In taking farewell of my reader after our twisting journey through a labyrinth of ambivalence, absurdity, and shifting perspectives, I seek to restore a measure of security. Safety and trust are foundational to our destabilizing adventures in the arts for, if life itself is felt to be sound, then the risks of art can not only be permitted but enjoyed. Yet, paradoxically, as I have tried to show, even a dense, disturbing, or elusive work of art may, as we grow with it over time, suffuse us with a sense that life is full, rich, and even good. Created by the mind, art reshapes the mind, and although we keep trying, the match between inside and outside is always askew. Who has words to fit the images of Magritte, or lines and colors with which to represent the insect of Kafka's "Metamorphosis"? In despair but also in unending hope, the artist cries out with Hopkins:

Mine, O thou lord of life, send my roots rain.

References

Abarbanel, Andrew. 1988. A note on Magritte's use of the shroud. In *Psychoanalytic Perspectives on Art*, edited by Mary M. Gedo, vol. 3. Hillsdale, N. J.: Analytic.

Abraham, Karl. 1924. The influence of oral erotism on character formation. In *On Character and Libido Development: Six Essays by Karl Abraham*, edited by Bertram D. Lewin. New York: W. W. Norton, 1966.

Achenbach, Joel. 1993. Blood. Guts. Mayhem. Cool! *Washington Post*, 28 June, sec. B.

Andrews, Edmund L. 1993. Mild slap at TV violence. *New York Times*, 1 July, sec. A.

Ariès, Philippe. 1960. *Centuries of Childhood: A Social History of Family Life*, translated by Robert Baldick. New York: Vintage, 1962.

Arlow, Jacob. 1969. Unconscious fantasy and disturbances of conscious experience. *Psychoanalytic Quarterly* 38:1–27.

Barthes, Roland. 1957. *Mythologies*, translated by Annette Lavers. New York: Hill and Wang, 1972.

Battin, Margaret; Fisher, John; Moore, Ronald; and Silvers, Anita; eds. 1989. *Puzzles about Art: An Aesthetics Casebook*. New York: St. Martin's.

Baudrillard, Jean. 1988. *Baudrillard: Selected Writings*, edited by Mark Poster. Stanford, Calif.: Stanford University Press.

Bawer, Bruce. 1989. Poetry in motion. *American Spectator*, August 1989, 39–41.

Beckett, Samuel. 1957. *Endgame*. Reprint. New York: Grove Weidenfield, 1983.

Bergmann, Martin. Personal communication, 1 March 1993.

Bick, Ilsa. 1989. Aliens among us: A representation of children in science fiction. *Journal of the American Psychoanalytic Association* 37:737–59.

Bouwsma, William J. 1988. *John Calvin: A Sixteenth-Century Portrait*. New York and Oxford: Oxford University Press.

Brenner, Charles. 1982. *The Mind in Conflict*. Madison, Conn.: International Universities Press.

Breslin, James E. B. 1991. Modernizing biography. Paper delivered at the College Art Association annual meeting, Washington, D.C.

Brown, Lyn Mikel, and Gilligan, Carol. 1992. *Meeting at the Crossroads*. Cambridge, Mass.: Harvard University Press.

Burgin, Victor. 1990. Geometry and abjection. In *Abjection, Melancholia, and Love*, edited by John Fletcher and Andrew Benjamin. London and New York: Routledge.

Camus, Albert. 1955. *L'Etranger*, edited by Germaine Brée and Carlos Lynes, Jr. New York: Appleton-Century-Crofts.

Carroll, Lewis. 1865. *Alice's Adventures in Wonderland*. Reprint (with *Through the Looking Glass*). Kingsport, Tenn.: Grosset and Dunlap, 1946.

————. 1872. *Through the Looking Glass*. Reprint (with *Alice's Adventures in Wonderland*). Kingsport, Tenn.: Grosset and Dunlap, 1946.

Carton, Evan. 1989. Better dead than read: The society of poets. *Tikkun*, November/December, 64–67.

Caruth, Cathy. 1991. Unclaimed experience: Trauma and the possibility of history. *Yale French Studies* 79:181–92.

Caws, Mary Ann. 1989. *The Art of Interference*. Princeton, N.J.: Princeton University Press.

Chekhov, Anton. 1887. The bear. In *Chekhov Plays*, translated by Elisaveta Fen. Baltimore, Md.: Penguin, 1959.

Chodorow, Nancy J. 1989. *Feminism and Psychoanalytic Theory*. New Haven, Conn.: Yale University Press.

Danto, Arthur. 1980. *The Transfiguration of the Commonplace*. Cambridge, Mass.: Harvard University Press.

Deleuze, Gilles, and Guattari, Félix. 1972. *Anti-Oedipus*, translated by Robert Hurley, Mark Seem, and Helen R. Lane. Minneapolis, Minn.: University of Minnesota Press, 1983.

Donaldson, Margaret. 1978. *Children's Minds*. New York: W. W. Norton.

Duckworth, Eleanor. 1972. The having of wonderful ideas. *Harvard Educational Review*, May 1972.

Eisen, George. 1988. *Children and Play in the Holocaust: Games among the Shadows*. Amherst: University of Massachusetts Press.

Ellman, Richard, ed. 1976. *The New Oxford Book of American Verse*. New York: Oxford University Press.

Esman, Aaron H. 1990. *Adolescence and Culture*. New York: Columbia University Press.

Ferenczi, Sandor. 1912. Symbolism. In *First Contributions to Psycho-Analysis*, translated by Ernest Jones. New York: Brunner/Mazel, 1952.

————. 1913. On eye symbolism. In *First Contributions to Psycho-Analysis*, translated by Ernest Jones. New York: Brunner/Mazel, 1952.

Foucault, Michel. 1973. *The Order of Things*. New York: Vintage.

————. 1983. *This Is Not a Pipe*. Berkeley: University of California Press.

Fraiberg, Selma. 1959. *The Magic Years*. New York: Charles Scribner's Sons.

Freud, Sigmund. 1895. Obsessions and phobias: Their psychical mechanism and their aetiology. *S.E.*3:74–84.

————. 1900. *The Interpretation of Dreams*. *S.E.*4 and 5.

References

References

————. 1905a. *Three Essays on the Theory of Sexuality, S.E.*7:125–243.

————. 1905b. *Jokes and Their Relation to the Unconscious. S.E.*8.

————. 1909. Notes upon a case of obsessional neurosis. *S.E.*10:153–318.

————. 1910. *Leonardo da Vinci and a Memory of His Childhood. S.E.*11:59–137.

————. 1914. On narcissism: An introduction. *S.E.*14:73–102.

————. 1917. Mourning and melancholia. *S.E.*14:239–58.

————. 1918. From the history of an infantile neurosis. *S.E.*17:3–122.

————. 1919. The "uncanny." *S.E.*17:219–56.

————. 1920. *Beyond the Pleasure Principle. S.E.*18:3–64.

————. 1922. Medusa's head. *S.E.*28:273–74.

————. 1923. The ego and the id. *S.E.*19:3–66.

————. 1937. Analysis terminable and interminable. *S.E.*23:209–53.

Gablik, Suzi. 1976. *Magritte.* Boston: New York Graphic Society.

Gamwell, Lynn, and Wells, Richard, eds. 1989. *Sigmund Freud and Art: His Personal Collection of Antiquities.* Binghamton: State University of New York.

Gardner, Helen, ed. 1972. *The New Oxford Book of English Verse, 1250–1950.* London: Oxford University Press.

Gardner, Howard. 1983. *Frames of Mind: The Theory of Multiple Intelligences.* New York: Basic.

Gardner, Tom. 1993. Moral energy in the young. *Harvard Graduate School Alumni Bulletin,* June 1993.

Gedo, Mary M. 1985. Meditations on madness: The art of René Magritte. In *In the Mind's Eye: Dada and Surrealism,* edited by T. Neff. New York: Abbeville Press.

Geertz, Clifford. 1973. *The Interpretation of Cultures.* New York: Basic.

Gilligan, Carol. 1982. *In a Different Voice: Women's Conceptions of Self and Morality.* Cambridge, Mass.: Harvard University Press.

Golomb, Claire. 1992. *The Child's Creation of a Pictorial World.* Berkeley and Los Angeles: University of California Press.

Goodman, Nelson. 1976. *Languages of Art.* Indianapolis: Hackett.

Gopnik, Adam. 1990. Comics. In *High and Low: Modern Art and Popular Culture,* edited by K. Varnedoe and A. Gopnik. New York: Museum of Modern Art.

Nancy Graves: A Survey, 1969–1980. (Catalogue for exhibition at the Albright-Knox Gallery, Buffalo, New York, 3 May–15 June 1980.) Buffalo: Albright-Knox Gallery.

Green, Gerald. 1978. *The Artists of Terezín.* New York: Schocken.

Greenacre, Phyllis. 1955. "It's my own invention": A special screen memory of Mr. Lewis Carroll, its form and its history. In *Emotional Growth: Psychoanalytic Studies of the Gifted and a Great Variety of Other Individuals,* ed. Phyllis Greenacre, vol. 2. New York: International Universities Press, 1971.

Greenberg, Mark S., and Kolk, Bessel A. van der. 1987. Retrieval and integration of traumatic memories with the "painting cure." In *Psychological Trauma*, edited by Bessel A. van der Kolk. Washington, D.C.: American Psychiatric Press.

Hammacher, A. M. 1985. *René Magritte*, translated by James Brockway. New York: Abrams.

Hartmann, Heinz. 1958. *Essays on Ego Psychology*. New York: International Universities Press.

Hasan, Judith Wershil. 1980. Museum modernizes tours for children. *New York Times*, 2 November.

Hayman, Ronald. 1981. *Kafka: A Biography*. New York and Toronto: Oxford University Press.

Heilman, Robert B. 1989. The great teacher myth. *American Scholar* (Summer 1989): 417–23.

Hirsch, Marianne. 1989. *The Mother/Daughter Plot: Narrative, Psychoanalysis, Feminism*. Bloomington: Indiana University Press.

Hobbes, Thomas. 1651. *Leviathan*. Reprint. Edited by C. B. Macpherson. Harmondsworth: Penguin, 1951.

Hopkins, Gerard Manley. 1889. Thou art indeed just, Lord. In *Poems and Prose*, edited by W. H. Gardner. Harmondsworth: Penguin, 1979.

Hurwitz, Al, ed. 1983. *The Gifted and Talented in Art*. Worcester, Mass.: Davis.

Isenberg, Arnold. 1973. *Aesthetics and the Theory of Criticism: Selected Essays of Arnold Isenberg*, edited by W. Callaghan, L. Cauman, C. Hempel et al. Chicago: University of Chicago Press.

Jean, Marcel, ed. 1980. *The Autobiography of Surrealism*. New York: Viking.

Jelavich, Peter. 1993. *Berlin Cabaret*. Cambridge, Mass.: Harvard University Press.

Kant, Immanuel. 1790. *The Critique of Judgement*. Reprint. Translated by James Creed Meredith. Oxford: Oxford University Press, 1978.

Karas, Joža. 1985. *Music in Terezín, 1941–1945*. New York: Beaufort.

Kestenberg, Judith. 1990. Children under the Nazi yoke. In *Mind and Human Interaction* 2, no. 2 (October 1990):39–45.

Kivnick, Helen Q., and Erikson, Joan M. 1983. The arts as healing. *American Journal of Orthopsychiatry*, 53, no. 4 (October 1983):602–18.

Klein, Melanie. 1964. *Contributions to Psychoanalysis, 1921–1945*. New York: McGraw-Hill.

———. 1975. *Envy and Gratitude and Other Works, 1946–1963*. New York: Delacorte Press/Seymour Lawrence.

Kolk, Bessel A. van der. 1987. *Psychological Trauma*. Washington, D.C.: American Psychiatric Press.

Kovel, Joel. 1978. Things and words: Metapsychology and the historical point of view. In *Psychoanalysis and Contemporary Thought*, edited by Leo Goldberger.

References

Kuspit, Donald. 1988. Surrealism's re-vision of psychoanalysis. In *Psychoanalytic Perspectives on Art*, edited by Mary M. Gedo, vol. 3. Hillsdale, N.J.: Analytic.

Lacan, Jacques. 1970. Of structure as an inmixing of an Otherness prerequisite to any subject whatever. In *The Structuralist Controversy*, edited by R. Macksey and E. Donato. Baltimore: Johns Hopkins University Press.

Langer, Susanne. 1953. *Feeling and Form*. New York: Charles Scribner's Sons.

Laub, Dori. 1991. Truth and testimony: The process and the struggle. *American Imago* 48:75–91.

Leith, John H. 1989. *John Calvin's Doctrine of the Christian Life*. Louisville, Ky.: Westminster/John Knox Press.

Liebert, Robert S. 1983. *Michelangelo: A Psychoanalytic Study of the Man and His Images*. New Haven: Yale University Press.

Loraux, Nicole. 1987. *Tragic Ways of Killing a Woman*, translated by Anthony Forster. Cambridge, Mass.: Harvard University Press.

Lyotard, Jean-François. 1984. *The Postmodern Condition: A Report on Knowledge*, translated by Geoff Bennington and Brian Massumi. Minneapolis, Minn.: University of Minnesota Press.

René Magritte: Paintings. 1986. Catalogue for Arnold Herstand Gallery exhibition, 6 November–20 December 1986. New York: Arnold Herstand.

René Magritte. 1987. Catalogue for exhibition, Fondation de l'Hermitage, Lausanne, 19 June–18 October 1987.

Mahler, Margaret S. 1968. *On Human Symbiosis and the Vicissitudes of Individuation*. Vol. 1, *Infantile Psychosis*. New York: International Universities Press.

Marcus, Leah Sinanoglou. 1978. *Childhood and Cultural Despair: A Theme and Variations in Seventeenth-Century Literature*. Pittsburgh, Pa.: University of Pittsburgh Press.

Miller, Alice. 1981. *The Drama of the Gifted Child*, translated by Ruth Ward. New York: Basic.

Milner, Marion. 1957. *On Not Being Able to Paint*. New York: International Universities Press.

Morstein, Petra von. 1983. Magritte: Artistic and conceptual representation. *Journal of Aesthetics and Art Criticism* 41:369–74.

Nagel, Thomas. 1979. *Mortal Questions*. New York: Cambridge University Press.

Nietzsche, Friedrich. 1874. On the uses and disadvantages of history for life. In *Untimely Meditations*, translated by R. J. Hollingdale. Cambridge: Cambridge University Press, 1983.

Nussbaum, Martha C. 1986. *The Fragility of Goodness: Luck and Ethics in Greek Tragedy and Philosophy*. Cambridge and New York: Cambridge University Press.

181

O'Connor, John J. 1990. Cartoons teach children, but is the lesson good? *New York Times*, 20 February, sec. B.

Oldenburg, Claes. 1967. *Store Days*. New York: Something Else Press.

Opie, Iona, and Opie, Peter. 1969. *Children's Games in Street and Playground*. Oxford: Oxford University Press, 1985.

Orwell, George. 1949. *1984*. New York: Harcourt, Brace.

Otto, Rudolf. 1979. *The Idea of the Holy*. London: Oxford University Press.

Passeron, René. 1972. *René Magritte*. Chicago: J. Philip O'Hara.

Paulson, Ronald. 1974. *Hogarth: His Art, Life, and Times*. New Haven: Yale University Press.

Piaget, Jean, and Inhelder, Barbel. 1969. *The Psychology of the Child*, translated by Helen Weaver. New York: Basic.

Pirsig, Robert M. 1974. *Zen and the Art of Motorcycle Maintenance*. New York: Bantam.

Pynoos, Robert S., and Nader, Kathi. 1990. Children's exposure to violence and traumatic death. *Psychiatric Annals* 20(6):334–44.

Sartre, Jean-Paul. 1956. *Being and Nothingness*, translated by Hazel E. Barnes. New York: Philosophical Library.

Saussure, Ferdinand de. 1916. *Course in General Linguistics*, edited by Charles Bally and Albert Sechehaye and translated by Wade Baskin. New York: Philosophical Library, 1959.

Schneede, Uwe M. 1973. *René Magritte: Life and Work*, translated by W. Walter Jaffe. Woodbury, New York: Barron's, 1982.

Schorske, Carl. 1980. *Fin-de-siècle Vienna*. New York: Alfred A. Knopf.

Scutenaire, Louis. 1947. *René Magritte*. Brussels: Librairie Selection.

———. 1958. *Magritte*. Chicago: William and Noma Copley Foundation.

———. 1977. *Avec Magritte*. Brussels: Lebeer Hossmann.

Seven Artists. Catalogue for exhibition, 5 October–4 January 1980. Purchase: Neuberger Museum, State University of New York.

Snow, Edward. 1983. "Meaning" in *Children's Games*: On the limitations of the iconographic approach to Breugel. *Representations* 1, no. 2 (Spring):27–60.

Spector, Jack. 1972. *The Aesthetics of Freud: A Study in Psychoanalysis and Art*. London: Praeger.

Spitz, Ellen Handler. 1984. Toward the separation of memory and hope: Applications of psychoanalysis to art in the writings of Martha Wolfenstein. *Hillside Journal of Clinical Psychiatry* 6:91–104.

———. 1985. *Art and Psyche: A Study in Psychoanalysis and Aesthetics*. New Haven: Yale University Press.

———. 1991. *Image and Insight: Essays in Psychoanalysis and the Arts*. New York: Columbia University Press.

————. 1993. Promethean positions. In *Freud and Forbidden Knowledge*, edited by Peter L. Rudnytsky and Ellen Handler Spitz. New York: New York University Press, 1993.

Spitz, René. 1965. *The First Year of Life*. New York: International Universities Press.

Steiner, George. 1986. *Antigones*. Oxford: Oxford University Press.

Sylvester, David. 1978. Portraits de Magritte. In *Retrospective Magritte*. Exhibition catalogue, Brussels, Palais des Beaux Arts, 1978; Paris, Musée National de l'Art Moderne, 1979.

————. 1992. *Magritte*. London: Thames and Hudson.

Terr, Lenore, 1987. Childhood trauma and the creative product: A look at the early lives and later works of Poe, Wharton, Magritte, Hitchcock, and Bergman. *Psychoanalytic Study of the Child* 42:545–72.

————. 1991. Childhood traumas: An outline and overview. *American Journal of Psychiatry* 148:10–20.

Theoharides, Catherine T. 1981. Museums and children: A natural connection. *Journal of the New York School Boards Association*. May 1981.

Thoreau, Henry David. 1854. *Walden and Other Writings*. Reprint. Edited by Joseph Wood Krutch. New York: Bantam, 1962.

Thurber, James. 1945. The secret life of James Thurber. In *The Thurber Carnival*. Harmondsworth: Penguin, 1953.

Torczyner, Harry. 1979. *Magritte: The True Art of Painting*, translated by Richard Miller. New York: Abrams.

Tormey, Judith Farr. 1990. Art, interpretation, and animation: Commentary on Ellen Handler Spitz's "Calvin and Hobbes." Paper read at meeting of the American Society for Aesthetics, Austin, Texas, October 1990.

Varnedoe, Kirk, and Gopnik, Adam. 1990. *High and Low: Modern Art and Popular Culture*. New York: Museum of Modern Art.

Viederman, Milton. 1987. René Magritte: Coping with loss—reality and illusion. *Journal of the American Psychoanalytic Association* 35:967–98.

Volaková, Hana, ed. 1993. *. . . I never saw another butterfly . . .* Revised edition. New York: Schocken.

Waldberg, Patrick. 1965. *René Magritte*, translated by Austryn Wainhouse. Brussels: André De Rache.

Watterson, Bill. 1987. *Calvin and Hobbes*. Kansas City, Kans.: Andrews, McMeel and Parker.

————. 1988. *Something under the Bed Is Drooling*. Kansas City, Kans.: Andrews and McMeel.

————. 1989. *Yukon Ho!* Kansas City, Kans., and New York: Andrews and McMeel.

—————. 1990. *Weirdos from Another Planet!* Kansas City, Kans., and New York: Andrews and McMeel.

—————. 1991. *Scientific Progress Goes "Boink."* Kansas City, Kans.: Andrews and McMeel.

Weissberger, Ella. 1990. Personal interview.

Whitfield, Sarah. 1992. *Magritte.* London: South Bank Centre.

Whitman, Walt. 1983. *Leaves of Grass: The 1892 Edition.* New York: Bantam.

Winnicott, D. W. 1956. The antisocial tendency. In *Through Paediatrics to Psycho-Analysis.* London: Hogarth, 1987.

—————. 1965. *The Maturational Processes and the Facilitating Environment.* New York: International Universities Press.

Wittgenstein, Ludwig. 1953. *Philosophical Investigations.* New York: Macmillan.

Wolfenstein, Martha. 1951. A phase in the development of children's sense of humor. *Psychoanalytic Study of the Child* 6:336–50.

—————. 1954. *Children's Humor: A Psychological Analysis.* Reprint. Bloomington: Indiana University Press, 1978.

—————. 1966. How is mourning possible? *Psychoanalytic Study of the Child* 21:93–123.

—————. 1969. Loss, rage, and repetition. *Psychoanalytic Study of the Child* 24:432–60.

—————. 1973. The image of the lost parent. *Psychoanalytic Study of the Child* 28:433–56.

—————. 1974. The past recaptured in the work of René Magritte. Unpublished manuscript prepared for the Margaret S. Mahler Symposium, Philadelphia, May 1974.

—————. *The Man in the Bowler Hat.* Unpublished manuscript (referred to in text as MS).

Wolfenstein, Martha, and Kliman, Gilbert, eds. 1965. *Children and the Death of a President.* Garden City, New York: Doubleday.

References

Index

Index

Magritte, René (*continued*)

and parodies, 37–40; immobility of forms in the art of, 22, 28, 34, 51; obsession with blocked looking, 19, 29, 47, 49; repetition in the art of, 4, 50; suicide of mother, 3, 19, 26–29, 34–35, 41; titles of works of, 44–45; works of, as puzzles, 6–7, 17–18, 25, 36, 44, 54, 61, 62

—works: *Anniversary, The,* 50; *Attempting the Impossible,* 34; *Blank Signature, The,* 58; *Blood of the World,* 42; *Central Story, The,* 34; *Childhood of Icarus, The,* 29, 46; *Collective Invention,* 27, 28, 38; *Curse, The,* 34; *Dangerous Relationships,* 30, 33; *Daydreams of a Solitary Walker,* 29, 30; *Discovery,* 52; *Discovery of Fire,* 9, 34, 51; *Empire of Lights,* 35; *Eternally Obvious, The,* 33; *Evening Falls,* 41, 51; *Explanation, The,* 23, 70; *False Mirror, The,* 19, 38, 47; *Flood, The,* 24, 30, 34; *Fortune Made,* 52; *Giantess, The,* 39; *Girl Eating Bird,* 23, 27, 53; *Glass House, The,* 29; *Great War, The,* 38, 40, 48; *Hegel's Vacation,* 41; *Homesickness,* 42; *Human Condition, The,* 38, 50, 62; *Idea, The,* 38, 48; *Key of Dreams,* 42; *Legend of the Centuries,* 8; *Listening Chamber, The,* 14, 49, 50; *Magician, The,* 18; *Memory,* 26; *Menaced Assassin, The,* 27, 34; *Month of the Grape Harvest, The,* 21, 28, 62; *Palace of Curtains,* 44, 47, 52; *Pandora's Box,* 51; *Personal Values,* 42, 65; *Perspective: Mme Récamier of David,* 34, 52; *Philosophy in the Boudoir,* 35, 52; *Pilgrim, The,* 37, 38; *Pleasure Principle, The,* 40; *Postcard, The,* 49; *Rape, The,* 27, 32, 33, 40; *Red Model, The,* 41; *Secret Double, The,* 14; *Smile of the Devil, The,* 3, 39; *Son of Man, The,* 20, 47, 48; *Spirit of Geometry, The,* 24, 30, 47; *Spoiler, The,* 42; *Spy, The,* 42; *Survivor, The,* 47; *Thief, The,* 52; *This Is Not an Apple,* 37, 47; *Time Transfixed,* 22; *Titanic Days,* 25, 39, 51; *Tomb of the Wrestlers,* 49; *Treachery of Imagery, The,* 47; *Unexpected Answer, The,* 38, 39; *Waterfall, The,* 54; *When the Hour Will Strike,* 35, 51, 52; *Where Euclid Walked,* 23

Mahler, Margaret S., 9, 23, 71

Mapplethorpe, Robert, 85

McKay, Winsor, 82

Mead, Margaret, 8

Medusa, 21, 54

Memory (Magritte), 26

Menaced Assassin, The (Magritte), 27, 34

Menil Collection, 33

Metamorphosis as surrealist theme, 79, 92

"Metamorphosis" (Kafka), 3, 4, 176

Miller, Alice, 110

Milner, Marion, 5

Minotaur, 44, 45, 55

Mirror, as symbol, 30, 31

Month of the Grape Harvest, The (Magritte), 21, 28, 62

Moore, Ronald, 146

Mourning, 26

Mouth-eye equation, in Magritte's art, 21, 40, 48, 49, 53

Suicide, 110, 112; parental, 3, 19, 26, 29, 34–36, 39, 44
Surrealism, 6–25 passim, 78; game of the "corps exquis," 10, 33, 158; and thralldom to childhood, 16
Survivor, The (Magritte), 47
Sylvester, David, 9, 26, 30, 35, 36, 38, 45

Teaching, 104–106, 109, 113–115, 124, 147, 149; Latin, 153–154; in museum education, 155–160; Wolfenstein as teacher, 8
Terr, Lenore, 22, 26, 35, 36
Thief, The (Magritte), 52
This Is Not an Apple (Magritte), 37, 47
Thoreau, Henry David, 115
Thurber, James, 43
Time Transfixed (Magritte), 22
Titanic Days (Magritte), 25, 39, 51
Titles, of Magritte's works, 45
Tomb of the Wrestlers, The (Magritte), 49
Torczyner, Harry, 42
Transference, 79, 80
Trauma, 7, 41, 130; childhood and adolescent, 11, 18, 19, 22, 27, 43
Treachery of Imagery, The (Magritte), 47
Tudor, Anthony, 152

"Uncanny," the, 8–9, 41, 42, 63, 80
Unexpected Answer, The (Magritte), 38, 39

Van der Kolk, Bessel A., 19, 20
Varnedoe, Kirk, 37

Vermeer, Jan, 28
Viederman, Milton, 35
Visual-oral equation. *See* Mouth-eye equation
Voyeuristic urges, 48

Waldberg, Patrick, 23, 46
Walden (Thoreau), 115
Warren, Robert Penn, 111
Waterfall, The (Magritte), 54
Watterson, Bill, 81–101
Wharton, Edith, 99
When the Hour Will Strike (Magritte), 35, 51, 52
Where Euclid Walked (Magritte), 23
Whitfield, Sarah, 9, 24, 34, 46, 48, 49, 58
Whitman, Walt, 105, 107, 113
Winnicott, D. W., 23, 54, 95, 126, 127, 128
Wittgenstein, Ludwig, 123
Wolfenstein, Martha, 7–10 passim, 18, 26, 28, 30, 35, 36, 39, 42, 46, 53, 63, 65, 68–72 passim
Women: ambivalent portrayals of in Magritte's art, 30–35; denigration of, 10, 52, 78
Words and deeds, 112, 130; in aesthetic education, 150–152
Words and images, 42–43, 44, 47, 51; incompatibility of, 3–4

Zen and the Art of Motorcycle Maintenance (Pirsig), 117–128